SCIENCE FICTION ROOTS AND BRANCHES

Science Fiction Roots and Branches

RHYS GARNETT
Principal Lecturer in English
Staffordshire Polytechnic

and

R. J. ELLIS
Senior Lecturer in English
Staffordshire Polytechnic

St. Martin's Press   New York

First published in the United States of America in 1990

Printed in Hong Kong

ISBN 0–312–03598–5

Library of Congress Cataloging-in-Publication Data
Science fiction roots and branches: contemporary critical approaches
  /edited by Rhys Garnett and R. J. Ellis.
        p.   cm.
     Includes index.
     ISBN 0–312–03598–5
     1. Science fiction—History and criticism.   2. Feminism in
literature.   I. Garnett, Rhys, 1935–   . II. Ellis, R. J., 1949–   .
PN3433.5.S34   1990
809.3'8762—dc20   89–36454
                                                          CIP

To Pamela and Maggie

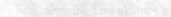

Contents

Notes on the Contributors   ix

1 Introduction   1
   R. J. Ellis and Rhys Garnett

   PART ONE   SOME ROOTS: VICTORIAN SCIENCE
   FICTION AND FANTASY

2 Counter-Projects: William Morris and the Science   7
   Fiction of the 1880s
   Darko Suvin

3 H. G. Wells's *The War of the Worlds*   18
   Stanislaw Lem

4 *Dracula* and *The Beetle*: Imperial and Sexual Guilt and   30
   Fear in Late Victorian Fantasy
   Rhys Garnett

   PART TWO   SOME BRANCHES: POSTWAR SCIENCE
   FICTION

5 Scientists in Science Fiction: Enlightenment and After   57
   Patrick Parrinder

6 The World as Code and Labyrinth: Stanislaw Lem's   79
   Memoirs Found in a Bathtub
   Jerzy Jarzębski

7 The Neglected Fiction of John Wyndham: 'Consider   88
   Her Ways', *Trouble with Lichen* and *Web*
   Thomas D. Clareson and Alice S. Clareson

8 Frank Herbert's *Dune* and the Discourse of Apocalyptic   104
   Ecologism in the United States
   R. J. Ellis

9   Ursula Le Guin and Time's Dispossession   125
    Robert M. Philmus

    PART THREE   SOME BRANCHES: CONTEMPORARY
    FEMINIST RESPONSES

10 Men in Feminist Science Fiction: Marge Piercy, Thomas   153
    Berger and the End of Masculinity
    Marleen Barr

11 The Destabilisation of Gender in Vonda McIntyre's   168
    Superluminal
    Jenny Wolmark

12 Man-Made Monsters: Suzy McKee Charnas's *Walk to*   183
    the End of the World as Dystopian Feminist Science
    Fiction
    Anne Cranny-Francis

    Index   207

Notes on the Contributors

Marleen Barr is Associate Professor of English at Virginia Polytechnic Institute and State University. She has edited issues of *Women's Studies*, *Women's Studies International Forum*, *Future Females: A Critical Anthology* and the forthcoming *Discontented Discourses: Feminism/Textual Intervention/Psychoanalysis*. Her book *Alien to Femininity: Speculative Fiction and Feminist Theory* has been recently published. She is currently completing another book, *Feminist Fabulation: Space and Postmodern Fictions*.

Alice S. Clareson has taught at both high school and college levels. She is now a reference librarian at the Wayne County Public Library in Wooster. She is collaborating with her husband Tom on the first book-length study of the fiction of John Wyndham.

Thomas D. Clareson, Professor of English at the College of Wooster (Ohio), has edited *Extrapolation* since 1959. One of the founders of the MLA Seminar on Science Fiction in 1958, he was also the first president of the Science Fiction Research Association from 1970 to 1976. His publications include *Science Fiction: The Other Side of Realism*, *A Spectrum of Worlds*, *Science Fiction: An Annotated Checklist* and two books on Robert Silverberg. He is the editor of both *Science Fiction Periodicals, 1926–1978* and *Science Fiction in America: 1870s to 1930s*. He is at present completing an overview of contemporary American science fiction, from the 1950s to the 1980s.

Anne Cranny-Francis lectures at the University of Wollongong in New South Wales. An authority on Victorian and Australian literature, and the author of articles on the work of James Tiptree Jr, *Dracula* and Arthur Conan Doyle, she is preparing a study on Christina Stead.

R. J. Ellis lectures at Staffordshire Polytechnic, and has published articles on, amongst other topics: Mark Twain; 'Publishing, Pornography and Censorship'; 'The Frontier Myth in Popular Culture'; 'Little Magazines and Small Presses'. He is also the editor of *Sow's Ear* poetry series. Present research interests focus on evolving practical methods to interrelate writing, ideology and contexts.

Rhys Garnett is Principal Lecturer in English at Staffordshire Polytechnic. He has published articles on Malcolm Lowry, and his current research interests are in the areas of Victorian popular fiction, late Victorian fantasy, and the sensation novels of Mary E. Braddon.

Jerzy Jarzębski is Assistant Professor of Polish Literature in Craców, and author of many books and articles on contemporary Polish literature, including 'The Gombrowicz Game' and 'The Novel as Autocreation'. His studies have focused particularly on Gombrowicz, Bruno Schulz, Czesław Miłosz and Stanislaw Lem. His recent book on Lem, *Chance and Order*, is at present only available in a German translation.

Stanislaw Lem has now been translated into 36 languages. From over forty published books some twenty are available in English translations. Lem is considered to be the most prominent science fiction writer residing in Eastern Europe, and was the recipient of the Austrian State Award for European Literature in 1985. His major piece of science fiction theoretical speculation, *Fantastyka i Futurologia*, unfortunately remains untranslated.

Patrick Parrinder, Professor of English at the University of Reading, is author of *Science Fiction: Its Criticism and Teaching* and editor of *Science Fiction: A Critical Guide*. He is Chairman of the H. G. Wells Society, and has received the 1987 President's Award of World Science Fiction. His latest book is a collection of essays, *The Failure of Theory*.

Robert M. Philmus has co-edited three books on H. G. Wells (*H. G. Wells: Early Writings in Science and Science Fiction* with David Y. Hughes; *H. G. Wells and Modern Science Fiction* with Darko Suvin; and *H. G. Wells's Literary Criticism* with Patrick Parrinder). He has also published *Into the Unknown*, a study of the evolution of science fiction from Francis Godwin to H. G. Wells, and numerous articles. He is Professor of English at Concordia University in Montreal, and edits *Science Fiction Studies*.

Franz Rottensteiner is editor of the 'Fantastic Library' series published by Suhrkamp. He has compiled numerous anthologies, and has published several essays of science fiction criticism. His recent editing work includes the anthology *The Slaying of the Dragon* and an edition of Stanislaw Lem's *Microworlds*.

Darko Suvin, F.S.R.C., taught in Yugoslavia until 1967, and is now Professor of English and Comparative Literature at McGill University in Montreal. His numerous writings include *To Brecht and Beyond, Metamorphoses of Science Fiction, Victorian Science Fiction in the United Kingdom* and, most recently, *Positions and Presuppositions in Science Fiction*.

Jenny Wolmark is Senior Lecturer in Media and Cultural Studies at Humberside College of Higher Education. Her research interest is women in popular culture, and she has contributed articles on science fiction and feminism to *Foundation* and *Cultural Studies*.

1

Introduction

R. J. ELLIS and RHYS GARNETT

science fiction has become a dialect for our time
Doris Lessing[1]

The essays in this volume are arranged in two broadly chronological groups, focusing on crucial periods in the historical development of the genre. The first explores some features of the genre's complex Victorian origins; the second consists of a larger number of essays examining post-Second World War science fiction's equally diverse developments. Common to all these essays, to a greater or lesser extent, and underlying any variations they display in their methods and objectives, is a concern with the nature and disposition of power in modern societies – whether in its overtly political distribution, its ideological reinforcement, its subversion, its scientific and technological deployment, or its expression within gender relations. This common concern flows from the generically pivotal interaction between on the one hand science fiction's exploration of alternative/oppositional models of social organisation (with all of its implied loading of social criticism), and on the other the very diversity of its origins and evolving identity as a genre which characteristically draws on elements of the fantastic. This interaction has recurrently enabled it to slide duplicitously in and out of a negotiation with realist precepts when examining power – a process of exploration that, apparently set in other (alternative) time/space continuums, can gain a directness or penetration that, in part, marks it out as a genre. This capacity has made it fundamentally amenable to what might be called post-post structuralist critical analyses, which themselves have recurrently confronted the issue of how power is represented in literature.

These considerations plainly emerge within the essays in this volume, not least because they stand in implicit or explicit positions of negotiation with the current proliferation of exegesis of post-structuralist critical theories. In some instances this negotiation is

1

a matter of innovation – as when Darko Suvin maps out a way of identifying what he describes as 'counter-projects', shaping one segment of the field of discourse in which science fiction texts operate. In other cases this negotiation has resulted in an evident commitment to the implementation of a particular nexus of theoretical positions: Rhys Garnett draws on the theories of Frederic Jameson in his exploration of the fantasies of Richard Marsh and Bram Stoker; R. J. Ellis uses a technique of discourse analysis drawing on the theories of Pierre Macherey and Michel Foucault to drive his analysis of *Dune*; Jenny Wolmark mobilises feminist theories in her examination of Vonda McIntyre's *Superluminal*, as does Anne Cranny-Francis when exploring Suzy McKee Charnas's *Walk to the End of the World* as an interrogation of patriarchal discourses. Sometimes the interaction is more a matter of ambience, as when Patrick Parrinder considers how science fiction has interacted with discursive representations of the role of the scientist in Western culture, or when Marleen Barr's comparison of Thomas Berger and Marge Piercy is enabled both by a clear familiarity with the field of gender relations defined by feminist debates and by her attendant recourse to the employment of a transactive critical analysis. A key example of the beneficial results of exploring this middle ground is the profit realised by Jerzy Jarzębski in his analysis of Stanislaw Lem, through building his analysis on the recognition that language as a sign system on the one hand, and reality on the other, are in an unstable, potentially ludic, relationship. Elsewhere such interaction with post-structuralist exegesis is made available by the juxtaposition of essays within this volume, as when Thomas and Alice Clareson's analysis of the pioneering feminist perspectives in John Wyndham's lesser-known fiction is read in conjunction with the debates about gender roles and hence about power and ideology, conducted by Marleen Barr and Jenny Wolmark.

Of course, the overview that this volume provides is not as integrated as this brief resumé might suggest, and two essays do not so readily fit into this depiction of negotiation at various removes. Robert Philmus's essay points to intriguing intertextual links between Ursula K. Le Guin's *The Dispossessed* and Eliot's *Four Quartets*, in its complex analysis of the novel's interactions with various philosophies of temporality, thereby demonstrating that science fiction as a genre can establish concrete narrative explorations of the highly abstract theories of more 'privileged' areas of discourse. This essay, along with Stanislaw Lem's on H. G. Wells's *The War of the Worlds*, also provides a useful reminder that the evolution of post-structuralist critical theory challenges (in a multiplicity of ways), but has by no means dislodged or as yet fundamentally disrupted, the development of longer-established mainstream theories of literary analysis.

Lem's creative re-reading of Wells's seminal text reminds us strongly of Joseph Skvorecky's comparably creative interpretation of the significance of the harlequin Russian's admiration for Kurtz in Conrad's *Heart of Darkness*.[2] Lem's resulting essay could be categorised as a species of interactive criticism, perhaps (an idea gaining authority from the fact that Lem subsequently has turned away from science fiction writing or criticism), but this would be to neglect the meta-textual national and political implications of this 1974 Polish commentary upon Wells's themes of conquest, dominance and subordination. Even in this, however, it can be seen that a dialogue is available between Lem's essay and the other contributions in this volume, in which the investigation of such themes is recurrent.

The principles of selection informing this collection necessarily absolved us from attempting to achieve what was never effectively attainable – a comprehensive survey of the genre. This volume does not investigate the genre's development in the period between 1900 and 1950 – of the (multi-stemmed) 'trunk' into which our roots feed and from which our branches have developed. Science fiction critics' depiction of this 'trunk' have always, in a sense, been 'ahead' (if relatively untheoretically) of the critical game in their recurrent focus on the significance of not only production, the reader and reader response (fanzines and the concept of a horizon of expectation might, for example, be held to be inextricably interwoven in what has to be regarded as a most interesting symbiosis), but also in the contribution genre studies can make to the process of comprehending a text's location in its multiple contexts.[3]

These justifications, however, do finally leave the full dimensions of the 'trunk' to be guessed at. All this collection offers in this area is an outline of some of its significant features, via the useful unitary perspective offered in Patrick Parrinder's essay. What is gained, we feel, more than compensates. Placing branches next to roots makes very apparent the way in which science fiction's mongrel origins in Victorian fiction's sub-genres provide, at a deep-structural level, the generic resources for this form of fictional writing to function in the post-Second World War period as a flexible platform for discursive representations of issues and problems confronting the societies in which they were written. Science fiction's interrogative capacity is thus recurrently enabled in ways which, whilst not always coherent, amount (symbolically or allegorically) to defamiliarisations – a capacity that brings the wheel round full circle, since the genre's Victorian progenitors precisely functioned in this way. We believe this recurrent capacity of science fiction comes through in all of the analyses in this volume. And this is also why we find ourselves in fundamental agreement with Doris Lessing's aphorism, which we also offer as the epigram to this whole collection.

NOTES

1. Doris Lessing, quoted in 'Sayings of the Week', *Observer*, 13 November 1988, p. 15, cols 3–4.
2. Joseph Skvorecky, *The Engineer of Human Souls* (London: Chatto and Windus, 1984); Joseph Conrad, *Heart of Darkness* (1902; rpt. Harmondsworth, Middx: Penguin, 1973).
3. See, in particular, Brain W. Aldiss, *Billion Year Spree* (London: Weidenfeld and Nicolson, 1973); Kingsley Amis, *New Maps of Hell* (London: Gollancz, 1961); Paul A. Carter, *The Creation of Tomorrow* (New York: Columbia University Press, 1977); Patrick Parrinder (ed.), *Science Fiction: A Critical Guide* (London: Longman, 1979); Patrick Parrinder, *Science Fiction: Its Criticism and Teaching* (London: Methuen, 1980); Robert Scholes and Eric S. Rabkin, *Science Fiction: History, Science, Vision* (New York: Oxford University Press, 1977); Darko Suvin, *Metamorphoses of Science Fiction* (New Haven, Conn.: Yale University Press, 1979).

Part One
Some Roots: Victorian Science Fiction and Fantasy

2

Counter-Projects: William Morris and the Science Fiction of the 1880s

DARKO SUVIN

This essay is based on two of my books, *Metamorphoses of Science Fiction* and *Victorian Science Fiction in the UK*.[1] In the first, I argue at length for a theoretical and historical definition of science fiction as a fictional genre 'whose necessary and sufficient conditions are the presence and interaction of estrangement and cognition, . . . whose main formal device is an imaginative framework alternative to the author's empirical environment', and which is narratively dominated by a hegemonic 'fictional *novum* (novelty, innovation) validated by cognitive logic' (*MSF*, pp. 7–8, 63). I further argue that this means a feedback oscillation between two realities. The science fiction narrative actualises a different – though historical and not transcendental – world corresponding to different human relationships and cultural norms. However, in science fiction the 'possible world' induced by the narrative is imaginable only as an interaction between two factors: the conception which the collective social addressee of a text has of empirical reality, and the narratively explicit modifications that a given science fiction text supplies to this initial conception. The resulting alternate reality or possible world is, in turn, not a prophecy or even extrapolation but an *analogy* to unrealised possibilities in the addressee's or implied reader's empirical world; however empirically unverifiable the narrative agents, objects or events of science fiction may be, their constellation in all still (literally) significant cases shapes a parable about ourselves.

If this is accepted, then utopian fiction is not only, historically, one of the roots of science fiction, it is also, logically if retroactively, one of its forms, that validated by and only by sociopolitics; it is 'the sociopolitical subgenre of science fiction' (*MSF*, p. 61, and cf. the whole chapter leading up to this). Whether this is accepted or not, the historically very intimate connection of Utopian fiction with other forms of science fiction (extraordinary voyage, technological anticipation, anti-Utopia and dystopia, and so on) is surely neither accidental nor insignificant: it reposes, in fact, on the cultural interpenetration of the validating intertextual category of Utopian fiction (sociopolitics) with the validating categories of the mentioned cognate forms (foreign otherness, technocracy or wrong politics). Secondly and possibly more illuminating, the even more intimate connection of the narrative logics at hand is also lawful and significant. Utopian fiction is, narratologically speaking, science fiction in which the always necessary element of explicating the novum (the 'lecture'), which is usually both masked and distributed into various narrative segments, is systematically discursive – that is, is almost the whole plot. As Barthes has indicated in *Sade, Fourier, Loyola*, the plot of utopian fiction is a panoramic sweep conducted along the well-known, culturally current sociopolitical categories (geography, demography, religion, constitution, economics, warfare, and so on).[2]

I hope this introduction may at least sketchily indicate a context more significant than simple facticity or accident for a discussion of some not insignificant relationships between Morris and the science fiction of Victorian Britain of the decade preceding *News from Nowhere*.[3] No doubt, I am thereby just broaching and, in the best case, identifying some foci of the theme which could be called 'Morris and Intertextuality', worthy of a monograph on *News from Nowhere* in itself. My essay will have two different but, I hope, complementary parts, both of them arising from data presented and works whose context is discussed at more length in my *Victorian Science Fiction*. I shall deal first with the image of William Morris found in two brief science fiction 'alternative histories' which postulate a bad socialist government in a near-future UK. Secondly, I shall discuss two works of dystopian science fiction, elements from which I believe were refunctioned in *News from Nowhere*. This may allow some more general conclusions about a two-way relationship between Morris and the science fiction discourse of his time, which appears to have been more intimate than heretofore assumed.

I MORRIS AS A NARRATIVE AGENT IN 1880s' SCIENCE FICTION

(i) A booklet of 35 pages was published in 1884 under the title of *The Socialist Revolution of 1888, by an Eye-Witness.*[4] Two of the main investigators of the domain identify its author as 'Fairfield', no first name, an attribution which I have been unable to confirm or disprove by going through all the biographical handbooks and annual lists of Victorian professions from 1848 to 1900 inclusive. It belongs to the form or sub-genre I have called the 'Alternative History'. I have defined it as that science fiction sub-genre in which an alternative locus, sharing the material and causal verisimilitude of the writer's empirical world, is used to articulate different possible solutions to such societal problems which are of sufficient importance to require an alteration in the overall history of the narrated world. After 1880, with the rise of social tensions in the whole of Britain, this form became dominant within science fiction at the momentary expense of the Future War and the more lasting expense of the moribund Extraordinary Voyage form. More precisely pinpointed, *The Socialist Revolution of 1888* is, as its title spells out, a near-future variant of this small but recognised form of social discourse. In fact, it is the best from half a dozen short-range historical alternatives which sprang up suddenly in 1884–5, whose choice of fictional form, as well as relative brevity and absence of the author's true name, testifies in all cases to an urgent intervening into the suddenly strengthening British political conflicts.

The plot of the booklet is not unshrewd nor unhumorous: Socialists led by Hyndman and Burne-Jones(!) revolt through mass demonstrations and seize London, the troops fraternise with them. After one week, they hold a plebiscite which votes in Socialism as against Individualism with 7.5 against 5.5 million votes. The new, clearly quite legal government repeals private property, at which – in a transposition of the Paris Commune events – all British ships flee the country with the rich and their possessions on board. Morris is appointed Minister for Industries in the Socialist government of 1888 as the only practical person in the whole crowd who knows how to keep the expenses of production down. This is not what one might call a 'Cold Civil War' text, since it gives explicit credit to the Socialists for genuine goodwill and also implies that their mass support stems from their addressing genuine grievances. Further, it is written from the vantage-point of a high civil servant who, as secretary of the Cabinet, sees the personal working out of political manoeuvres. However it has an anti-Socialist horizon, and it depicts how societal confusion results from the loss of affluence, international financial pressures and increase of State meddling *à la* Henry George. The government therefore becomes generally detested and, in particular, all the women turn unanimously against it. The passive resistance of the people, as well as of the army and police, forces Hyndman's government to call another plebiscite which abolishes Socialism by a vote of 9.5 million to 100 thousand (it is unclear what happened to the *c*.3.5 million voters who have disappeared since the first plebiscite; presumably they are those who fled the country, rather than abstainers). The new Liberal parliament eschews vengeance against the toppled regime, and in fact keeps one important measure enacted under it: Irish Home Rule. We must today sigh at the bloodless and, except for the initial catalysis, genuinely democratic nature of all the events, shaped within a fair-minded and, for this sub-genre, unusually even-tempered, if somewhat ironical, liberal ideology. My initial parallel to 1871 Paris (always a presupposition in such UK Alternative Histories) must be therefore amended to the effect that this is a counter-project to the Paris Commune: the British, having a genuine parliamentary tradition, would deal with such an emergency better. This brief text implies, rather than openly states, that even within the 'extravagant doctrinaries' that Socialists notoriously are, there is one queer (but very British) chap, namely Morris, who actually knows that production means. I will refrain from making obviously possible twentieth-century parallels, and only remark that we hear nothing else of interest about Morris: one must assume he carries on in the now liberal England, suitably chastened. At any rate, this text establishes that the theme of a possible non-violent change of regime was current in the social discourse prior to Morris's text.

(ii)   My second text is another booklet of 36 pages, *The Next 'Ninety Three* by W. A. Watlock, published in 1886.[5] It belongs to the same sub-genre of near-future Alternative History, and the discrepancy of there being a writer's signature may be only apparent, since another fruitless search through all the Victorian biographical sources for Britain and its Empire in the British Library (*VSF,* pp. 128–36) turned up no evidence of such a person, so that this might well be a pseudonym. Its discursive strategy can be seen from the subtitles: . . . *or, Crown, Commune, and Colony: Told in a Citizen's Diary*. The *diary* of a *supporter* of the egalitarian regime introduced in Britain by the 1893 Equable Distribution of Property Act is used to present the reader with its thus doubly authenticated results: Ireland is divided into 38 kingdoms, the canny Scots proceed to fuse employers and employed, but the diary naturally focuses on the woes in England. Though divided into Communes, it is subjected to an all-meddling State, which introduces an equal four-hour working day for all, including the intellectuals, who are obliged to do manual work. It is mentioned in passing that William Morris rebels at the iniquities of State oppression and interference and insults the power that be (no particular consequence results from this). Finally, the ground having been prepared by universal discontent, a Colonial Legion from Australia brings about the Restitution of the old regime. This is a much less fair-mind and condemnatory rather than even-tempered companion to the previous booklet, but it will serve to indicate the second, 'conservative' rather than 'liberal', end of the anti-socialist spectrum. It is quite interesting that the liberal took Morris's democratism for granted and focused on his competence in production, while the conservative focused on his (obviously well-known) enmity toward centralised State authority. The strong-arm methods ascribed to all political factions are of a piece with the rhetorical expedient of 'double negation' in which a supporter of the opposed faction both testifies to its illusions and (mis)deeds, and to the inevitable disillusionment. It is a cruder piece of work than the first booklet (possibly written by a sometime Australian?), but it is again not without a certain polemical, anti-revolutionary shrewdness.

II TWO NOVELS OF THE 1880s: SCIENCE FICTION REFUNCTIONED IN *NEWS FROM NOWHERE*

It is well known that Morris wrote *News from Nowhere* among other things (to keep to the science fiction context only) as a counter-project to Bellamy's *Looking Backward*, and it has also been mentioned that he was certainly stimulated by Jefferies's *After London* and possibly by W. H. Hudson's *A Crystal Age* (*MSF*, pp. 187–8).

However it seems to me that these indispensable correlations display a one-sided emphasis on 'high lit.'. We do not have a full overview, I believe, of what Morris read, but it is quite possible that even had he usually read no semi-political or other (by Victorian bourgeois standards) 'lower' fiction – which is a dubious assumption – the mention of his figure and behaviour in these two samples of Alternative History would have been pointed out to him by political comrades or opponents. The case seems much strengthened by his possible (and, in the second case, highly probable) use of two 'farther future' science fiction works by Dering and Besant, the first of these being sufficiently obscure.

(i)   The first work, *In the Light of the Twentieth Century* by Innomina-tus, whom I was able to identify as Edward Heneage Dering, is less interesting.[6] Published in 1886, it is a dream-vision of 155 pages, with a first-person narrator transferred to 1960. Dering himself (1827–92), though the son of an Anglican parson, converted to Catholicism with his wife, novelist Lady Georgiana Chatterton, in 1865, and lived the life of a recluse in a mediaeval country home, reputedly dressed in seventeenth-century costumes. He wrote seven novels to further his views, also one book on Esoteric Buddhism, a pamphlet on philosophy and a book of poems, and he translated from the Italian books on philosophy and political science. (Many more particulars could be found in these books as well as in a memoir of his and another by his wife edited by him, all of which I confess to not having read – cf. *VSF*, pp. 160, 227, 238.) His book is accordingly an eccentric ultramontane tract or anatomy very loosely allied to a novel, which fulminates against 'Corporate freedom' (that is, state control), paganism, free-love flirtation, the outlawing of caritative endeavours, and other pet Catholic horrors. There is much religious discussion on a high philosophical level, and the narrative ends in uprisings of the mob.

However unlikely a companion to Morris's radically different Utopia this might be, there are two elements in it which strike me as significantly similar. First, *the framework*: at the beginning, when the *Ich-Erzähler* comes to the future, his translation is explained to him – by interlocutors who belong to those better, *ergo* unsatisfied, people that even in this soul-destroying future long for happiness – as due to 'the force of your will against the actual state of things at the time, [which] affected your own state of being *in* that time' (*LTC*, p. 8). He had therefore 'reduce[d] the action of the heart', as the fakirs do, and slept his way to the future (*LTC*, p. 9). Further, at the end, as the narrator is being killed by the mob, he awakes: '"Was it a dream? or am I delirious?"', he asks (*LTC*, p. 151). Secondly, *the jump over a second generation*: Dering's narrator is expressly identified as being two generations into the future by the expedient of meeting the grandson of an old friend. This has no constitutive signification in his text, whereas in Morris it is meaningfully refunctioned into an enmity (as Middlebro' put it) against the generation of the fathers, and by metonymy against patriarchal authority (cf. *MSF*, p. 186). None the less, the fact that Morris's main narrative agents are either old men (Old Hammond and William Guest, who is in some powerful ways identified as Hammond's alternative twin) or a range of young people, from children to rather young adults, introduces a discrepancy into the supposed realistic verisimilitude of *News from Nowhere*: the absence of fathers, or for that matter mothers too, that is, of the whole parental or adult generation. This might be partly explained by the incomplete refunctioning of Dering in Morris, due to powerful psychological pressures in the latter. A similar situation might obtain with the fuzziness of the 'dream's' validation: Morris obviously would want to use neither an esoteric 'force of the will' nor a fakir-like catalepsy, but he was too much in a hurry, and probably too little interested, to supply a better motivation. Since I am in this paper not at all interested in positivistic 'sources', I cheerfully acknowledge that this last element is most probably over-determined. Beside and before Bellamy, this was a commonplace of fantasy arrivals into the future, ever since Washington Irving, Edmond About and John Macnie (cf. *VSF, passim*). Most important, Morris's affinity for this feature was probably extra-literary, since it manifested itself from his earliest prose tales and poems onward. Something similar might therefore be said about the verbal parallels describing the narrator's puzzlement upon awakening. 'Was it a dream?' is an utterance to be expected in this situation. Furthermore the famous 'Was it a vision, or a waking dream? / . . . – do I wake or sleep?' ending from Keats's 'Ode to a Nightingale', Morris's great verse exemplar, would in itself have sufficed. None the less, the exact semantic inversion of the second half of Dering's sentence, signalled by Morris's italicisation of *was*, seems more than acciden-tal:

Or indeed *was* it a dream? If so, why was I so conscious all along that I was really seeing all that new life from the outside . . . ?   (*NN*, p. 182)

This 'deconstruction' would fit well with the putative relation Morris–Dering, which I submit is in some ways analogous to the relation Morris–Bellamy: in linguistic terms, semantico-pragmatic opposition coupled with syntactic parallelism: in ideological terms, a counter-project based on the stimulating irritation supplied by some significant formal elements.

(ii)   My most interesting exhibit is Walter Besant's novel *The Inner House*, published by Arrowsmith's as their 1888 Christmas Annual. Popular novelist, historian, and do-gooder, Besant was a well-known Victorian figure so that I need not recount his biography, except to mention that I found him to be the clearest example within this genre – and possibly Victorian fiction as a whole – of social climber as pillar of Establishment, of novelist as virulently reactionary ideologist (cf. *VSF*, pp. 146, 401, 406, *et passim*). The novel begins with the discovery of immortality by the Carlylean Professor Schwarzbaum from Ganzweltweisst am Rhein in 1890. By some unexamined and perhaps burlesquely-meant analogy, this arrests decay in all domains, so that from the second chapter on, the plot moves within an ironic 'perfect Socialism' (*IH*, p. 103). In it there is no property and little work, people all live and dine together and dress uniformly (the famous antheap of petty-bourgeois anti-Socialism), births are allowed only to compensate for a mortal accident, and finally, all emotions – that is, religion, art, love, suffering and competition – are suppressed, so that life carries on in calm stupor. In a narratively clumsy move (perfectly consonant with the other aspects), the story is told in first person by the arch-villain, an ex-servant and – horrors! – scientific egalitarian, the mainstay of the ruling College of Physicians. Of course, this alone would not establish a sufficient parallel between Besant's and Morris's texts, since the whole tradition of future Alternative History (for example, Bellamy and my four texts here) used a first-person narrator for the obvious reason of needing to counteract strangeness.

However, there is another element which suggests this is

employed as another refunctioning by Morris. Almost all the older generation were liquidated in a Great Slaughter at the beginning of Besant's 'socialist' epoch. One of the few left is 'the Curator of the Museum' in the new capital, who lives with his granddaughter Christine. Perusing old books in the Museum, she rediscovers love, honour in battle (sic!), and the dignity of Death. With the help of a sailor who is 'curiously unable to forget the old times' (*IH*, p. 88), she revives the discontent of the quondam 'gentle class' (p. 89) – it is unclear why that class survived the Great Slaughter of the propertied, but Besant is above such petty consistencies since he wants to have both a horrible warning and a happy ending. This class revolts to regain leadership, land, wealth and, for good measure, arts, amusement and love. The 'Inner House' of the title is where the Secret of Life is kept; the rebels, not being able to bring the people over to their side, secede from the rule of the College of Physicians. I think it is beyond doubt that Old Hammond and Clara, as well as their location at the country's central Museum – the only source of a historical memory otherwise absent from the new society – are, once more, a refunctioning of the old curator and his granddaughter. Possibly, a few other touches in *News from Nowhere* may also be counter-projects to Besant's; for example, the emphasis on revival of love and jealousy may have suggested Morris's throwback murderer in Chapter 24, as well as the backsliding due to book-reading by the grumbling *laudator temporis acti* in Chapter 22, who is so eloquently put down by Clara in favour of the Book of Nature.

III SOME CONCLUDING INDICATIONS ON MORRIS AND ON COUNTER-PROJECTS

I hope to have indicated the possibility, and perhaps the probability or the near-certainty, of a few matters which might fruitfully engage further attention by the community of Morris critics. First, it is well known that Morris used some elements from the More-to-Bellamy Utopian panoramas or the Jefferies-cum-Hudson devolutionary anticipations. But in addition, beyond the testimonies to Morris's image to be gleaned from the two works considered in Section I, these works also suggest the possibility that Morris was alerted through them (if in no other ways) to the existence of para-literary forms such as the Alternative History or the science fiction genre as a whole. The discussion in Section II suggests, secondly, that Morris indeed knew at least the very 'middlebrow' work of Besant and probably that of Dering. Further, it shows that Morris found ways to use at least Besant's 'keeper of past knowledge' motif in the same way as he used the 'sleeping into the future' frame of Bellamy's, and possibly also of Dering's and some other writers – in a 'contrary' proceeding of subversion and inversion to which I have applied the term of *counter-project*. Finally, I suspect he may also have in the same manner reused the evacuation of the adult generation from Dering's text.

Of course, Morris not only stood the elements which he had (entirely or incompletely) refunctioned from Dering and Besant ideologically on their heads but also, and just as important, made triumphant sense of most of them. But this does not prevent us from using the insights obtained from the existence of such refunctionings for two purposes: first, to explain some minor but not uninteresting discrepancies in *News from Nowhere*; and secondly, to follow Morris's very process of refunctioning. It is instructive on its own as the work of an artist who refuses the fetish of individualist originality. He proceeded, in my opinion quite rightly too, as all the great creators have done: he made lion-flesh of digested mutton. With Molière, he could have indeed exclaimed: *Je prends mon bien où je le trouve.*

Morris's stance is also, last but not at all least, instructive as a formal procedure originating in the *ethos* of dialectical negation and sublation which seems common to consistent socialists, from Marx to Brecht (from whose playwriting practice I borrowed the term), and which includes William Morris as one of its best practitioners. I would like to end this essay – appropriately enough for one on Morris – with a pointer to possible genera discussions about this procedure. A counter-project can, I think, be provisionally defined as *the use of some significant aspects or relationships from one universe of discourse for contrary axiological conclusions in and by means of another universe of discourse; the induced value-judgements being intended to shape the reader's pragmatic orientation.* As a rule, the discursive aspects will be narrative agents and/or narrative spacetime – for example, in this case, a grandfather–granddaughter pair in a future country's only museum and repository of information about the past. However, the notion of a universe of discourse is not limited to fictional 'possible worlds', but comprises also non-fictional (doxological) 'possible worlds'. As suggested, this will be particularly clear in the case of writers strongly committed to a salvational doctrine or belief about human relationships in everyday 'reality' – for example, Socialists. The counter-project is obviously always some kind of inversion, and I would further speculate it might have an affinity with the rhetorical trope of *chiasmus*, for example, Marx's *Poverty of Philosophy* as counter-project to (rebuttal of) Proudhon's *Philosophy of Poverty*. It must be added, none the less, first, that we are here entering into extremely complex philosophical debates about 'possible worlds', and secondly, that I know of no sustained discussion of the discursive form of counter-project; these first notes of mine are thus mainly a call for such a discussion, in an informed feedback with social history. In any such discussion, the whole opus of William Morris, and in particular *News from Nowhere*, will be a fulcrum.

NOTES

1. Darko Suvin, *Metamorphoses of Science Fiction* (New Haven, Conn.: Yale University Press, 1979); Darko Suvin, *Victorian Science Fiction* (Boston, Mass.: G. K. Hall, 1983). Future references to these two books will appear in the text, preceded by the initials *MSF* and *VSF* respectively.
2. Roland Barthes, *Sade, Fourier, Loyola*, trans. R. Miller (New York: Hill and Wang, 1976).
3. William Morris, *News from Nowhere* (1890) rpt., ed. James Redmond (London: Routledge and Kegan Paul, 1970). Future references will appear in the text, preceded by the initials *NN*.
4. Anon., *The Socialist Revolution of 1888, by an Eye-Witness* (London: Harrison, 1884); cf. Suvin, *Victorian Science Fiction*, pp. 25, 127.
5. W. A. Watlock, *The Next 'Ninety-Three* (London: Field and Tuer, 1886).
6. Innominatus [Edward Heneage Dering], *In the Light of the Twentieth Century* (London: Hodges, 1886). Future references will appear in the text, preceded by the initials *LTC*.
7. Walter Besant, *The Inner House* (Bristol and London: Arrowsmith, 1888). Future references will appear in the text, preceded by the initials *IH*.

3

H. G. Wells's *The War of the Worlds*[1]

STANISLAW LEM

The War of the Worlds, H. G. Wells's most brilliant work, is at the same time one of the few novels which have transcended the fantastic nature of their premises and become a part of world literature.[2] This double assertion requires justification. Indeed, my opening claim may come as a surprise, since Wells wrote many books, of which this is one of the earliest – the fourth, following *The Time Machine* (1895), *The Invisible Man* (1897) and *The Island of Dr Moreau* (1897).[3]

According to the book's dedication, Wells owed the idea of the work to his brother; the 28-year-old writer planned his work very carefully over a long period, during extensive walks and bicycle rides through the countryside around Woking, in order to acquaint himself with the terrain that his Martians were to invade first, inspecting the topography of the region like a strategist on the day before a battle. One can only envy such a scrupulous approach to the matter, but from this alone one is unable to comprehend the visionary achievement of *The War of the Worlds*. Thousands of writers have since tackled the theme that Wells introduced – humanity in collision with extra-terrestial intelligence – and yet, nearly a century later, this book still rises above the multitude of science fiction works like a peak, conquered only once. That is why one can say without exaggeration that the more one becomes familiar with modern fiction, the more one can admire the superior vantage point which this work secured. The achievements of later authors, who could rely upon a range of knowledge unknown to Wells and artistic techniques developed subsequently over nearly a century, have not surpassed his.

Thus it is that we face a double riddle, unable to grasp why Wells himself never again produced a work as monolithic and dynamic as *The War of the Worlds*, or why the book from which it might be said modern science fiction originated still remains unsurpassed. This riddle has intrigued me, or perhaps one should rather say, unnerved me over the years. Vision must blend with intellect in a specific way, in a distinctly risky balance, to produce a masterpiece not only recognisable to and never fading in the eyes of future generations, but rather still accumulating new levels of meaning unavailable to his contemporaries. The passage of historical time acts upon literature like a wind on a fire; it extinguishes small flames and helps fan the large. In fiction this process takes on peculiarly drastic forms: realistic works of limited aspirations become dated to the point of inauthenticity; fantasy, on the other hand, undergoes a more vicious process of degeneration, in that what was originally supposed to be serious, or even sinister, can now only cause ridicule. While such degradation occurs gradually, books do not disappear, but change readership, like those novels by Jules Verne written for adults but predominantly read today by children.

The War of the Worlds was not however ousted from the position it attained – certainly the Second World War, which proved to be such a destructive proving-ground for so many realistic works, revealed a new, cruel, contemporary relevance, by validating, in unforeseen circumstances, its interpretation of the philosophy of history. So it was, for people of my generation in Poland, that few works of fiction could be read without the reader having to flinch – the result of a sense of malignancy, of fatalism and, at the same time, of superiority deriving from personal experience, intimating to us the secrets of the mechanism of cultural destruction. It did not matter that what was crushing us was an invasion of creatures of our own species filled with a doctrine of genocide, whilst in Wells's novel annihilation on this scale had come from an imaginary invasion from Mars. The young man composing *The War of the Worlds* was gifted with a rare sociological comprehension in creating his work without any experience of war. It is precisely those who have experienced modern Fascistic total war – including attempts to secure the complete destruction of the conquered – who *recognised* in this 'fictional' work what they themselves had undergone: unforgettable scenes of chaotic mass retreat; social disintegration; the rapid destruction of a way of life and of national traditions; the reduction to ashes of what we believe to be fundamental human rights; how in such social agony symptoms of dishonourable meanness conjoin with equally unlimited heroism; and to what extreme attitudes this complete calamity leads. Wells managed, epically, to reach out from his own time, intuitively, to both individual and collective responses within a crushed culture, and not simply to the conditions experienced in a society defeated in war – which has, ultimately, some bounds to its attendant cruelty. A work which is able to attain such subsequent validation of what were, when it was written, hypothetical representations, must be counted as great literature.

The war which we experienced was incontrovertibly real, leaving behind piles of documents, and yet I often cannot read books by writers of the postwar generation without anger, because I have a strong feeling that they are full of lies. It also seems that no effort of imagination – in the sphere of realistic writing – can substitute for personal experience of the fracturing and destroying of an era. Yet Wells's novel undeniably gives the lie to such views. I thus want to emphasise Wells's laconic down-to-earth ability to portray both the collapse of civilisation and the nightmarish ease of its destruction, the essential fragility of the structure of our heritage, and how a very few precisely aimed blows are sufficient to demolish it. (The reason why I dwell on this relatively 'non-fantastic' side of the problem is that *The War of the Worlds* owes its viability to such verisimilitude. As we can see, only a tale based on the absolute realism of every detail, credible in its every depiction of individual and collective reactions, can attain the rank of a masterpiece. The visionary character of fantasy may thus be verified – if it manages to concoct out of its fictitious elements a reality that will be confirmed by historical experience. The fictive may indeed create a portrait that turns out to be truly authentic and inescapable – and in this resides the concise formula for Wells's greatness.)

Consequently I identify the human race – treated as an 'inferior race', a species which cannot demand or expect anything from its conquerors – as the hero of *The War of the Worlds*. I make this claim, of course, looking at the book with knowledge gained from personal experience, not from other, more abstract perspectives, which for me are secondary to reality, for reality functions as the ultimate assessor of literary worth as much as any other worth. Therefore I conclude that *The War of the Worlds* owes its vitality to its visionary realism, its enduring capacity to advance beyond the terms of reference available to it at its time of composition. This is the reason why for me the novel is now less fantastic than it was 30 years ago, when I first read it, and why I still find it relevant.

In inventing the invaders from Mars, Wells in turn faced another exceedingly difficult task, because the realist venture embarked upon demanded simultaneously hard facts and the creation of a fantastic 'otherness' that prevents the reader responding to the cosmic invaders as no more than scarecrows, mere mummery. This means that both they and their equipment had to be provided with a sense of inhumanity at the same time as functionality. As the creator of Martian war technology, Wells again is unsurpassed. Their War machines and Work machines are for us today the sort of things that we might expect to be able to create in the near future – not in terms of exact appearance, but in terms of their function. Hence the original Work machines are pediculatory mobiles, and prototypes for these are actually now in existence. The Work machines would be recognisable to a modern cybernetist as a type of 'symbiotic': a union of a machine and a living being, designed to undertake a whole range of functions, not merely locomotion, through the abilities granted by its 'sham musculature of discs in an elastic sheath' (*WW*, p. 138). In the Heat-Ray one can recognise the power of the laser; Wells's 'Black Smoke' equates with poison gas. It should be emphasised that these figments of his technological imagination not only achieve authenticity futurologically, but also because of the graphically shocking realisation given to them.

As for me, I confess that there is nothing more weird in the Martians' depiction than the incredible contrast between their individual, physiologically ponderous helplessness, and the agility of their colossal Fighting Machines, those tripods resembling nothing on earth. A modern expert will see in these machines the incorporation of the most advanced concepts, above all in bionics – artificial imitation of and improvement upon such solutions as have been created by the process of the evolution of life.

And yet it is not this technological set of ideas, foreseeing potential inventions in the future, upon which the novel stands, but upon a faultless merging of all its 'realities' into a whole, because each aspect singly serves the whole, and each has also an individually appropriate scale. I touch here upon a certain, incontrovertible yet elusive dimension of creative writing, which cannot in the final analysis be explained discursively, but which I will nevertheless attempt to describe from two different angles of approach. From one angle, it can be seen that a successful work, in a sense, objectifies itself: now 'independent' from its creator, it gains progressively in authority, and is able – as I have tried to emphasise previously – to tell future readers things that even the author himself could not at the time have known with clarity. Thus it achieves a certain kind of kinship with universal scientific theory, which the future will verify on the basis of facts yet to be discovered at that time. Approaching this elusive dimension from a second angle, it can be seen that, in all spheres of activity, in the social whole, in its constituent groups, and in individual cases, the structure that always manifests itself is order admixed with chance, accident with predictability, the planned with the unforeseen yet predestined. Reality has its own iron laws, and its whims, order in chaos, and chaos in logic. Necessarily this complicated mixture of heterogeneous elements is difficult to signify in narrative, and in fiction this task is most difficult of all. Nobody, as far as I know, has analysed Wells's account of the Martians' war tactics in defeating the human race, as a historian would in his description of great battles. Thus I can only venture to say that the actions on both sides seem to me to be underpinned by a weight of probability; Wells introduced the means, strategy and tactics in the book's action as are necessary to achieve convincingly the Martian victory so disastrous to the human race.

Since I have paid such homage to this masterpiece, let me be allowed to point out what I regard as its only fault: I am struck by the Martians' total lack of culture, understood, of course, not in anthropocentric terms of cultural solidarity, because that would be a nonsensical postulate. The conception of the Martians' social organisation in this novel is collective. They are sexless creatures, breeding by germination, and they do not appear to recognise any ethics apart from the strictly objective ethics of co-operation; consequently, on the Earth this means they become completely militarised, because their co-operative objective here is to work together to effect the planet's conquest. Creatures so completely reduced down, in the motivations that can be deduced to be underlying their actions and thoughts, to values that can only be termed instrumental, seem to me impossible, or at least unconvincing. The mind, if it is really to be regarded as a mind, must show a propensity to extend beyond the instruments which it generates in order to sustain life. The mind then must be *curious*, and this characteristic categorically contains some measure of disinterestedness. This may be supported by reference to the history of science; if it were concerned always and exclusively with what seemed to promise the discovery of something with practical utility, it would not get far in its evolution. Thus, the Martians should at least be interested in humans, to the extent that we ourselves are interested in apparently useless crustaceans or vegetation, studying them as much out of intellectual curiosity as from a physiological viewpoint, and not simply sucking out their juices once this has been identified as tolerable nourishment. Yet the Martians behave in what seems to be a purely instinctive way, as if they were creatures akin to vampires, and this just does not equate with my concept of the mind, even were this to be exercised within the framework of an extremely cruel morality. Nor do they leave behind any trace of their own culture, no significant monuments, no documents – absolutely nothing, apart from mysterious machines. Wells reduces them down to a purely aggressive functionalism, as though they themselves were programmed machines, not great intelligences. I presume that he did this because he was simply not interested in the nature of a civilisation from another planet, its values and its possible goals. Here at last we unearth – deeply hidden! – an allegorical intention of this work, revealed in the complete indifference of the writer to the questions just raised. The Martians function as a tool, committing a horrific experiment on behalf of the writer, in order to open his readers' eyes – that is, to place their insignificant achievements in the context of history, terrestial as well as cosmic. This line of thought enables us to identify certain recurrent concerns in Wells's novels. The artilleryman, one of the novel's 'heroes', in conversation with the narrator, foresees a division in humanity: after the defeat, one half, remaining under Martian rule, will become their 'beasts' for slaughter, as well as their servants, falling into a form of mystic psychosis, as a last asylum of the mind, consequently degenerating into immediate promiscuity or sinking into degradation. The other half will hide underground, in old sewers, and these fugitives will be hunted down by human beings especially trained as slaves for the task.

The deservedly high critical esteem enjoyed by Kafka's story, 'In the Penal Settlement',[4] which has been justified by the observation that it foresaw the concentration camps (and therefore the *extent* of the betrayal which human beings are capable of perpetrating on each other), encourages me to observe that Wells had already suggested a quarter of a century earlier the same extremity, in his artilleryman's vision of people hunting down others for the Martians; certainly it is clear that, despite his melioristic humanism, Wells did not fundamentally hold a very high opinion of human nature.

This division of humanity, only fleetingly outlined in the artillery-man's desperate reaction to catastrophe, Wells had already depicted more extensively in his earlier *The Time Machine*, in its portrait of humanity 'Eight Hundred Thousand Years hence' (*TM*, p. 52), when the Eloi live in an apparent Arcadia, above an underworld swarming with Morlocks. One may thus presume that in such binary divisions Wells adopts a mythical schema – Arcadia/Hades, Heaven/Hell. However, *The Time Machine* presents not a real paradise but an ironic caricature, since the innocent and beautiful Eloi are also the dull and thoughtless descendants of the ruling class, whilst the Morlocks, degenerate proletarians, in maintaining civilisation's mechanical infastructure, only sustain the Eloi's existence in order to feed off their flesh. *The War of the Worlds* expresses the antithesis of this concept: only underground can humanity retain the remnants of independence, after its defeat. Within this binary schema, and also common to both these books, is the alarming motif of cannibalism: Morlocks consume Elois as Martians do humans.

No denigration of Wells's achievement is intended if I now say I find this excessive – and not on the basis of sanctimonious moralising, since no writer or critic, particularly in our own era, has the *right* to shut his eyes against indications of the emergence of cruelties that are always potentially present in any civilisation. But in this case, the vampire-like physiology of the Martians is unneccessary; first, because it would be completely improbable that a creature evolving in one planetary environment could serve as nourishment for an organism that derives from a different planet. Even on the Earth, with its single evolutionary tree with common roots, not every kind of species can prey on every other, and, by extrapolation, this must be held to be even more the case with species that are evolutionarily discrete, both anatomically and physiologically. Secondly, though this might sound trivial, any biologist knows the low nutritional value of blood; an organism the size of a man or a Martian would have to consume a minimum of a dozen litres of blood daily to survive. Moreover, the direct transmission of this alien blood into the Martians' blood vessels is biologically implausible. These are purely scientific objections; more important to me is that, from the narratological point of view, the bloodthirstiness of the Martians is absolutely unnecessary, achieving, in my view, only a cheap, but calculated, dramatic effect. But here we are dealing with problems of preference in composition that are not subject to verification by any objective criteria.

Perhaps I will now allow myself, at the end of this section of criticism, a shameless authorial invasion of the text: if it were I who had written *The War of the Worlds*, I would have created Martians who would have *investigated* humanity, if necessary by means of vivisection, rather than make them cannibalistic; and, more importantly, I would not have introduced the conquest of humanity as the objective of the invaders – a conquest which now seems so similar to the genocidal projects of Fascists. Rather, I would overtly describe only the Martians' military activities; their actual motives would be camouflaged. The Martians' objective would not be the conquering and destruction of human civilisation, nor enslavement of the population, nor the creation of a 'food reservoir'. Instead, their objective would not be crudely anthropomorphic. In attempting this project, one would need to depict an interaction between humans and Martians somewhat analogous to the events which occurred on the Bikini atoll in 1946. When the Americans evacuated the inhabitants of Bikini prior to the nuclear explosion, the latter were not fully aware of and could not comprehend the nature of the activity occurring around them, even though in a brief moment they were being deprived of all their territory and their livelihoods. Thus, in my hypothetical novel, the Martians would not act as in Wells's novel, but simply deceive humanity, to prevent any interference with their plan to turn the Earth into their base. The rationale for this 'plot-reconstruction' would be the principle that different societies' paths of social evolution create quite distinct behaviour patterns. Consequently, the outcome of interactions between radically different societies is an asymmetric lack of understanding: those who become swept up into the course of historical events at a particular juncture cannot comprehend the objectives of those who have intervened, because the former lack the necessary knowledge and concepts. Such a schema seems to me more rational and artistically restrained, since in the resulting scenario, civilisation on the Earth is simply swept away by the invader as an obstacle to be annihilated – and for no other reason. I realise, of course, how 'ahistorical' my remarks are; such a conception was not a real possibility in Wells's time.

Wells declined as a writer in his subsequent fiction, although he continued to produce inventive work. However, he never again achieved such an enduring and penetrative exploration, and I now wish, albeit tentatively, to advance a hypothesis as to the reason for this. At the time of Queen Victoria's jubilee, representing as it did the apogee of Victorianism, when the British Empire appeared to be the mightiest power on this planet at its very fulcrum of cocksureness, yet bearing within it the seeds of incipient stagnation, when nineteenth-century English bumptiousness had reached a peak of self-satisfaction, Wells, in order to escape from these narrow, coagulating horizons, inflicted blow after blow upon the jingoistic pride of his contemporaries. The first blow – from the time dimension – came with the novel *The Time Machine*, in which he envisaged the disappearance of an epoch – of a social structure, which, although apparently enduring, will yet vanish. At the same time, he extrapolated from the order which he found – bourgeois and proletariat – the evolution of Eloi and Morlocks. Then, via the fictional protrait of an extra-terrestial invasion, he inflicted another blow – from the space dimension – *The War of the Worlds*. In this novel, we discover, he clearly intimates in the form of mock citations from scientific periodicals that his representation of the Martian invasion (their outward appearance and behaviour), whilst overtly the manifestation of the catastrophic impact of another, extra-terrestrial culture upon Earth's, was also a representation of a possible future for humanity.

Thus, in these works, Wells has twice cast the same basic idea into the form of a realistically presented allegory. With these visions he strikes at fossilising Victorianism, like an Archimedes of literature, searching for such points of leverage as would enable him to disturb the dominant, though not universal, torpor of Victorian social complacency. But this was still insufficient for Wells. From the visionary artist, conveying his argument allegorically, he changed into a proponent of social meliorism. With this change, his artistry became subordinated to his intellectual preoccupations: his literary masterpieces gave way to belletristic tracts describing social Utopias and anti-Utopias in which critical analysis and a discursive rationality displaced the deployment of imaginative insight (as, for example, in *The First Men in the Moon*,[5] a book openly directed against the Earth's social structures, which, just because this is so overtly its subject, ultimately disintegrates narratologically, becoming ever less convincing as it becomes more discursive). The intellectual achievement of these later works must command some respect, but his polemical intention had given his writings a distinctly Utopian leaning. In this way, he acted as though he believed in the possibility of changing the world through literature. Such dreaming, the most ambitious that a writer can aspire to, must unfortunately remain only a dream. Wells broke the backs of his later fictions by imposing upon them this polemical weight, which they could not bear. His books became instruments through which he directly sought to convert, through persuasive instruction.

Subsequently he again switched direction, from polemical narratives rooted in a belief about the potential of art, to the production of what amounted to sociological and anthropological discussions, themselves generating such great masterpieces as his *A Short History of the World*.[6] But, throughout these transitions, he never again produced as great a novel as *The War of the Worlds*. Thus one may say that he offered up his creativity and talent to the world in such a way that it never received the full benefit. Rather, he sacrificed his highest abilities – as a writer of fiction – and instead sought to persuade, lecture, reprimand and provoke thought through his writings. These projects caused him, by the end of his life, to sink into a profound pessimism about the future of our species. This became particularly acute after he had witnessed the explosive release of atomic energy, and proved to be a species of pessimism to which nobody, or rather almost nobody, wished to listen. This sort of commitment, based on a desire to see society's organisation given some moral grounding, was, of course, Utopian. Wishing too much to help humanity through his writing, Wells had in fact, in his masterpiece, instead advanced only a devastating analysis of its potentialities.

This is of course only my own hypothesis, based on a belief that one can expect quite a lot from literature, but only within certain bounds. Demanding more forces fiction beyond these limits, yet should it stray beyond these only minimally, its potential as serious literature will suffer drastically, and cause it to risk the charge of being no more than a childish imagining of disaster.

In an attempt to solve the second riddle mentioned at the very start of this essay – namely, why only Wells, and no one subsequently, achieved a perspective upon civilisation comparable in its penetration to that realised by *The War of the Worlds* – I was tempted to write a monograph on science fiction writing.[7] My resulting debate extended over almost a thousand pages, and it is pointless to attempt to rehearse it here, though it is necessary to make a brief allusion to the fact that it analysed some contributory factors of a literary historical nature, to which need to be added others, such as commercial considerations. These cumulatively played a part in the degeneration of fantasy, until it sunk to the level of being artistic trash, intellectual rubbish; but to understand this process more fully it is necessary to add that, during the period of 90 years which divides us from the genesis of *The War of the Worlds*, the situation of European society has undergone a series of radical transformations. Wells wrote in a world by and large convinced of its own stability and permanence, so much so that it discounted the risk of cataclysm or metamorphosis. That is why his first, most astute masterpieces sought to broaden horizons, and foretell a forthcoming disruption of civilised order. We, however, live in a world in which nothing is as certain as this: that tomorrow will not be a repetition of today. The present-day consciousness of change – a consciousness promoted by the very acceleration of the rate of change (which in itself does not show any tendency to stand still, nor is it apparently amenable to social restraint) – is now a common possession.

Given such radical alterations to the rate of change, and of consciousness of such change, it is therefore not really possible for subsequent works to emulate to any significant degree *The War of the Worlds*, written in an age predominantly convinced of its own stability, just as one cannot awaken the already awake, nor discover America for the second time. Therefore successors to *The War of the Worlds* can only possess an epigonic continuity with their model; seen from the perspective of the philosophy of history, they are irrelevant, for to search in the depths of space for the origins of the catastrophe that has befallen mankind subsequent to Wells's work would be like using a match for illumination in the full glare of searchlights. It would certainly be possible to tackle in literature the problems of the collapse of civilisations, and their intellectual attainments, on *other* planets, but not in the same kind of (terrestrial) conjunction established by H. G. Wells. The very growth of our own terrestrial powers threatens us more than sufficiently, so that allegorical tales, which childishly try to reverse the tide of history by beating it with a stick, now seem useless. Wells, as I have stated, prophesied continuous wholesale change in an epoch of relative stagnation. We are now inhabitants of Wells's prophesied world of change, and consequently cannot turn to guidance from the originator and creator of the epitome of the genre. We can only admire his youthful masterpiece, and learn to derive instruction from the conscientiousness it incorporates and the power of vision achieved by the intelligence it brings to bear upon the issues it raises. For all other, supposedly free-wheeling, flights of fancy are basically escapes from the burning issues of the world, evasions which refuse to recognise that they are desertions.

Translated by John Coutouvidis, assisted by Franz Rottensteiner, R. J. Ellis and Rhys Garnett.

NOTES

1. H. G. Wells, *Wojna Swiatów*, with an epilogue by Stanislaw Lem (Krakow: Wydawnictwo Literackie, 1974).
2. H. G. Wells, *The War of the Worlds* (1898; rpt. London: Pan Books, 1980). Future references will appear in the text, preceded by the initials *WW*.
3. H. G. Wells, *The Time Machine* (London: Heinemann, 1895); H. G. Wells, *The Invisible Man* (London: Pearson, 1897) H. G. Wells, *The Island of Dr Moreau* (London: Heinemann, 1897). Future references to *The Time Machine* will appear in the text, preceded by the initials *TM*.
4. Franz Kafka, 'In the Penal Settlement', in *In the Penal Settlement: Tales and Short Prose Works*, trans. E. Kaiser and E. Wilkins (London: Secker and Warburg, 1949).
5. H. G. Wells, *The First Men in the Moon* (London: Newnes, 1901).
6. H. G. Wells, *A Short History of the World* (London: Cassell, 1922).
7. Stanislaw Lem, *Fantastyka i Futurologia* (Kraków: Wydawnictwo Literackie, 1970) 2 vols.

4

Dracula and *The Beetle*: Imperial and Sexual Guilt and Fear in Late Victorian Fantasy

RHYS GARNETT

I IMPERIALISM, GENDER AND GENRE

Richard Marsh's supernatural horror novel, *The Beetle*, was – like *Dracula* – published in 1897, the year of Queen Victoria's Diamond Jubilee.[1] To the Jubilee celebrations, sustained and strident, of England's imperial supremacy and of the New Imperialism's apparent irresistibility, came tributaries from all of England's manifold colonies and conquered and 'protected' territories. To the London of Marsh's novel comes, also, a representative of those territories. He comes, however, not to pay tribute but to exact retribution. His is a terrorist campaign, mounted from within a territory desecrated and currently repenetrated by British imperialism; he seeks revenge through the destabilisation of the centre of British power, by means of the appropriation and destruction of symbols of the moral, spiritual and racial 'superiority' of England's ruling class – its women.[2] (Those unfamiliar with this novel will find a synopsis under note 2.) Simultaneously, in his Transylvanian castle, Count Dracula practices his English and studies the geography and railway timetables of England. He too seeks to appropriate those symbols, as the first step in a vampiric conquest of England, and then the entire world – an expansionist campaign to end all such campaigns. When his plans are complete, he too will set forth to penetrate 'the heart of the empire'.[3] Marsh's protagonist reveals the guilty fear of an imperialist class that its greedy expropriation of alien territories may *deserve* punishment; Dracula represents its fear of the logic of its own doctrines and practices, a fear of the emergence of a superior and necessarily antagonistic rival; fear, in a sense, of imperialism itself.

Both Stoker and Marsh were members of, and functioned

30

within, the upper-middle ranks of late-Victorian cultural-ideological production and reproduction.[4] Both chose, in the mid-1890s, to write novels that are shaped within the same sub-genre of popular fiction, using very similar methods and structures of narrative, character-disposition and symbolic formation, to serve closely related ideological functions. They can be seen in these novels to be pursuing 'various strategies of legitimation' of the power positions of their own class and gender, and to have produced narrative forms which have 'the function of inventing imaginary . . . "solutions" to unresolvable social contradictions'.[5] In pursuing these 'strategies of legitimation', Marsh and Stoker unwittingly expose the guilty conscience of their class through the very processes by which they seek to assuage that conscience, justify their power and exorcise their sexuality.

The forms of transgression and danger which they release, and then attempt to expel, in these fictions are those in which the power relations of dominance and subordination, upon which the patriarchal ruling class depends for the maintenance of its superiority, are shown to be inversive. British imperial penetration into alien lands and disruption of ancient cultures is inverted into Oriental/Eastern European penetration and desecration of London and its ruling class; the sexual dominance of the patriarchal Englishman over woman *and* his morally superior capacity for sexual repression and sublimation, in contrast to degraded, libidinous aliens of all kinds, is inverted through a range of transgressive sexual relations, in all of which English 'manhood' is destroyed or displaced (passive submission to rapacious female sexuality; usurpation of sexual primacy by superior alien potency; homosexuality; lesbianism).

The primary mechanism by which imperial and sexual fear and guilt are able to take such forms is that of projection. By this means the unacceptable is converted into more or less acceptable forms. In both novels, guilt and fear are projected primarily – though *not* exclusively – on to non-English, non-bourgeois and (therefore) non-human figures, 'archetypes of the Other'. These figures are listed by Jameson as the stranger, the barbarian and also the Woman, 'whose biological difference stimulates fantasies of castration and devoration' and 'the avenger of accumulated resentments from some oppressed class or race, or else that alien being, Jew or communist' (*J*, p. 115). In the figures of Stoker's vampire Count and Marsh's 'Egypto-Arabian' priest of Isis, the stranger, the barbarian, the avenger, the alien being and the releaser (Dracula) or embodiment (the Beetle-priest/ess) of voracious female desire are compounded. In each novel, however, evil is discoverable *also* within even the most ideally and rigorously virtuous of bourgeois psyches, thereby exposing tensions inherent in the texts' authorial projects. The projection of guilt and desire on to the Other exonerates the self; the additional and secondary location of guilt and desire within the self 'retracts' and even contradicts that projection; the subsequent expulsion of guilt and desire in the (still projected) form of the Other once more exonerates the self. These contradictions are caused by conflicting yet inseparable impulses: (1) to repress, and (2) to release guilt and desire *in order to* exorcise them.

A further contradiction is exposed within these novels. It is, like those inherent in imperial and sexual dominance/guilt, integral to the ideological legitimation of the late-Victorian patriarchy. Jameson states that 'the ethical binary opposition of good and evil [is] . . . one of the fundamental forms of ideological thought in Western culture' which 'lives by exclusion and predicates certain types of Otherness as evil' (*J*, pp. 86, 61). This binary opposition has been historically constituted in Western culture primarily through the symbolic structures of Christian mythology, in the name and with the authority of which successive ruling power groups have armoured themselves ideologically. But by the 1890s this armour has been worn and fissured, even fragmented, by the growth of scientific rationalism, by a counter-faith in the capacity of science to penetrate all mysteries and possess all knowledge. Between the simultaneous validations of the late-Victorian patriarchy on both 'scientific' and ethical-metaphysical grounds – proclaiming the biological and 'evolutionary' necessity *and* the moral legitimation of its dominance – many spaces reveal themselves, within which both ideological contradictions and the consequent need for their symbolic resolution are exposed. Both *The Beetle* and *Dracula* enter into this deeply-fissured territory, where representatives of '"our scientific, sceptical, matter-of-fact nineteenth century"' (*D*, p. 242) encounter and attempt to comprehend '"things which you cannot understand"' through '"faith: that which enables us to believe things we know to be untrue"' (*D*, pp. 194, 196).

Dracula and *The Beetle* were published without penalisation – indeed, without controversy. This was possible, in a society which had reacted with hostility to (for example) Hardy's modestly heterodox realist treatment of sexual relations in *Tess* and *Jude*, for several reasons.[6] First, as Jameson explains:

> It is in the context of the gradual reification of realism in late capitalism that romance once again comes to be felt as the place of narrative heterogeneity and freedom from that reality principle to which a now oppressive realistic representation is the hostage. Romance now again seems to offer the possibility of sensing other historical rhythms, and of demonic and Utopian transformations of a real now unshakeably set in place. (*J*, p. 104)

The use of the supernatural in popular middle-class late-Victorian fiction does allow the writer more freedom than is otherwise normally available. This is because it automatically causes the text in which it appears to be marginalised into a cluster of categories of insignificance (popular, sensational, 'mere' fantasy, un-realistic, and so on) – a process which defuses through its reception any transgressive charge the text may be capable of providing. This can take place, however, only if the text itself conceals what it reveals, ensuring that its transgressions, 'presupposing the laws or norms or taboos against which they function', at least *appear* to 'end up precisely reconfirming such laws' (*J*, p. 68).[7]

II IMPERIAL DIMENSIONS

The debate concerning the political, economic and moral validity of imperial expansionism had been proceeding throughout the lifetimes of Stoker (1847–1912) and Marsh (1857–1915). It had however reached a crescendo in the 1890s when the voices of Chamberlain, Curzon, Lord Roseberry and Rhodes, proclaiming the doctrines of unlimited expansionism as justified by racial superiority, manifest destiny and divine mission, and celebrating the triumph of the new Imperialism, almost – but not entirely – drowned the voices of the doubters and opposers of such doctrines.[8]

At its most immediate level, *The Beetle* is a product, in its imperial dimension, of the author's awareness and processing of contemporary, even topical, imperial ventures and attitudes. The

Beetle-priest has emerged, it transpires, from 'a dog-hole in the desert – the Wady Halfa desert' and 'it was during the recent expeditionary advance towards Dongola' that the apparently spontaneous combustion of this 'den of demons' (*B*, p. 714) is heard and its fragmented remains discovered. Kitchener's expedition 'to reconquer the Sudan had started South from Egypt in 1896';[9] the Dongola campaign began in March of that year,[10] and during the summer of 1897 the expeditionary force was 'gloriously revenging the death of Gordon'[11] and thereby satisfying '"the honour of England"'.[12] In *The Beetle*, the honour of England – or that of representatives of its ruling élite – is very much endangered as a consequence of analogous, though symbolically displaced and reduced, imperialist intrusions: those of Paul Lessingham and of 'two sisters and their brother . . . members of a decent English family' (*B*, p. 688), who foolhardily venture into the native quarter of Cairo 'in search of amusement' with 'a spice of adventure' (*B*, p. 629). 'In the eyes of the colonised', writes Memmi, 'all Europeans . . . are potential colonisers. All they have to do is set foot in the colonised's land.'[13] Egypt and the Sudan were indeed appropriate topical locations for the release and formulation of themes of imperial guilt. England's seizure of control over Egypt, its continued occupation after 1882, and the economic and political motives for this, had provoked much debate and much shifting of ideological ground in the 1880s and 1890s. During this period, an embryonically aggressive anti-British natonalist movement had sputtered briefly;[14] Egypt was a key stepping-stone for further expansionism[15] and was a particularly prominent focus of European cultural depredations, not least by British explorers, archaeologists, entrepreneurs and potentates.

Marsh's *Beetle*, however, is a response not merely to a specifically topical area and sequence of events, but to the whole process of late nineteenth-century British expansionism. Eventually located as a priest/priestess of the ancient, obscene but still potent cult of Isis, the alien intruder is variously described as an Algerian, an 'arab of the Soudan', an 'unbaptised Mohammedan', an 'Egypto-Arabian' and, later, as 'Oriental to his finger-tips' yet 'hardly an Arab . . . not a fellah', perhaps not 'a Mohammedan at all' and, because of his 'thick and shapeless lips', as having 'more than a streak of negro blood' (*B*, pp. 500, 504, 534, 537) – appropriate enough for an inhabitant of the Sudan, yet suggestive also of other areas of conquest. Because he is none of these things specifically, he is all of them approximately: a composite symbol, primarily of a dominant European constitution of the Oriental – of ancient Oriental depravity and power – with undertones of African primitivism. 'The Orient is not only adjacent to Europe; it is also . . . one of its deepest and most recurrent images of the Other.'[16] This mechanism – the projection of Western guilt, fear and desire, on to the Oriental (African) – as Other – carries with it a considerable in-built penalty. It invests him with the power of the repressed: 'Deep within himself the colonialist pleads guilty', states Memmi.[17] The forms of inversion of imperial power which this guilt produces include defeat by alien technological superiority (Wells's Martians, for example), and not only the revenge, in appropriately dehumanised forms, of imperial subjects, but also the return of, or regression to, the metaphysical realm of transcendental religion, displaced, and debased, by the advance of scientific positivism. Thus Benita Parry writes that 'the obverse to these disparaging images is the conception of colonial peoples as possessed of privileged insights into the transcendental realm and endowed with magic powers'.[18] These 'privileged insights' are the product in *Dracula* of anti-Christian, and in *The Beetle* of pre-Christian, sources of knowledge and power – sources that Western science cannot penetrate or possess. Sydney Atherton, Marsh's upper-class experimental scientist is, before the novel's end, forced to recognise the limitations of his science in the face of Oriental 'magic':

> In matters of prestidigitation, Champnell, we Westerners are among the rudiments, we've everything to learn – Orientals leave us at the post. If their civilization's what we are pleased to call extinct, their conjuring – when you get to know it – is all alive oh! (*B*, p. 655)

Atherton's role is that of heroic leader of civilisation's resistance to the terror (and terrorism) of the Beetle-priest. All other representatives of his society – from indigent ex-clerk to leading radical statesman and, of course, woman are rendered instantaneously helpless before and subject to this representative and wielder of the ancient powers of the East.

Dracula is descended from 'a conquering race' (*D*, p. 36); he has a history of attempted invasions: '". . . once before . . . he went back to his own country from the land he had tried to invade. . . . He came again, better equipped for his work; and won. So he came to London to invade a new land . . ."' pp. 346–7). It is primarily but not only England that is in peril. Humanity at large is in danger of colonisation by the mutant sub-species of which Dracula is the source and centre:

> they cannot die, but must go on age after age adding new victims or multiplying the evils of the world; for all that die from the preying of the Un-Dead become themselves un-Dead, and prey on their kind. And so the circle goes on ever widening . . .   (*D*, p. 217)

He is '"the father . . . of a new order of beings, whose road must lead through Death, not Life"' (*D*, p. 306) and must be defeated '"for the sake of humanity"' (*D*, p. 323).

That Dracula has imperialist ambitions – initially, to conquer and colonise '"your great England"' (*D*, p. 27) – is, therefore, fully recognised by his antagonists; it is demonstrated also by his elaborate plans to infiltrate England and cumulatively possess its inhabitants: '"My revenge has just begun! I spread it over centuries, and time is on my side. Your girls that you love are mine already; and through them you and others shall yet be mine . . ."' (*D*, p. 311). His role, consequently, is not that of resistance-group terrorist, punitively raiding the home territory of an imperial aggressor, but that of rival to and potential conqueror of Britain and its empire. Yet whereas the Beetle-priest overtly represents prominent and topical areas of British 1890s expansionism, *Dracula*'s imperialist themes relate only partially, and obscurely, to a contemporaneous situation in which England's main imperial rivals were primarily Western European, led by Germany, and secondarily (imminently) the USA. The latter 'threat' is acknowledged, and disarmed. The former is excluded – or displaced.

Quincey Morris, a wealthy Texan and master-explorer of foreign lands, is the only one of Dracula's opponents to die. He has, we are told by the admiring Dr Seward, born himself throughout '"like a moral Viking. If America goes on breeding men like that she will be a power in the world indeed"' (*D*, p. 177). A similar tribute is paid later in the novel to America's imperial potential, by Dracula's disciple, Renfield:

> Mr Morris, you should be proud of your great State. Its reception into the Union was a precedent which may have far-reaching

effects hereafter, when the Pole and the Tropics may hold allegiance to the Stars and Stripes . . . [and] when the Monroe doctrine takes its true place as a political fable.   (*D*, p. 247)

Quincy's fate, however, is *reassuringly* not to figure in the imminent rise to imperial dominance of the USA, but to be incorporated (as a valued contributor rather than potential rival) into the restabilised, repurified and fortified power of the British ruling classes, in the symbolic person of their heir:

It is an added joy to Mina and me that our boy's birthday is the same as that on which Quincey Morris died. His mother holds . . . the secret belief that some of our brave friend's spirit passed into him. His bundle of names links all our little band together: but we call him Quincey.   (*D*, p. 334)

On the much more immediate threat of the rapidly growing economic and military power of Germany, however, the text is silent. Stoker's European imperial enemy is not located in the historical present, but displaced to a mythical-historical past. A descendant of Attila the Hun, yet hereditary defender of the Holy Roman Empire against the Turks (*D*, p. 36), Dracula appears primarily to embody ancient but still potent eastern European feudal power, which now seeks unholy, anti-Christian means to rise from the dead and usurp modern Anglo-Saxon imperial supremacy (he scorns yet seeks to emulate the Hapsburgs and the Romanovs [*D*, p. 37] and has been perceived as representing the fast-fading power of the Austro-Hungarian Empire).[19] As with his treatment of class relations and conflict, Stoker here appears to have erected residual, obsolescent formations, thereby displacing (silencing) dominant formations of a much more immediate and threatening kind.[20] However displaced, the imperial threat to Britain is nevertheless seen to lie within Europe – in archaic beliefs and superstitions – and to embody expansionist ambitions as insatiable as those of Cecil Rhodes: '"History has taught me that expansion is everything."'[21] What has been done by imperialist Britain will be done to imperialist Britain. The greatest of ninet-eenth-century imperial powers is itself to be colonised, by the undead powers of feudal Europe, against which all of its scientific knowledge and technological strength may prove to be unavailing.

In *Dracula*, Stoker creates a threat to arch-imperialist England that is potentially more absolute and final than any process of conquest and domination achieved under the British (or any other) flag. Dracula plans to conquer mind and body totally: to achieve instantaneous conversion of his victims to his culture, creed and personality-structure, by means of a system of conquest that necessitates unlimited expansion and unfailing, ever-recurrent rewards. The novel is, in this aspect, a nightmare of the logic of imperialism carried to its extremist limits – an imperialism which, in seeking to convert and consume the entire human species, must thereby ultimately destroy both that species and itself.

III   SEXUAL TRANSGRESSIONS

The growth of European imperialism in the nineteenth century coincided with what Edward Said describes as the 'increasing embourgeoisement' of Europe, with its intensified institutionalis-ation of sex:

> On the one hand, there was no such thing as 'free' sex, and on the other, sex in society entailed a web of legal, moral, even political and economic obligations of a detailed and certainly encumbering sort . . . so the Orient was a place where one could look for sexual experience unavailable in Europe.[22]

An intensified need for adequately distanced figures of *sexual* Otherness combined with the increased visibility and availability of figures of *racial* Otherness, figures made more available through the much extended contact between members of the British ruling class and alien cultures, and through the multiplicity of late nineteenth-century discourses relating to imperialism. That which was repressed as 'evil', unnatural, inhuman, inferior, was provided with a whole range of richly supplemented locations for the projection of repressed desire – in the demonstrably heterodox sexual attitudes, practices and 'freedoms' of subject, alien races.

In *Dracula* and *The Beetle*, a malevolent, alien creature invades 'the citadel of white purity with intent to ravish':[23] to gain domi-nance over its representative owners by seizing the symbols of their purity and superiority, their women. The alien is aided by hitherto concealed moral deficiencies within these symbols, and within the owners themselves. In each case, the owners rally, combine, purge themselves of individual (and therefore collective) guilt and fear, and can organise the pursuit and expulsion of the Other – a pursuit much complicated by the revealed fragility of these symbols. In Marsh's novel, those women who through foolhardiness or rejection of male authority venture, unwittingly, into the territory of the Other, pay the ultimate penalties of violation and death, unless, like Marjorie Lindon, they can be repossessed in time to be reconstituted in more docile form. The woman who does not transgress by challenging male authority (Dora Grayling) remains untouched by the Other, to reward the hero with marriage and considerable wealth. A similar though more complex and suggestive process takes place in *Dracula*, where both female protagonists embody idealised female purity *and* innate female vulnerability to corruption. Mina, both before and after her pollution and part-conversion by Dracula, and Lucy, as she is initially perceived to be by her chivalrous admirers and after her final purification, symbolise the chastity and morally inspirational nature of the ideal bourgeois female (although Lucy does so always more ambiguously than Mina). And Mina demonstrates also how such New Womanish tendencies as lead to Marjorie London's downfall in *The Beetle* can and should be harnessed to, and *incorporated* into, orthodoxly submissive and supportive channels.[24] Both women are also shown, however to have within them elements which find their most polarised forms in the trio of vampire females who cluster avidly over Harker's prone and quivering body: woman as demonic sexual aggressor and polluter of male virtue. In *The Beetle*, this role is confined to the demonic and supernatural. Marjorie and her co-victims are not shown themselves to become 'sexualised' by their violation. Indeed, the experience appears (most painfully) to purge Marjorie of 'aggression'. She is punished, essentially, for challenging male authority. Stoker's Mina and Lucy are punished for possessing sexual desires.[25] Mina submits, and then resists: Lucy submits, completely. Mina, who is after all the finest flower of English womanhood – ' "one of God's women" ' (*D*, p. 192) – is, like Marjorie Lindon, redeemable; Lucy, who has actively collaborated with the enemy and herself become the Other, can be repurified only in death; just as Marjorie's predecessors have undergone a process of despoliation so extreme that their fate worse than death can be followed only by death. For Marjorie and Mina, the process is arrested at a point before that from which there can be no return to true womanhood as bourgeois wives and mothers. Where *The Beetle* demonstrates how foolish and weak even the best of women are (particularly when they believe themselves to be strong-minded and independent), *Dracula* reveals a parallel though more extreme conviction that even the best and least consciously sexual of women contain the potential for surrender to desire, and therefore for moral and social destruction. Even 'one of God's women' may be periodically unstable, untrustworthy and (albeit unconsciously) liable to collusion with the enemy.

Yet in both novels the men are also shown to be vulnerable and corruptible; they too must struggle against an enemy within. Frequently in Victorian novels female deviancy occurs at least in part as a consequence of failures or abuses of patriarchal responsibility.[26] Marjorie Lindon's abduction and despoliation occur only partly because she has rejected the authority of her father and honorary brother, Atherton, and insisted on taking an active part in the pursuit of the monster. It occurs also because Atherton *allows* her to overrule his authority, and because he leaves her unprotected in the monster's London lair by rushing off in pursuit of the erratic 'double-agent' Holt (a failure of responsibility which has its parallel in *Dracula*, when Dr Seward falls asleep while guarding Lucy – with literally fatal consequences for her). Both novels indicate that sexual desire is a source – perhaps *the* source – of weakness in men, when not sublimated into romantic/chivalric love. Harker fails twice to behead the coffin-bound Count Dracula, after his too-willing submission to the desires of the vampire women. These failures impair his ability to defend his wife thereafter; during the scene of Mina's violation by Dracula, Harker lies unconscious – inert and impotent – on the bed beside her. Similarly, Paul Lessingham's two-month submission to the obscene embraces of the priestess of Isis signifies the surrender of his manhood and renders him again helplessly vulnerable and ineffective in defence of his fiancée when, twenty years later, the Beetle-priest reappears seeking vengeance. Even Sydney Atherton, the least vulnerable opponent of the Beetle-priest, is *most* vulnerable when led to desire and possess Marjorie sexually;[27] and Lord Godalming, Stoker's ideal English gentleman, has twice to be physically prevented from polluting himself by responding eagerly to the vampire-Lucy's unmaidenly solicitations.

It is, nevertheless, the power of released *female* sexuality which is perceived to be overwhelmingly offensive – indeed, to be a potentially revolutionary force which can overthrow patriarchal dominance and invert gender roles. The only proper response to this – both novels demonstrate – is the recovery and most extreme use of superior and 'legitimate' masculine force. Lessingham regains his manhood, at least partially, by strangling the priestess to death as she once again descends lasciviously upon him (*B*, pp. 635–6). Lord Godalming most emphatically reasserts male dominance and repossession of Lucy as, looking like the supreme patriarchal 'figure of Thor', he hammers his phallic stake 'deeper and deeper' into Lucy's heart, providing her with her ultimate and definitive climax (*D*, p. 219). In effect, male sexuality paradoxically represents the extreme source and manifestation of superior male power as well as, elsewhere, of male weakness. On the one hand, male surrender to female sexuality causes impairment or loss of manhood; on the other, as reprisal against and reconquest of dominance over the female, the violent reassertion of male sexuality constitutes the recovery and reaffirmation of manhood.

In both novels, however, the greatest and least resistible sexual power is possessed by the Other, and thus identified with the monstrous, the un-natural; not with reproduction and life, but with loss of self and death. Dracula embodies this most dangerous power, released from its bondage, un-neutered by repression or sublimation. His power releases that in others. He is for the men an object of bitter envy, and for the women of irresistible desire. But while Dracula operates in an almost exclusively heterosexual world,[28] the sexual identity of Marsh's Other is very much more ambiguous. After Robert Holt has broken into an apparently deserted house, he is first – like Dracula's victims – 'stricken by a sudden paralysis of fear', and then graphically mounted in deep darkness by a 'monstrous' insect which 'gained my loins' and climbs further until 'it enveloped my face with its huge, slimy, evil-smelling body, and embraced me with its myriad legs' (*B*, p. 452). That this assault has a pronounced sexual element is evident; but of what kind? A light is struck: 'I saw someone in front of me lying in a bed. I could not at once decide whether it was a man or a woman. Indeed at first I doubted whether it was anything human. But, afterwards, I knew it to be a man – for this reason, if for no other, that it was impossible that such a creature could be feminine' (*B*, p. 453). It is either male or female; it may be neither: it is a man (or is it? – the reasons given are hardly conclusive). It is nevertheless *as a man* that this creature then commands Holt to strip naked and then smiles at him with 'a satyr's smile . . . which filled me with a sense of shuddering repulsion. "What a white skin you have – how white! What would I not give for a skin as white as that – oh yes!" He paused, devouring me with glances' (*B*, p. 456). Like Harker before the vampire women and Lessingham in the power of the Isis-priestess, Holt becomes 'feminised'. Already reduced to less than a 'man' economically and socially, he is resistlessly overwhelmed in these scenes by the sexual desire, racial envy and supernatural powers of the Oriental-African Other.[29]

Just as in *Dracula* the supernatural mode allows the thinly disguised expression of sado-sexuality, so in *The Beetle* this mode makes possible the transgression of an even stronger taboo: that of sado-sexuality in homosexual form – a transgression protected only by its brief attribution to a non-human cause ('this could be nothing human' – *B*, p. 458). The extremely hazardous nature of the territory into which Marsh has ventured here is emphasised by his attempts to obscure or retract the homosexual significance of these scenes. When Holt next sees the creature it has become much younger and 'the most outstanding novelty was that about the face there was something essentially feminine'. Holt wonders: 'if I could by any possibility have . . . mistaken a woman for a man' (p. 462). If so, since aggressive female sexuality (as in *Dracula*) is not merely unwomanly but un-human, then 'she' must be 'some ghoulish example of her sex, who had so far yielded to her depraved instincts as to have become nothing but a ghastly reminiscence of womanhood' (ibid.). A very *Dracula*-like contradiction is discernible here: woman has the innate (instinctual) capacity for sexual desire, yet the activation of this capacity reduces her to something less or even other, than a woman.

However, the sexual ambiguity of this monster's role and signification is by no means yet resolved. It receives yet another disorientating twist in a slightly later scene when the creature, lying in bed, says: ' "Is it not sweet to stand close at my side? You, with your white skin, *if I were a woman*, would you not take me for your wife?" ' (*B*, p. 486; my emphasis). If 'he' is not a woman, then these sexual advances and assaults are homosexual, and the line of transgression is crossed yet again, albeit in demonic form. But the crossing is again conditional, for Holt then comments, 'there was something about the manner in which this was said which was so essentially feminine that once more I wondered if I could possibly be mistaken in the creature's sex' (*ibid.*) – only for the line to be crossed yet again, when the creature springs upon Holt, 'clasping my throat with *his* horrid hands bearing me backwards onto the floor; I felt *his* breath mingle with mine . . . and then God, in his mercy, sent oblivion' (p. 488; my emphasis).

The perceived nature of the sub-genre of the Gothic-supernatural in Victorian fiction, and the relative licence allowed to it, enables Marsh to break into the general area of sexual transgression. Within that territory he develops a strategy – the persistent uncertainty about, and fluctuations in, the creature's sexual identity – which gives him access to an inner area of extreme transgression, where it can be indicated (in a novel written for a popular middle-class Victorian readership) that a homosexual rape has taken place. The strategy, although somewhat repetitively (even obsessively) used, is in itself very economical. Holt can be violated simultaneously by a figure representing the release of both male and female desire, indeed of desire itself – a release which reveals it to be (when released) intensely perverse, destructive and, savingly, non-human.

In its most spectacular series of transformations, the creature changes, before the 'stupified' eyes of the scientist Atherton, from an Oriental male into 'a monstrous creature of the Beetle tribe' with a 'smooth head and throat [which] seemed to suggest that it was female', and then, when Atherton attempts to capture it, it bursts 'naked from top to toe' into the shape of 'my truly versatile Oriental friend', revealing that Atherton 'had been egregiously mistaken in the question of sex. My visitor was not a man but a woman, and . . . by no means old or ill-shaped either' (*B*, pp. 546–7). What is it, then, that shortly thereafter in *beetle* form drives Marjorie 'in the madness of terror' into her bed and creeps 'between the sheets' (p. 599)? Marjorie is here violated by male-female-and-insect, with the implicitly lesbian aspect of the violation taking Marsh's novel (even though still screened by the supernatural-insect form that perpetrates the act) into yet another area of 'unthinkable' sexual depravity and gender-role confusion. The novel's final act of gender-reversal is performed by the creature on Marjorie Lindon. She is stripped of her (elaborately itemised) clothes, shorn of her hair, and forced to wear male clothing, a dislocation of sexual identity which precedes and accelerates her loss of identity, and of self, in madness. Would-be rebellious or sexually deviant females in Victorian fiction suffer a variety of retributions; few are more punitive than those inflicted on Marsh's self-willed heroine, or Stoker's too susceptible Lucy Westenra.

In *The Beetle*, a representative of Oriental sexual deviancy and potency penetrates to and ravishes those inhabitants of 'the citadel of white purity' whose social or sexual weakness, or whose dislocations of 'natural' gender roles, exposes them to the power of the Other. European fear of and desire for the 'alien' sexuality of the Oriental/African Other is projected in the form of the libidinous monster's envy of and sexual desire for the 'white' bodies of English men and women. In both Beetle-priest and Dracula, vengeful victim and predatory rival of British imperialism, the sexual fear and guilt of the late-Victorian patriarchy can find a habitation and a name for desires distanced in extreme forms of Otherness – distanced, however, only to be brought home to where they really belong, within the heart of those 'citadels of white purity' from which they can only with great difficulty once more be re-expelled.

IV CLOSURE: SCIENCE AND RELIGION

If the primary ideological function of *Dracula* and *The Beetle* is to provide 'the imaginary resolution' of real contradictions, then the processes of closure in these novels are liable to come under particular strain. Once released in such texts conflicts must – almost invariably – be resolved, even if they, and the contradictions that underly them, may have been released in such potent and disturbing forms that their resolution can be achieved only by demonstrably inadequate means.

The two novels follow similar narrative structures towards closure. Once the presence of the Other has declared itself within the citadels of English civilisation, and the nature of the threat that it represents has begun to be understood (its power and the limitations of that power), then the protectors of this civilisation can turn from reactive and defensive measures to attack and pursuit. They have by this stage bonded themselves into a cohesive, aggressive class unit – extensively and uniformly in *Dracula*, belatedly and less coherently in *The Beetle*. Then follows, in both novels, the attempt to locate, entrap and destroy the invader in the base or bases it has established within the heart of the Empire. The procedures are very much more elaborate in *Dracula*, but they serve the same function as in *The Beetle*. They are the first steps towards the expulsion of the Other from British soil. In each case the creature escapes, and it escapes in order to be pursued. Again, the pursuit of Dracula is more extensive and elaborate. It carries the righteously vengeful band of bourgeois warriors into the home territory of the invader, there to neturalise the central locus of his power, his castle, and destroy him in a climactic confrontation.

The Beetle-priest and his captive are also pursued, but only as far as 'somewhere in the neighbourhood of Luton' (*B*, p. 700). He too is (possibly) destroyed, but only by accident – by a catastrophic and fortuitous failure of the very technologies by means of which he has been pursued (a railway collision). What appear to be the remains of the creature's clothes and bedding, together with foul-smelling blotches of 'some sort of viscid matter' are discovered in 'the first third-class compartment' (pp. 711–12). That this by no means indicates the conclusive extermination of the Beetle-priest, or what he represents, is made evident by Champnell: 'What became of the creature . . . who he was – if it was a "he", which is doubtful; whence he came; whither he went; what was the purpose of his presence here – to this hour these things are puzzles' (p. 712). Nor is the central locus of the creature's power penetrated and sanitised. Its apparently spontaneous combustion merely *coincides* with the passing of Kitchener's punitive expedition to the Sudan. No explanation for its destruction is provided, and Champnell declares: 'That the den of demons . . . had, that night, at last come to an end, and that these things that lay scattered . . . on that treeless plain, were the evidence of its final destruction, is not a hypothesis I should care to advance with any degree of certainty. . . . It cannot be certainly shown that the Thing is not still existing – a creature born of neither God nor man' (pp. 714, 715).

Dracula is entrapped and destroyed as a direct consequence of the courage, clear-headedness, organisational capacity, methodological adaptability and – above all – the revived 'faith' of his pursuers. The imperial rival is defeated; the sexual superior is himself symbolically raped and castrated.[30] His potency is thus simultaneously, if paradoxically, destroyed and possessed. It is after this that Jonathan and Mina can produce a child. The only hint of ambiguity in the apparent finality of this exorcism is that Dracula's body dissolves into dust – a material form into which he has several times transformed himself and from which reconstituted himself. But this tiny fissure is soon sealed over. On a celebratory return visit to Transylvania, to go 'over the old ground', the obliteration of the Other is confirmed: 'Every trace of all that had been blotted out'; and on their return home; 'we got to talking of the old time – which we could look back on without despair' (*D*, p. 334).

Both authors make use of a mechanism of closure indispensable to the restabilisation of destabilised social groups in Victorian fiction: their multiple reintegration through marriages and the formation of totally harmonious micro-societies. In *Dracula*, this procedure is integrated into and mutually supported by the exorcism of the Other. In *The Beetle*, it is undermined by the text's inability to exorcise the Other. Lessingham is married at last to Marjorie, who has inherited her father's wealth and forms a hegemonically unifying class unit with the now fully-risen middle-class Lessingham. Yet both continue to have 'what seems to be a constitutional disrelish for the subject of beetles' and 'cannot be induced to speak of them', and there are still moments when Lessingham harks backs, 'with something like physical shrinking, to that awful nightmare of the past' (*B*, pp. 713–14). In contrast to *Dracula*, therefore, there are three gaps in the closure of *The Beetle*: the arbitrary nature of the mechanisms of 'expulsion' of the Other; their inconclusiveness; and the incomprehension of the protagonists before a mystery which, as witnesses, they must admit to exist, but cannot explain (or explain away).

Throughout the Victorian era religious belief – belief in the realm of the metaphysical – was under assault from positivistic science. These two very powerful and extensive conceptual and institutional formations each functioned ideologically primarily as mechanisms through which a dominant class could fortify, extend and continuously revalidate its dominance. Yet each did so from premises which subverted and invalidated the claims of the other.[31] In both *Dracula* and *The Beetle*, science is shown to be inadequate, in itself, to defeat the power of the Other. The blood-transfusions that Van Helsing and Seward carry out delay but do not prevent Dracula's vampiric pollution and appropriation of Lucy, or his corruption of Mina. Atherton's new secret weapon of imperial conquest – a poison gas of deadly potency – can only briefly deter the Beetle-priest. The technological means used to pursue and entrap Dracula (telegrams, trains, a power-boat, rifles) are impotent to destroy him; for his destruction, arcane, unscientific knowledge of and belief in the metaphysical realm are indispensible. While admitting the failure of his advanced scientific knowledge and methods to 'pin-down' the Beetle,[32] Atherton – unequipped with the symbols of faith – pursues the alien by exclusively rational and material means (cabs, telegrams, a special train). The 'rational' pursuit of Dracula is most usefully supplemented by Mina Harker's vampire-induced telepathic capacity for tracking the Count's progress. No such extra-scientific aids are available to Atherton (even though he claims an open mind and some knowledge of ancient religions). Indeed, the realm of the metaphysical appears to be almost exclusively appropriated by the Other in *The Beetle*, the only significant exception occurring when Marjorie begs Atherton to pray, so that she may get away from '"the presence of evil . . . back into the presence of God"'. Initially sceptical and reluctant: 'At last I did what she wished. . . . At least there is no harm in praying – I never heard of it bringing harm to anyone', Atherton repeats the Lord's Prayer, 'the first time for I don't know how long'. And when the prayer is ended, he feels 'something tugging at my heart-strings which I had not felt there for many and many a year, almost as though it had been my mother's hand' (B, p. 564). Atherton represents the best type of Englishman in the novel, and he possesses the highest and broadest sources of knowledge in this society. Yet religious belief – here associated with the emotional and spiritual capacities of women, rather than the intellectual 'superiorities' of men – has for him only a retrospective and briefly-kindled power. Hereafter, he and his fellow defenders of the Victorian patriarchy seek no further aid from such an obsolescent and de-potentised source, failing even to attribute the apparently entirely arbitrary 'destruction' of priest and temple to the workings of an ultimately benevolent Providence. Indeed, for Champnell, by implication, Christian mythology offers no explanation for a mystery which is, after all, pre-Christian in origin. The creature is 'born of neither God nor man', explicable neither within the framework of Christian metaphysics nor that of rational science, and he and Atherton remain mystified to the end, aware only that 'there are indeed more things in heaven and earth than are dreamed in our philosophy' (B, p. 715).

Neither religious faith nor the materialistic belief system of empirical science is validated in *The Beetle*. Not so much a contradiction as a vacancy appears in their place. The surface of this society initially appears, to its male ruling-class inhabitants, to be essentially ordered and secure in its proper structuring and distribution of power relations, ruffled only by apparently superficial and resolvable disturbances. Beneath this surface, however, and appropriately broken into by the descending Holt, is a dark space, wherein the Other can manifest itself to exert a pressure that expands seemingly tiny surface fissures into fractures and gaps, exposing the radical (Lessingham) alternative to the archaic Toryism of Lindon to be also rotten at its core, the New Woman tendencies of Marjorie Lindon to be a potential source of profound destabilisation of patriarchalism, the sexuality of the patriarchs and their females to be deeply insecure, and their imperial ventures to be productive not only of further economic and political power, but also of guilt, fear and retribution. Against this, the novel's 'imaginery resolutions' of 'real conflicts' seem flimsy indeed.

In *Dracula*, contrastingly, it is the revitalisation of religious faith that restores morale and provides the weapons with which – and only with which – the Other, identified as the Anti-Christ or his agent, can be defeated. The inspirer of this religious revitalisation of the English bourgeoisie is not, however, himself English, but a Dutch collaborator, Van Helsing. His arcane, un-English knowledge and *belief* enable him to combine decidedly heretical '"traditions and superstitions"' (*D*, p. 241) with the apparatus of Christian worship, and to supplement both with medico-scientific expertise and technological proficiency. All the Englishmen have to offer initially is Seward's medical and psychiatric knowledge, ready access to technology and a vague awareness that they are Christians as well as gentlemen. It is as though in this '"scientific, sceptical, matter-of-fact nineteenth century"' (p. 242), the sources of 'true' faith have dried up, and require a benevolent and powerful *external* agent to cause them to flow again. Van Hesling, closer to and in contact with the East, has kept '"an open mind"' (p. 189). He has first to convince the rational man of science, Dr Seward, to open *his* mind: '"Do you not think that there are things which you cannot understand, and yet which are; that some people see things that others cannot?"' The fault however is not entirely Seward's: '"It is the fault of our science that wants to explain all"' (p. 194). Van Helsing wants Seward to *believe*: '"To believe in things that you cannot"' (p. 196). Still, there is resistance ('"Dr Van Helsing, are you mad?"'), which is disarmed as Van Helsing produces:

'The Host. I brought it from Amsterdam. I have an Indulgence.'

It was an answer that appalled the most sceptical of us. . . . In the presence of such earnest purpose . . . which could thus use the to him most sacred of things, it was impossible to distrust. (*D*, p. 213)

These 'things' are, however, still the 'most sacred' to *him*. There is a distance still between the Anglican Englishmen with their 'matter-of-fact' religion and the superstitious/idolatrous Catholic beliefs of the Dutchman. Indeed for the Anglo-Saxon gentlemen further proof is needed: the witnessing of a travesty-miracle, when they see the undead Lucy pass through the interstices of the locked door of her tomb. After this, Godalming can with full conviction 'Strike in God's name' as he drives 'the mercy-bearing stake . . . deeper and deeper' into Lucy's wildly contorting body: 'His face was set, and high duty seemed to shine through it' (p. 214).

Now the enemies of Dracula can form themselves into what is both a committee of directors,[33] and a quasi-mediaeval order of Christian Knights:

> Thus we are ministers of God's own wish: that the world, and men for whom his son die, will not be given over to monsters, whose very existence would defame him. He has allowed us to redeem one soul already, and we go out as the old Knights of the Cross to redeem more. Like them we shall travel towards the sunrise; and like them, if we fall, we fall in a good cause. (*D*, p. 324)

Similarly, 'ancient' and modern join in combinations of rifles and crucifixes, telegraphy and telepathy, and of the 'philosophy of crime' (Lombroso, Nordau) with the Eastern European vampire lore that Van Helsing has acquired: '"We have on our side power of combination – a power denied to the vampire kind; we have the resources of science."' And what science can now combine with its faith: '"because, after all, these things – tradition and superstition – are everything"' (pp. 241, 242).

Dracula, states Rosemary Jackson, 'remains one of the most extreme inversions of the Christian myth. . . . It blasphemes against Christian sacraments – Renfield, the Count's disciple, chants "The blood is the life!"'[34] The vampire baptism in which Mina is 'tainted' (*D*, p. 370) has elements of a travesty of the Mass. What both these inversions of Christian ritual and the conversions to active belief of Seward and his companions confirm is that the contradiction between faith and science resolves itself in this novel in the victory of faith, to which science becomes secondary and subordinate. It is, nevertheless, the hollowest of victories: a resolving of a 'real contradiction' at the most facile level of wish-fulfilment. For it is the darkness beneath the surface of late-Victorian patriarchal dominance that these two novels most powerfully and convincingly reveal – a darkness of imperial, sexual and existential guilt. In his inventing of 'imaginary "solutions" to unresolvable social contradictions', Marsh provides 'solutions' that are demonstrably unconfident and incomplete, and Stoker's 'solutions', though formally complete, are ideologically obsolescent. They are constructed from materials that are not merely residual but historically regressive. Stoker seeks reassurance in a past when religion was ideologically dominant, by projecting the Other *and* its antidote into the more archaic regions and currently fragmenting formations of 'one of the fundamental forms of ideological thought in Western culture . . . the ethical-binary opposition of good and evil' (*J*, p. 88). In these novels, 'Romance' does indeed function as 'the place of . . . freedom from the reality principle', and offers 'the possibility of sensing other historical rhythms [and] . . . demonic or Utopian transformations'. It does so, however in forms that reveal, beneath the surface of 'a real now unshakeably set in place' (*J*, p. 104), a deep confusion and fear in the imperial, sexual and ethical core of late-Victorian patriarchal ideology.

NOTES

1. The edition of Bram Stoker's *Dracula* used for this chapter is that published by Arrow Books (London, 1970; 3rd impression 1973). Future references will appear in the text preceded by the initial *D*. *The Beetle* can be found in Graham Greene's and Hugh Greene's selection, *Victorian Villainies* (Harmondsworth, Middx.: Penguin, 1984). This is the edition referred to and quoted from in this essay. Future references will appear in the text preceded by the initial *B*.

2. *The Beetle* begins with Robert Holt, an indigent and starving ex-clerk, breaking into an apparently empty house in a west London 'wasteland' of half-finished speculative building. He is there terrified and mesmer-ised into complete subjection by a monstrous creature, later revealed to be a priest of the cult of Isis, seeking revenge upon Paul Lessingham, a one-time desecrator of the cult's desert temple. Lessingham, of obscure lower-middle-class origin, is now a leading Radical politician,

secretly engaged to the daughter (Marjorie Lindon) of a reactionary Tory aristocrat. The priest's revenge takes the form, primarily, of seeking to abduct, violate and ritually murder Lessingham's fiancée (the cult has a particular penchant for the sacrificial violation of middle/upper-class English women). He is aided by the mesmerised Holt and by the guilty weakness and terror of Lessingham, and opposed by 'Sydney Atherton, Esquire' and, belatedly, 'the Hon. Augustus Champnell, Confidential Agent'. Atherton, in love with Marjorie and hostile to Lessingham, is an advanced experimental scientist; he is repeatedly out-manoeuvred by the Beetle-priest's Oriental 'prestidigitation', eventually allowing the creature to abduct Marjorie. Atherton, Champnell and Lessingham are in pursuit by special train, when a railway crash apparently destroys the monster and enables them to recover the deeply-traumatised Marjorie. After several years of recovery in an asylum, she inherits her father's wealth and marries the politically successful Lessingham; Atherton also marries a rich heiress (Dora Grayling). Learning that the cult's temple has seemingly exploded, Champnell is by no means convinced that 'the den of demons' is finally destroyed or that 'the Thing is not still existing'. The mystery of 'The Beetle' remains, finally, unresolved. *The Beetle's* narrative methods (a series of first-person narratives from Holt, Atherton, Marjorie Lindon and Champnell) is broadly similar to that of *Dracula*. The model for both is likely to have been Wilkie Collins.

3. C. F. G Masterman (ed.), *The Heart of the Empire* (London: Fisher Unwin, 1901) is mainly concerned with the plight of the inhabitants of the working-class ghettos of London. It also contains E. P. Gooch's essay 'Imperialism', which questions the moral basis for 'non-colonial expansion' (pp. 310–11), opposing the Social Darwinism of Karl Pearson (p. 312) and pointing to the exploitative nature and dislocating effects of 'English rule of men with dark skins' (p. 356). To Cosmo Monkhouse in *Punch* (26 June 1887) the 'Jubilee of Jubilees' was being celebrated at the 'Heart of the World' (James Morris, *Pax Brittanica: The Climax of an Empire* (London: Faber and Faber, 1968) p. 19).

4. Stoker came from an Anglo-Irish middle-class professional family, attended Trinity College, and worked as a Dublin civil servant (like his father), before becoming Henry Irving's business manager. See Harry Ludlam, *A Biography of Bram Stoker, Creator of Dracula* (London: New English Library, 1977), and Daniel Farson, *The Man Who Wrote Dracula: A Biography of Bram Stoker* (London: Michael Joseph, 1975) – both are seriously inadequate as biographies. Marsh, described by P. Haining as 'a rather underrated early master of mystery and detective novels' (*Mystery!* (London: Souvenir Press, 1977) p. 73), was educated at Eton and Oxford and 'had written over sixty novels of very uneven quality by the time of his death' (Greene, 'Introduction', *Victorian Villainies*, p. 10).

5. Frederic Jameson, *The Political Unconscious: Narrative as a Socially Symbolic Act* (London: Methuen, 1981) pp. 83, 79. Future references will appear in the text preceded by the initial *J*.

6. Thomas Hardy: *Tess of the d'Urbervilles* (London: Osgood, McIlvaine, 1891); and *Jude the Obscure* (London: Osgood, McIlvaine, 1895).

7. '". . . perverse desire could not have been acceptable as content in the literary work without the latter's also accepting *the formal model capable of filtering it.*" This formal model is the monster metaphor, the vampire metaphor. It "filters", makes bearable to the conscious mind those desires and fears which the latter has judged to be unacceptable and has thus been forced to repress, and whose existence it consequently cannot recognize. The literary formalization, the rhetorical figure, therefore has a double function: it *expresses* the unconscious content and at the same time *hides* it' (Franco Moretti, 'The Dialectic of Fear', *New Left Review*, no. 136 (1982) p. 81).

8. 'It is not to be doubted that this country has been invested with wealth and power, with art and knowledge, with the sway of distant lands and mastery of restless waters, for some great and important purpose in the government of the world. Can we suppose otherwise [than] that it is our office to carry civilization and humanity, peace and good government, and, above all, the knowledge of the true God, to the uttermost ends of the earth?' (Lord Curzon). Underlying and opposing such assertions of British imperial *hubris*, however, could be heard voices expressing 'a deep-seated uneasiness at the role adopted by Britain', a ' "sense of guilt and desire for atonement . . . a gnawing doubt . . . that could not be quelled by the passion for fanfare and pride in grandeur that reached their climax under Curzon"' (Alan Sandison, *The Wheel of the Empire": A Study of the Imperial Idea in Some Late Nineteenth and Early Twentieth Century Fiction* (London: Macmillan, 1967) pp. 7, 11).

9. Morris, *Pax Britannica*, p. 24 (footnote).

10. A. P. Thornton: *The Imperial Idea and its Enemies* (1959; rpt. London: Macmillan, 1963) p. 86.

11. Morris, *Pax Britannica*, p. 24.

12. Thornton, *The Imperial Idea and its Enemies*, p. 51.

13. Albert Memmi, *The Coloniser and the Colonised* (1957; rpt. London: Souvenir Press, 1974) p. 130.

14. Thornton, *The Imperial Idea and its Enemies*, pp. 57–71.

15. 'nothing . . . expands like this sort of expansionism; once it had been decided to take command of Egypt it was necessary to see to its defence – hence the Sudan, and hence Uganda' (Sandison, *The Wheel of Empire*, p. 2).

16. Edward Said, *Orientalism* (London: Routledge and Kegan Paul, 1978) p. 1.

17. Memmi, *The Coloniser and the Colonised*, p. 57.

18. Benita Parry, *Conrad and Imperialism: Ideological Boundaries and Visionary Frontiers* (London: Macmillan, 1983) p. 3.

19. 'When *Dracula* was written, Transylvania was part of Austria – hence of the Austro-Hungarian Empire, a vestige of feudalism and England's world-historical enemy at the turn of the century. In a sense *Dracula* is an allegorical rehearsal for World War I' (Richard Astle, 'Dracula as Totemic Monster: Lacan, Freud, Oedipus and History', *Sub-Stance*,

no. 25 (1980) pp. 98–103). See also Richard Wasson: 'Count Dracula . . . represents those forces in Eastern Europe which seek to overthrow, through violence and subversion, the more progressive civilization of the West' ('The Politics of *Dracula'*, *English Literature in Translation*, vol. IX (1966) pp. 24–7); and Geoffrey Wall, ' "Different from Writing": *Dracula* in 1897', *Literature and History*, vol. 10, no. 1 (Spring 1984) pp. 15–24 (p. 20).

20. The working class in *Dracula* is universally presented as unthreatening – childishly venal and placatable with the price of a pint of beer. Instead, the threat to bourgeois hegemony comes from an unregenerate aristocrat, 'dead and not dead', as David Punter points out in *The Literature of Terror* (London: Longman, 1980) p. 119.

21. Quoted by E. P. Gooch, 'Imperialism', in *The Heart of the Empire*, p. 389.

22. Said, *Orientalism*, p. 190.

23. Benita Parry, *Delusions and Discoveries: Studies on India in the British Imagination, 1880–1930* (Harmondsworth, Middx.: Allen Lane, 1972) p. 78.

24. 'Stoker appears from the text to be almost traumatised by a specific sexual fear, a fear of the so-called "New Woman" and the reversal of sexual roles which her emergence implies' (Punter, *The Literature of Terror*, p. 261). See also Carol A. Serf, '*Dracula*: Stoker's Response to the New Woman', *Victorian Studies*, vol. 26, no. 1 (Autumn 1982) pp. 33–49; Ann Cranny-Francis, 'Sexual Politics and Political Repression in Bram Stoker's *Dracula*', in C. Bloom, B. Docherty, J. Gibb and K. Shand (eds), *Nineteenth-Century Suspense: From Poe to Conan Doyle* (London: Macmillan, 1988) pp. 64–79; and Wall, ' "Different from Writing" ', pp. 15–23.

25. See Cranny-Francis 'Sexual Politics and Political Repression': 'The assumption underlying this sequence of significances [the behaviour of the vampire females in Dracula's castle] is that normal women . . . are passive and sexually receptive, not initiatory. The titillation value of these women . . . is precisely a function of their transgression of conventional behaviour, a transgression which will, inevitably, be punished' (p. 66). Thus: 'Lucy's sexual aggressiveness . . . will be seen as her greatest crime and will provoke a combined male assault and assertion of dominance' (p. 67); and 'Mina is eventually saved . . . because she colludes with the men, accepting her rape as a sign of her own guilt. . . . In her acceptance of patriarchal ideology Mina asks that if she transgresses patriarchal norms by becoming sexually assertive, the men should return her to normality – rendering her sexually passive, submissive, receptive' (pp. 71–2).

26. For example, in such diverse texts as *Wuthering Heights* and *Jane Eyre*, *Lady Audley's Secret* and *The Woman in White*; *Adam Bede* and *Tess of the d'Urbervilles*.

27. 'As my gaze met his, the lower side of what the conquest of this fair lady would mean, burned in my brain; fierce imaginings blazed before my eyes. To win her – only to win her . . . Rage took hold of me. "You hound!" I cried' (*B*, p. 540).

28. Dracula, apart from an involuntary spasm of desire for the blood that Harker's shaving-cut releases, feeds upon men only when imprisoned on an all-male sailing-ship. Stoker's vampire women prey on men and children.

29. The racial significance of Dracula's attempted conquest is emphasised by John Allen Stevenson, 'A Vampire in the Mirror: the Sexuality of *Dracula'*, *PMLA*, vol. 103, no. 2 (1988) pp. 139–49: 'inter-racial sexual competition is fundamental to the energies that motivate this novel. . . . The problem of inter-racial competition would have probably had especial resonance in 1897' (p. 140); Dracula 'is an imperialist whose invasion seeks a specifically sexual conquest' (p. 144), 'imperilling the racial integrity of the West' (pp. 146–7).

30. 'on the instant, came the sweep and flash of Jonathan's great knife. I shrieked as I saw it shear through the throat; whilst at the same moment Mr Morris's bowie knife plunged into the heart' (*D*, p. 382). See C. F. Bentley, 'The Monster in the Bedroom: Sexual Symbolism in Bram Stoker's *Dracula'*, *Literature and Psychology*, vol. 22 (1972) pp. 27–34 ('Dracula is rendered powerless, symbolically castrated, by having his head cut off', p. 31) and Astle, 'Dracula as Totemic Monster', pp. 102–103.

31. As Anne Cranny-Francis states: *Dracula* 'enacts . . . the clash of conflicting discourses which problematizes bourgeois ideology; the positivist discourse of technology and the new scientific world view and the Christian discourse which, nominally at least, governed the ethical and moral practices of that society' ('Sexual Politics and Political Repression', p. 77).

32. 'if only I had retained the normal attitude of a scientific observer, I should, in all probability, have solved the mystery of my Oriental friend, and . . . his example of the genus of COPRIDAE might have been pinned – by a very large pin! – on . . . a monstrous piece . . . of cork . . . he and I had played together a game of bluff – a game at which civilization was once more proved to be a failure' (*B*, p. 550).

33. 'we unconsciously formed a sort of board or committee. Professor Van Helsing took the head of the table. . . . He made me [Mina] sit next to him . . . and asked me to act as secretary' (*D*, p. 239).

34. Rosemary Jackson, *Fantasy: The Literature of Subversion* (London: Methuen, 1981) p. 119.

Part Two
Some Branches: Postwar Science Fiction

Part Two
Some British Postwar Science Fiction

5

Scientists in Science Fiction: Enlightenment and After

PATRICK PARRINDER

It is thirty years or so since scientists in general became aware of the image-making powers of science fiction. In the middle to late 1950s it was common to argue that science fiction 'of the more responsible sort' could be used to propagate scientific knowledge and to help recruit adolescents into the scientific professions. Scientists began to wonder whether they ought not to be represented more favourably in a genre which was rapidly spreading from books and magazines to new outlets in comics, cinema, radio and television. Typical of the time was a paper by the astronomer Patrick Moore which inspired a lengthy debate at the 1955 UNESCO conference on the dissemination of scientific knowledge. Moore argued that each country should set up a science fiction selection board, so that novels distinguished by 'scientific soundness' (together with a category of scientifically unsound novels thought to possess 'wholesome' qualities of literary merit) could be given a stamp of approval. If this were done, science fiction could play a useful part in the propagation of knowledge, thanks to its ability to reach readers in urgent need of instruction who seldom if ever read a factual work.[1]

Naïve though Moore's proposal may have been, the idea that people's enjoyment of science fiction deserves to be exploited for 'higher' ends seems irresistible to the more utilitarian commentators on the genre. 'High-tech' enthusiasts, for example, often complain that science fiction fails to present science and technology in a sufficiently favourable light. Science, it is said, is caricatured and vulgarised in the entertainment media while the stereotyped scientist, an 'egghead' or a 'boffin', is either a dangerous fanatic or a helpless nincompoop. Since there is a continuing shortfall in recruitment to science courses, science fiction, according to this argument, may even take its share of the blame for the sluggishness of the national economy.

At the other end of the spectrum are the radical critics who accuse science fiction writers of slavishly and unthinkingly endorsing scientific values. Neo-Marxists believe that orthodox science fiction reinforces the ideology of 'scientism', which serves the interests of the ruling élites of present-day capitalist society. The genre privileges and glamorises science by suggesting that 'technical fixes' on their own could transform human life. The popularity of imaginary futures in which scientific discoveries have made social conflict and class organisation unnecessary is, for these critics, a sign of science fiction's prevailing political complacency.

Linking these rival ideological positions is a crucial area of agreement about what science fiction is and does. Science fiction is seen as a propaganda medium worth capturing and, moreover, as one that has (or ought to have) a close and symbiotic relationship with science itself. To the extent that these premises are justified they are the product of the era (roughly, 1895–1945) during which scientific values and the scientific outlook were the common faith of intellectuals belonging in the vanguard of progress. It was during this period, the period of what I shall call the Scientific Enlightenment, that science fiction became a popular medium and acquired its modern label. This was also the great age of the scientist-as-protagonist. All this has changed, in ways that scientists commenting on science fiction have often been the last to recognise. One of the most striking features of the science fiction of the last twenty years is that scientists are far less commonly represented in it than they used to be.[2]

I SCIENCE FICTION AND THE SCIENTIFIC ENLIGHTENMENT

The Scientific Enlightenment had its roots in the positivist philosophy and the science-versus-religion debates of the Victorian age. Modern scientific materialism, like the eighteenth-century Enlightenment, defined the good society as one which was organised on rational lines, free of the superstitions and religious dogmas of the past. By the early twentieth century, scientists were accustomed to appeal to the scientific 'attitude' or 'method', rather than to 'facts' and 'laws' as their nineteenth-century predecessors had done. Measured by this yardstick, all sorts of social practices, from metaphysics to ornamental architecture and slum housing, were found wanting. The vision of a scientifically planned social order was close to the heart of every major political innovation of the time, from the New Deal in America to Leninism in Russia. Even the Nazi ideal of a racially-pure Thousand-Year Reich was dependent on the ruthless and methodical application of supposedly scientific ideas.

Science in these years was generally seen as a progressive, subversive and destabilising influence on society. As late as 1959, C. P. Snow could plausibly affirm that, statistically, 'more scientists [were] on the left in open politics', and that, whether left or right, 'they had the future in their bones'.[3] In the 1940s and 1950s Snow's statistical majority of left-inclined scientists included most of the world-famous leaders of the scientific profession, as well as numbers or popular-science writers and journalists (though not necessarily of science fiction authors). Some, like J. D. Bernal and J. F. Joliot-Curie, were pillars of the world Communist movement.[4] Other left-wing scientists criticised Communism in its Stalinist guise as not being 'scientific' enough. H. G. Wells, when he joined J. B. S. Haldane and Julian Huxley in contributing to a series of BBC talks on *Reshaping Man's Heritage* in 1944, described himself as an 'extreme revolutionary, who considers the doctrines of the Communist Party . . . fifty years behind the times'.[5] C. H. Waddington's popular exposition of *The Scientific Attitude* (1941) asserted that science itself was a crucial source of political values. Science, Waddington wrote, 'has certain social requirements on whose satisfaction it must insist'.[6]

In Britain the Scientific Enlightenment reached its apogee in the late 1930s, as can be seen, for example, from the output of Pelican Books, the Penguin non-fiction imprint founded in 1936 which included Wells, Haldane, Julian Huxley, Sir James Jeans, J. G. Crowther, A. N. Whitehead and Sigmund Freud among its first authors. (Still more remarkably, the third Pelican to be published was Olaf Stapledon's science-fiction novel *Last and First Men*.) But at the very same time that it was being so energetically propagated, the scientific ideal was being systematically deformed from without and corroded from within. The 1930s saw the emergence of 'Nazi science', culminating in the grotesque experiments performed in the death-camps, and 'Soviet science' which gave birth to the Lysenko scandal. In the 1940s, secret scientific developments in Britain and America played a vital part in the outcome of the

Second World War. The war in the Far East was ended by the dropping of the atomic bombs made in a laboratory – Los Alamos – which embodied the most sinister and tragic aspects of the Scientific Enlightenment. The scientists at Los Alamos were not forced to lie or cheat, nor were they criminals or psychopaths, nor was their work condemned by the rest of the scientific community. They were simply the victims of forces which (thanks in part to their scientific training) were beyond their comprehension and control. An unnamed central European researcher, interviewed at Los Alamos by Robert Jungk in 1949, summed up his experience in these terms: 'What an extraordinary and incomprehensible thing! My whole youth was absolutely devoted to truth, freedom, and peace; and yet fate has seen fit to deposit me here where my freedom of movement is limited; the truth that I am trying to discover is locked behind massive gates; and the ultimate aim of my work has to be the construction of the most hideous weapons of war.'[7] What an epitaph on the intoxications and delusions of the intellectual power which scientists had wielded!

The term 'science fiction' dates from the 1930s. The genre, however, first achieved popularity in the 1880s and 1890s when it was usually known as 'scientific romance'. The early writers of scientific romance, including such reputable literary figures as Nathaniel Hawthorne, Mark Twain and Edgar Allan Poe, often had no more than a smattering of actual science. Jules Verne was the first science fiction writer of the sort envisaged by Patrick Moore – an adventure-story writer who set out to sugar the pill of technical instruction for a largely juvenile readership. H. G. Wells, by common consent the greatest of science fiction writers, began by revolutionising science fiction at the turn of the century and went on to become a leading protagonist of the Scientific Enlightenment. The association between science and science fiction remained close from the period of Wells's early romances until the end of the 1950s. Indeed, the particuar type of science which had most inspired science fiction writers reached its baroque culmination in the 'space race', which was triggered off by the launching of the Soviet Sputnik in 1957.

The interrelationship of science and science fiction – which was nowhere stronger than in Britain – can be illustrated by some significant personal biographies. H. G. Wells's first book was *A Text-Book of Biology*.[8] His earliest published work appeared in the students' magazine of the future Royal College of Science (now part of Imperial College). T. H. Huxley, then Dean of the college, was the formative influence on Wells and his fellow-students. Huxley took evolutionary theory as the basis for a general descriptive science of natural phenomena, which he called 'physiography'; at the same time, he cautioned against the vogue for reductive Social-Darwinist theories by stressing that the ethical or civilising process in man was often opposed to the natural evolutionary process. Huxley's biology class of 1884–5 contained no less than four future authors of textbooks of physiography.[9] Wells's lifelong friendships with some of his fellow-students, such as R. A. Gregory, the future editor of *Nature*, were instrumental in maintaining his contacts with the scientific community. Later his eldest son became a zoologist, compiling *The Science of Life* (the encyclopaedic successor to the *Text-Book of Biology*) with his father and Julian Huxley.[10] Among the principal episodes of Wells's later career were his presidency of the Educational Section of the British Association for the Advancement of Science, and his unsuccessful bid to become a Fellow of the Royal Society.[11]

Among British science-fiction writers since Wells, Arthur C. Clarke and Naomi Mitchison have been noted for their extensive and visible contacts with the scientific community. Clarke (b. 1917) originated the idea of the communications satellite in a 1945 article.[12] He played a major part in the early years of the British Interplanetary Society, which was founded in 1933 and reconstituted in 1936 with Clarke as Treasurer and E. J. Carnell – later to become editor of *New Worlds*, Britain's leading science fiction magazine – as Publicity Director. Clarke did two stints as Chairman of the BIS (1946–7 and 1950–3), and he must have been ideally placed to observe its progression from a small group of 'crackpot' visionaries to a professional association of rocket engineers employed, for the most part, in government research establishments.Two of his most influential books, *Prelude to Space*, a novel, and *The Exploration of Space*, a non-fiction treatise later reprinted by Pelican Books, were written during this period.[13] Since his emigration to Sri Lanka in 1956 he has continued to pour out novels, films, books and articles on the prospects of space exploration. Clarke, who was awarded the UNESCO Kalinga Prize for science popularisation in 1962, is in many ways the last of the great science popularisers – the last prophet, in fact, of the Scientific Enlightenment.

Naomi Mitchison (b. 1897) was a friend of Aldous and Julian

Huxley and sister to the great geneticist J. B. S. Haldane. Of her many novels it is the science fiction books, especially *Memoirs of a Spacewoman* (1962) – in which she almost single-handedly invented feminist SF – which are most likely to be remembered.[14] Mitchison, like Wells, is a writer who has always lived in a scientific environment and kept up with scientific ideas. Her novel *Solution Three* (1975) is dedicated to James D. Watson, who described a weekend spent at the Mitchisons' home in *The Double Helix*, his personal history of the discovery of DNA.[15] Mitchison's interest in genetics was undoubtedly kindled by her brother, whose own scenarios of *Possible Worlds* and possible ends to the world influenced a whole generation of science fiction writers.[16] Haldane, an indefatigable scientific journalist, left an unfinished science fiction novel, *The Man with Two Memories*, among his posthumous papers.[17]

Other British scientists who belong in the history of science fiction are Sir Julian Huxley (b. 1887), J. D. Bernal (b. 1901), Sir Fred Hoyle (b. 1915) and Patrick Moore (b. 1923). But there, more or less, the tradition stops. Of the British 'New Wave' writers, J. G. Ballard (b. 1930) has been a medical student, an advertising copywriter, and an RAF pilot – but not a professional scientist. Brian Aldiss (b. 1925) worked as a bookseller and literary editor. Michael Moorcock (b. 1939), who took over *New Worlds* magazine from E. J. Carnell, has no scientific background and has specialised in heroic fantasy rather than science fiction. Of the newer generation of leading writers only one, the American Gregory Benford, stands out as a practising physicist.

The relationship of science fiction to science in the United States was once fairly close, though with significant differences from the situation in Britain. In the USA, pulp magazine science fiction was pioneered by Hugo Gernsback, an engineer and entrepreneur whose chief interests lay in electronics. The prevalence of an 'engineer's science fiction' is best illustrated by the literary cult of the robot or electronic man; this was invented by the Czech writer Karel Čapek but saved for the Free World by Isaac Asimov, whose robot stories began appearing in 1940. American science fiction writers and editors were much more cut off from the scientific and literary establishments than their British counterparts. The magazines tended to be owned and managed by commercial publishing houses; in Britain *New Worlds*, by contrast, was initially run as a small business launched by its editor. In the so-called 'golden age' the typical British science fiction writer was a science graduate who (like Wells) had given up scientific work for the precarious existence of a literary hack. Neverthless, writers and editors as often as not took it upon themselves to specify the social requirements of science (in Waddington's phrase) and to help recruit their teenage readers into the scientific careers which they themselves had abandoned. In America, as in Britain, the generation of writers formed by the Scientific Enlightenment – Asimov, James Blish, Robert A. Heinlein, John W. Campbell and others – was succeeded by a new generation in which the leading figures had received little or no scientific education. (This is true, for example, of Samuel Delany, Philip K. Dick, Harlan Ellison, Ursula K. Le Guin,[18] and Robert Silverberg.) Today the aspiring science fiction writer, a contributor to *Fantasy and Science Fiction*, *Interzone* or *Isaac Asimov's*, is more likely to be an English teacher than a research student in physics.

Though I have concentrated on writers' biographies, a critical factor in the relationship of science fiction to science is the nature of the science fiction readership. In recent years, with the explosion of popular fantasy literature, the material marketed under the science fiction label has diversified so much that it is possible there is no longer a single public for it. Nevertheless, there are plainly still numbers of science students and technically orientated readers who look to science fiction as their 'own' brand of fiction. What is hard to tell is the extent to which this is a residual taste, relying on the continuing consumption of 'classic' authors of the Scientific Enlightenment period – the endless reprints of Asimov, Heinlein, Clarke and their contemporaries and imitators. One would expect the newer and more experimental science fiction, written by authors with little scientific training and whom one does not imagine as regular readers of the *Scientific American*, to appeal to a rather different public. John Boyd's *The Last Starship from Earth* (1969) begins with a mathematics student, Haldane IV, who takes a symbolic wrong turning when driving to the university science museum and lands up instead in an art gallery. 'Self-respecting students of mathematics rarely visited art galleries: but there it beckoned',[19] we read, and the art gallery, not the science museum, is the source of the subsequent adventures. Harlan Ellison (b. 1934) may be the first new generation science fiction writer to have terminated his formal education by getting himself kicked out, not from a science laboratory, but from a creative writing class. Ellison and his generation of writers anxiously questioned the 'science fiction' label, and it is always possible that the next New Wave will wash it away altogether.

II SCIENCE FICTION, SCIENCE AND IDEOLOGICAL CRITIQUE

A historical and sociological sketch of British and American science fiction such as I have attempted leads to the conclusion that the association of science fiction with science has diminished, and is likely to diminish still further. With this in mind we may look more closely at the two opposing critiques of the ideology of science fiction outlined at the beginning of this essay. I shall refer to these respectively as a conservative and a radical critique, though it is only in the aftermath of the scientific Enlightenment, and by a process of historical irony, that these labels have come to seem the appropriate ones.

We have seen how it was borne in on nuclear scientists after Hiroshima that science had become the tool of the military establishment. The stirrings of an international peace movement among scientists in the late 1940s were quickly stifled by the onset of the Cold War. Any scientist felt to be disloyal or soft on Communism (that is, not accepting the need for the continuation of secret military science under virtual wartime conditions) was liable to lose his job. Soviet successes in space exploration and nuclear technology produced near-panic in the West, and concern was expressed over the future supply of military scientists. It was in this context that greater efforts were demanded of science fiction writers. Walter Hirsch, writing in the *American Journal of Sociology* in 1958, was convinced that the United States was falling behind the Soviet Union in its ability to attract young people into the scientific professions. (The same concern, in a British context, was forcefully expressed by C. P. Snow in his famous 'Two Cultures' lecture the following year.)[20] 'Several recent studies of high-school students', Hirsch wrote, 'indicate that their attitudes toward a scientific career are often negative and their views of scientific work unrealistic. The sources of these attitudes are still largely unexplored, but it is plausible that the reading of science fiction is such a source.'[21] Hirsch noted that propagandists for science fiction such as Isaac Asimov (cited for a 1956 article in *Chemical and*

Engineering News) tended to maintain that science fiction gave a highly sympathetic and positive view of science; other writers, however, were not so sanguine. Hirsch tried to resolve the question by empirical research, undertaking a content-analysis of 300 stories published in science fiction magazines between 1926 and 1950 and selected at random. Though his presuppositions, research methods and mode of presenting his conclusions strike us as naïve today, some of the conclusions themselves are of considerable interest. Over the 25-year period Hirsch notes a steady decline in the number of stories with scientists as major characters. The scientist-hero had declined in popularity rather more drastically than the scientist-villain, even though there were still twice as many heroes as villains (*IS*, pp. 508–9).

If science fiction, as Hirsch maintains, is more often than not favourable to scientists, it is nevertheless distinguished from other modes of popular culture by its vehement attacks on the business élite and its outlook (*IS*, p. 509). Moreover, in the later stories scientists are increasingly presented in a 'bureaucratic' rather than an independent setting, and social improvements are usually brought about, not by human action or by technological developments, but by alien intervention. In short, Hirsch believed that science fiction had outlived its phase of 'naïve adulation of the omnipotent and omniscient scientist' (*IS*, p. 510). He took comfort from the observation that American science fiction had not been unduly influenced by the polemical anti-scientific stance found in British writers like Aldous Huxley, George Orwell, and C. S. Lewis – though these authors had been disconcertingly popular on both sides of the Atlantic (ibid.). The article plainly implied (though Hirsch stopped short of spelling it out) that in the national interest American writers ought to redouble their efforts to produce positive – but also informed and 'realistic' – views of the scientist as hero. In the 1950s, similar goals were being much more explicitly set for science fiction writers in the Soviet Union.

By the early 1970s scientific apologists had perhaps come to expect less of the genre, and a 1974 article by Milton Millhauser on 'Scientists in Fiction from Swift to Stevenson' is notable for its indictment of the whole British science fiction tradition. From Swift to Stevenson, Millhauser wrote, 'the image of the scientist was either ludicrous or evil at a time when in fact British science achieved triumphs that were . . . universally renowned'.[22] Even in Wells there was 'a faint suggestion of the air of the "forbidden experiment"', a view of science as an 'unstable ally, disposed to press further than we had expected or to pursue its own ends in preference to ours' (*NH*, p. 297). The harmful effects of this early literary treatment of the scientist were, in Millhauser's view, still current in the form of the 'subliterary cliché which represents the scientists as at best eccentric and faintly comic, often alien, often somehow "unsound", and frequently positively evil' (*NH*, p. 288). Why, then, had British writers so blatantly refused to take a proper pride in the achievements of British scientists? Millhauser argued that this 'failure' was due to psychological factors – the comfort of stereotyped responses and defence mechanisms against the unknown (*NH*, p. 304). The nearest he came to a sociological explanation was in noting that science and its practitioners remained unfamiliar to nearly all nineteenth-century Englishmen, whose main point of contact with scientific thought was by way of the family physician. Since medicine and medical inspections were usually disagreeable, the figure of the scientist emerging from the nineteenth-century imagination was all too often a grotesque and nightmarish medical man, a Dr Jekyll or a Dr Moreau (*NH*, p. 301).

The neo-conservatism of Millhauser's approach is apparent when we consider how well it complements the much wider thesis of Martin J. Wiener's recent study of *English Culture and the Decline of the Industrial Spirit* (1981). Weiner, again using mainly literary evidence, argues that British culture has systematically denigrated the achievements of industrial capitalism. English literature and historical writing 'was not only hostile to unregulated capitalism, but also questioned the value of technological advance, and the pursuit of economic growth itself'.[23] Here cultural analysis, of a selective and oversimplified sort, offers a highly fashionable set of explanations for the decline of the British economy and its manufacturing base, leading to an endorsement of the policies of industrial regeneraton associated with Margaret Thatcher. Wiener implies that writers ought to show unquestioning loyalty to industrial capitalism, just as Millhauser demands loyalty to 'scientism'. Unsurprisingly, the radical left has counter-attacked by subjecting literature – in our case, science fiction – to equal and opposite demands.

In a 1985 article on 'Scientism in Science Fiction', Gavin Browning defines scientism as 'the uncritical acceptance of what is termed "science" as objective knowledge, and a belief in the absolute value of what is called scientific'.[24] Scientism, in Browning's view, is part of the economic and ideological apparatus of the present phase of capitalism. Waddington's assertion that science had 'certain social requirements on whose satisfaction it must insist' would now be seen as an example of the self-delusions of the earlier generation of 'progressive' scientists, which made their work an unresisting prey to capitalist appropriation. Browning goes further, however, arguing that the scientific project at any time and place is constituted by its underlying sets of social relations. On this basis it could doubtless be argued that the Scientific Enlightenment was always an élitist, an idealist and a male-chauvinist movement. Did not Wells, Haldane and Bernal hold that scientists ought to have the status of a privileged group, that social engineering would one day replace politics, and that it was 'mankind's' future that was at stake and 'man's' inequalities that had to be removed?[25]

On the brighter side, Browning holds that both science and science fiction have a subversive and revolutionary potential, even if that potential is doomed to languish unrealised or (in the case of science fiction) neutralised. He gives clear indications of the sort of science fiction he would like to encourage. 'The value of any literature for the socialist project of creating a more harmonious social order', he writes, 'lies either in a depiction of conditions as they are now, giving the motivation "something must be done", or in the depiction of conditions as they might be – dystopian "we must not let this happen" and Utopian "this is what we must work towards"' (*SSF*, p. 30). He notes how authors have failed to depict major aspects of present-day scientific reality, in particular the experiences of the vast number of people in science-based activities supporting the military-industrial complex (*SSF*, p. 29). He has an interesting, and sympathetic, discussion of the one widely-read recent science fiction novel which gives a detailed portrayal of laboratory scientists at work: Gregory Benford's *Timescape* (1980).[26] I think that Browning is right in concluding that *Timescape* tacitly supports the present-day ethos of science by creating a world where 'scientists are people doing important things, where a "scientific" understanding of what is going on is seen as the objective reality that we are led towards, and where there is no alternative presented to the practice of science as it now is in the West' (*SSF*, p. 31). Browning, however, seems unaware of the problems that this sort of analysis raises.

For example, he appeals to Ursula K. Le Guin's *The Dispossessed* (1974) as the novel besides which *Timescape*, and the other books with which he deals, are found wanting. As he rightly says, this is 'one of the few science fiction books that has taken a radically changed set of social relations and given us a picture of how the changed science and society might work' (*SSF*, p. 35). Nevertheless, *The Dispossessed* is also vulnerable to the sorts of criticism he brings against *Timescape*. Shevek, the theoretical physicist who is the hero of Le Guin's novel, is unquestionably a scientific genius engaged in important work. The Principle of Simultaneity which he discovers will change the history of the universe by making an intergalactic federation or Ekumen (portrayed in other novels by Le Guin) possible. The narrative drive of *The Dispossessed* depends on Shevek's determination to finish his work whilst other people and other forms of social relations (some Utopian and some dystopian) are trying to prevent him. The narrative is the more easily resolved because he is a theoretician requiring little more than time to think and access to computers and learned journals. He is not a laboratory scientist, and his dilemma is more akin to that of (say) a Soviet dissident writer than a scientific worker at Los Alamos.

The problems in Browning's position, however, go much deeper than the terms of his (understandable) preference for *The Disposses-sed* over *Timescape*. Like Hirsch and Millhauser, he seems to be a utilitarian who regards science fiction as a basically realist literature which ought to produce propaganda for the causes he believes in. Such a view, reminiscent of the Stalinist 'socialist realism', is now calculated to produce howls of derision among the literary left, however it is regarded in scientific circles. The 'reflection theory' holding that literature should mirror 'social reality' – whether the empirical reality or some form of alternative reality – is condemned by structuralist and post-structuralist critics as itself part of the ideological apparatus of contemporary capitalism. Here we have the cruel comedy of Marxist critics appealing to what Browning might regard as a form of bourgeois scientism while Marxist scientists appeal to the bourgeois canons of literary realism.

I am not myself a structuralist, and I am uneasy with the facility with which radical literary critics currently argue that only through linguistic and formal experimentation (often incomprehensible to its first readers) can writing evade the production-and-consumption circuits of modern society. Nevertheless, the Browning version of science fiction, along with those of Millhauser and Hirsch, founders on its failure to understand the nature of literary meaning. These latter critics analyse the science fiction they discuss for its 'tendency' or 'content', as if the content could be read off in isolation from the form. In addition, the positive enthusiasm for science and its values desiderated by Millhauser and Hirsch has an irredeemably old-fashioned ring. Nor is Gavin Browning's opposition to scientism, to judge by his article, quite as novel or as radical as he would wish us to believe. Most science fiction readers have encountered statements of the absurdity of uncritical belief in science, and of the criminal complicity of scientists with capitalism and the military–industrial complex, in the fiction of that grand old conservative C. S. Lewis. However illuminating they are in some (fairly limited) respects, it would seem that each of the ideological critiques of the image of the scientists that we have considered leads to an impasse.

III   SORCERER AND SORCERER'S APPRENTICE

What sort of transaction is taking place when an author constructs a story based on scientific ideas, with scientists among its characters? Here is one answer to this question:

> SF characteristically transforms scientific and technological ideas into metaphors, by which these ideas are given cultural relevance. It works very much like historical fiction in this respect. It takes a body of extratextual propositions believed to be true, with no inherent ethical-cultural significance, and endows it with meaning by incorporating it in fictional stories about characters representing typical values of the author's culture.[27]

The writer's task, according to Csissery-Ronay, is to endow scientific ideas with 'cultural relevance', 'meaning' and 'typical values'. It is not that the meanings already exist, although conventions and processes for generating these meanings certainly do. A puzzling aspect of the transaction is that it involves propositions believed to be true becoming part of stories known to be fictional. This development highlights the background of ambiguity and contradiction which is, I would say, essential to all meaning. Meanings and values do not come into existence to fill a vacuum-like original state of non-meaning (Csissery-Ronay's formulation is potentially misleading here). Rather, like succeeding hypotheses, they are chosen in preference to earlier meanings and values. A meaning, like an electric current, can only be generated against a resistance; but once generated it becomes part of the resistance against which further meanings are generated.

Images of the scientist in science fiction possess the latent ambiguity and ambivalence of all meaning – an ambiguity which is highlighted in any 'fictional' text, with the result that these texts can never be restricted to a single authoritative reading. Nor did the image of the scientist come into existence in a vacuum. In the early nineteenth century a number of words crucial to scientific culture were first coined: the word 'scientist' dates from 1840, 'expert' (used as a noun) from 1825, 'specialist' from 1856. The twentieth century has extended the range with a series of slang terms – 'egghead', 'boffin', 'backroom boy', 'whizz kid' – representing the sort of caricatured image of the scientist found in science-fictional stereotypes. Nevertheless, it is striking that literary images of the scientist have continued to allude to a much older conception of the savant, or master of esoteric knowledges, which dates from before the Scientific Revolution of the seventeenth century. This is not as surprising as it at first seems. If (as the above argument suggests) all meanings latently imply their own opposites, the literary image of the scientist is a tribute to science's own obsession with defining itself as the antithesis of mysticism, fairy-tales and magic.

Not only do scientists in science fiction often appear as lurid, melodramatic and evil, but they frequently (and usually quite explicitly) evoke the pre-scientific past. That is, the evil scientist – or the future scientist surviving into a post-industrial society – carries with him the trappings of sorcery, wizardry and alchemy. The good scientist will often relive the destruction of the alchemical tradition by experimental scientists such as Copernicus and Galileo. It is in stories of the triumph of empiricism over superstition, or of the Faustian nemesis of the scientist who proceeds from permissible to impermissible knowledge, that the 'typical values' of scientific culture are often asserted.

Two specific aspects of science fiction need to be borne in mind here. The first is that, to the extent that it expresses our sense of wonder at new technologies, it tends to endow them with the air of conjuration and magic. Arthur C. Clarke expressed this idea in his much-quoted statement that 'Any sufficiently advanced form of technology is indistinguishable from magic'. The time travel, antigravity, artificial intelligence and genetic engineering of science fiction stories are modern equivalents of the magic carpet of the fairy-tales and the alchemist's elixir of life. The second relevant aspect of science fiction is its tendency (in common with other literary forms since the mediaeval period) to pursue the adventures of an isolated, individual hero. This hero moves through a series of social relations which gradually unfold his or her individual identity. The social relations themselves are often presented under the aspect of a puzzle or a mystery – a convention which tests to the full the hero's, and the reader's, powers of observation. Because of these fictional conventions the isolated observational scientist, either a field-worker or a 'pure' researcher separated from what he observes by the lens of telescope or microscope, became the norm in science fiction. Very often one such scientist, representing the official values of science, will be portrayed observing another, whose observations have led to his discovery of the secret and demonic powers of nature. In each case the isolated individual with his appalling secret is tacitly contrasted with the absent body of normal workaday scientists.

The appeal of these stories lies in the ambivalence of the stereotypes they invoke. They touch on intoxicatingly attractive aspects of science (the possibility of individual heroism, the potential conversion of secret knowledge into power over others) which form little part of the experience of the ordinary scientific worker and which provoke suspicion and fear among non-scientists. The orthodox scientific establishment would very much like to repress these images. At the same time, the recruitment of potential scientists depends on the glamour of science just as recruitment into the army depends on the covert appeal of uniforms and bullets.

The old tale of the sorcerer's apprentice is a classic expression of the ambivalence we feel towards esoteric knowledge. This tale can be traced back to Lucian and is best known in the ballad-version produced by Goethe ('Der Zauberlehrling', 1797).[28] In the story the apprentice decides to use one of his master's spells to save himself from the menial tasks he has been instructed to perform while the sorcerer is away. He recites the magic formula and commands the broom to fetch the water to fill the tubs in the house. When the tubs are full he finds he has forgotten the spell his master would have used to stop the broom doing its work. Luckily, the master-sorcerer comes home in the nick of time to prevent the house and all its contents from being washed away.

The story depends heavily on a couple of might-have-beens. The apprentice would have scored a secret triumph if only he had remembered the second formula; and total catastrophe would have ensued if the master had not happened to come home early. We have no difficulty in reading this as a story about a scientist (cast as a sorcerer) and a technology (disguised as magic). But, by the same token, it brings home the impossibility of separating both scientist and technology from a network of social relations. It is not hard to find in it such implications as the apprentice's resentment and rebellious desire to take over from his master, the sexual form his initiative takes (command of the broom), and the social threat of a technology replacing domestic labour usually performed by juveniles and females. A large proportion of Scientific Enlightenment science fiction, I would contend, relies on evoking and rehandling stereotypes of the sort found in 'The Sorcerer's Apprentice'. For example, any reader of science fiction could project a recognisably Heinleinian or Asimovian version, or for that matter a *Star Wars* version, of Goethe's tale. Heinlein would probably have made the complacent master forget his own spell, so that the disobedient apprentice had to hit on the right formula by instinct. Asimov would have built in a fail-safe device so that the broom countermanded its human controller once it saw the house was in danger. In *Star Wars* the apprentice could have been hypnotised into remembering the formula at the last minute by the sound of his master's voice. And so on.

To say that Heinlein and Asimov, outspokenly pro-science writers, can be fitted into the 'sorcerer's apprentice' framework is to say that their stories tend to demonstrate ambivalence by undermining their own explicit meanings.[29] 'The Tissue-Culture King', a 1927 story by Julian Huxley – much better known as a scientist, UNESCO Director-General and scientific populariser than as a science fiction writer – is a splendid example of Scientific Enlightenment ambivalence. Whatever meanings we find in this story (which was published almost simultaneously in the *Yale Review* and in the science fiction magazine *Amazing Stories*) the author can hardly be accused of hostility to science.

'The Tissue-Culture King' tells of an endocrinologist who is captured by a fierce African tribe and saves his skin by showing them the 'magical' powers of contemporary biology. Pursuing his experiments, he soon becomes adopted as the tribal witch-doctor.

He revolutionises the tribe in ways which evidently parallel the industrial revolution in Western societies. The twist is that, while he comes to love his captivity, he is gradually outwitted by a member of the tribe who turns the new biotechnology to his own advantage. Hascombe, the endocrinologist, had hoped to indulge in unlimited research at the expense of his tribal hosts. By the end he is simply a tool of their internal power-struggles.

The story of Hascombe is told by an explorer who stumbles on his research laboratory in the jungle. His first intimation of Hascombe's experiments is the sight of a two-headed toad. To the narrator, Hascombe is a 'bent' individual whose research has taken a wrong turning. He has used science in the hope of gaining power over his captors but, the narrator asks, what end did all this power serve? This narrator is intended to reassure us and to represent the cautious, rule-bound and morally responsible face of science. But science has two, or perhaps three faces.[30]

Read as an allegory, Huxley's story is a hostile cautionary tale about the incorporation of science by a (capitalist) political world. The way in which Hascombe is outwitted by a member of the tribe could be seen, for example, as a prophecy of the way in which Los Alamos scientists were 'used' to develop a bomb which could then be dropped on Japan. Yet Huxley's story, despite its demonic scientist and its cautionary allegory, does nothing to diminish the glamour and lure of science – in fact, it probably increases it. The double focus of Hascombe and the narrator combines the thrills and risks of illicit science with sober, rational hard-headedness. Huxley's hero is indeed a king for a season, and by leaving the Middlesex Hospital, where he was once a research worker, for the jungle he has gained the sort of power that other men envy.

Writers of the Scientific Enlightenment often portrayed the scientist as a man of destiny who had left common scruples behind and was dangerously in league with the illicit. This is true of Verne's Captain Nemo, of Wells's Griffin and Dr Moreau, and of the scientific worker idealised in J. B. S. Haldane's *Daedalus: or Science and the Future.* (1923): 'If every physical and chemical invention is a blasphemy, every biological invention is a perversion. . . . The scientific worker of the future will more and more resemble the lonely figure of Daedalus as he becomes conscious of his ghastly mission and proud of it.'[31] A more recent novel on similar themes, though concentrating on social groups rather than demonically isolated individuals is Naomi Mitchison's *Solution*

Three. (The novel is dedicated 'To [James D.] Watson who first suggested this horrid idea'.) In *Solution Three* civilisation has been slowly rebuilt after a nuclear holocaust by means of three successive imposed 'solutions': world pacification, control of population and food production, and the cloning of the great majority of new births. The result is a society in which heterosexuality is almost extinct and homosexual lovemaking takes place everywhere in public. Reproduction is still grudgingly allowed to the Professorials, a bunch of social misfits who produce the technology which keeps society going. It was the Professorials, going back to the pioneers 'Watson and Mitchison', who introduced the process of cloning everywhere except among their own ranks. The world has been turned into an oppressive welfare state in which freedom is restricted not by the police but by the ubiquitous counsellors and social workers. The despised Professorials come to the fore once again when a mysterious blight attacks the wheat crop (which is cloned throughout the world). In the nick of time scientists discover a blight-resistant strain of wheat and begin to argue the need to maintain an adequate gene pool – for humans as well as cereals. The novel ends with Solution Four: let copulation thrive.

As it happens, knowledge of the importance of genetic diversity is as old as the science of genetics. *Solution Three* presents a world in which scientists, who have long been taken for granted, are suddenly called upon once again to play a heroic role and avert a threatening human destiny. At the same time, the impending catastrophe, which results from the universal adoption of a policy of cloning, is of the scientists' own making. Scientific social engineering has been pursued in the interests of the ruling élite (seen as the enlightened guardians of society at large) and in defiance of elementary technological safeguards. Once again a tendency to glamorise scientists and their work is combined with the moral that esoteric knowledge should be used responsibly. The scientists' Solution Four is, needless to say, what common sense would have urged all along.

Though its author is a veteran of the Scientific Enlightenment, *Solution Three* is a novel of the 1970s in that the scientists in it have to be rescued from social insignificance. A society increasingly dominated by technological developments and hence organised on 'scientific lines' leads, it would seem, not to the supersession of politics but to the overshadowing of the scientists themselves. Where it does not simply retreat into fantasy, the science fiction of the last twenty years seems to confirm the view that society suffers from a superfluity of 'experts' and their products, so that the 'boffin' or scientific genius is no longer a charismatic figure. The protagonists of the early novels of J. G. Ballard – arguably the most influential science fiction writer of the last two decades – are members of the scientific and technological professions who can do no more than helplessly look on as technological society brings about its own self-destruction. Ballard records the failure of the Scientific Enlightenment, typically through his scenarios of the end of the Space Age. In other stories the nemesis of biological engineering is shown, as humanity is destroyed by internal psychic mechanisms inadvertently triggered off in the cause of 'progress'. The most that Ballard's protagonists can do is to achieve some insight into the process of their own decay. Ballard's negative and passive image of the scientific worker is the more remarkable when we consider that almost none of the younger writers (he is now in his mid-fifties) can be said to have put their stamp on the image of the scientist at all.

The prospect of a science fiction without scientists does not necessarily mean that there will be no representation of scientific knowledge. In his book *The Soft Machine* (1985), David Porush studies the genre of 'cybernetic fiction', a type of fiction written by post-modernist novelists such as Kurt Vonnegut, William Burroughs, Thomas Pynchon, John Barth, Donald Barthelme and others. In cybernetic fiction there is characteristically a dissolution of literary realism, or the illusion that the novel depicts a consistent external reality. Instead, the book itself asks to be treated as a cybernetic machine, constructed by an author who invites the reader to take over the roles both of programmer and decoder. The human figures in these novels tend to be not scientists rationally and connectedly working things out, but lost individuals obsessively wandering around in the hope of stumbling across a coherent message. The premise of cybernetic fiction thus seems to be, not that knowledge is 'discovered' by individuals and then applied for the benefit (or otherwise) of humanity, but that knowledge is a consumer product sold or dumped in the market-place in the form of pre-processed cybernetic packages. The producers of this knowledge are invisible, and what they do is no longer of any interest; it is simply a form of magic, and what matters is what we do with it. The novel (which in this account curiously resembles a home computer) invites us, not to 'understand' something, but to sit back and learn the prepackaged games we are invited to play.

The cybernetic metaphor has penetrated very deeply into such fiction, to the extent that Porush can argue that 'the authors of cybernetic texts view themselves as machines'.[32] In such a context a 'serious' novel – in the old-fashioned humanist sense of a novel which offers moral, historical and psychological insight – can only be written by sleight-of-hand. (For example, Vonnegut's *Slaughterhouse-Five* is presented by the author not as a novel about the bombing of Dresden – of which Vonnegut himself was a survivor – but about the 'impossibility' of writing, or even attempting to write, a novel about Dresden.)

Though viewed by Porush as a minority avant-garde art, cybernetic fiction has many popular analogues, notably the recent genre of 'Cyberpunk' novels such as William Gibson's *Neuromancer* (1984). The typical Cyberpunk hero, a streetwise 'computer cowboy', is yet another version of the sorcerer's apprentice. I have argued that, in the period of the Scientific Enlightenment, scientists could draw considerable comfort from fiction which presented their work as potentially tyrannical, catastrophic and evil. Today, however, it would seem that the image of the hero as discoverer has given place to the hero as information-processor, operating on knowledge that already exists. The hacker's function is not to increase knowledge but to keep it circulating, sapping the power and wealth of the corporations which monopolise it. Science as social currency is taken for granted in these novels, but it is no longer seen as a disinterested pursuit and the age of the great discoverer has long vanished.[33] Science-fiction writers under fifty no longer seem to believe that scientists have the future in their bones. It could be that this message is getting through to the readers, too.

NOTES

1. Patrick Moore, *Science and Fiction* (London: Harrap, 1957) pp. 10, 186–9. An earlier version of the third part of this paper was published as 'The Scientist in Science Fiction – Sorcerer or Sorcerer's Apprentice?', in *Sci-Tech Report*, ed. Jon Turney (London: Pluto Press 1984).
2. See Brian Stableford, 'Scientists', in *The Science Fiction Encyclopedia*, ed. Peter Nicholls (Garden City, N.Y.: Dolphin Books, 1979) pp. 533–4; also T. Hosty, '"A Universe of Death": Images of Science and

Technology in Twentieth-Century Science Fiction', unpublished PhD dissertation, University of Exeter (1983).

3. C. P. Snow, *The Two Cultures: And A Second Look* (New York: Mentor Books, 1964) p. 16.

4. On scientists and Communism, see Gary Werskey, *The Visible College* (London: Allen Lane, 1978).

5. H. G. Wells, 'Man's Heritage', in J. S. Huxley *et. al.*, *Reshaping Man's Heritage: Biology in the Service of Man* (London: Allen and Unwin, 1944) p. 7.

6. C. H. Waddington, *The Scientific Attitude*, 2nd ed. (Harmondsworth, Middx.: Penguin Books, 1948) p. 35.

7. Robert Jungk, *Brighter than a Thousand Suns* (Harmondsworth, Middx.: Penguin Books, 1960) p. 11.

8. H. G. Wells, *A Text-Book of Biology* (London: W. B. Clive, 1893).

9. R. A. Gregory and H. G. Wells, *Honours Physiography* (London: Joseph Hughes, 1893); A. Morley Davies, *First Stage Physiography* (London: University Correspondence College Press, 1897); A. T. Simmons, *Physiography for Beginners* (London: Macmillan, 1896), and *Physiography for Advanced Students* (London: Macmillan, 1897).

10. H. G. Wells, in collaboration with Julian Huxley and G. P. Wells, *The Science of Life* (London: Amalgamated Press, 1930).

11. See C. P. Snow, 'H. G. Wells', in *Variety of Men* (London: Macmillan, 1967), and the forthcoming biography of Wells by David C. Smith.

12. Arthur C. Clarke, 'Extra-Terrestrial Relays', *Wireless World*, vol. 51, no. 10 (October 1945) pp. 305–8.

13. Arthur C. Clarke, *Prelude to Space* (London: Sidgwick and Jackson, 1953), and *The Exploration of Space* (1951; revised edn, Harmondsworth, Middx.: Penguin Books, 1958).

14. Naomi Mitchison, *Memoirs of a Spacewoman* (1962; London: New English Library, 1977).

15. Naomi Mitchison, *Solution Three* (London: Dennis Dobson, 1975); James D. Watson, *The Double Helix* (London: Weidenfeld and Nicolson, 1968).

16. J. B. S. Haldane, *Possible Worlds* (London: Chatto and Windus, 1927).

17. For a fuller discussion of Haldane and Mitchison, see my article 'Siblings in Space', *Foundation*, vol. 22 (June 1981) pp. 49–56.

18. Though Le Guin was the daughter of two famous anthropologists, she took her degree in romance languages and wrote a thesis on French Renaissance poetry.

19. John Boyd, *The Last Starship from Earth* (London: Pan Books, 1972) p. 7.

20. Snow, *The Two Cultures*, pp. 37–43.

21. Walter Hirsch, 'The Image of the Scientist in Science Fiction: a Content Analysis', *American Journal of Sociology*, vol. 43 (1958), p. 506. Subsequent references are given in the text, preceded by the initials IS.

22. Milton Millhauser, 'Dr Newton and Mr Hyde: Scientists in Fiction from Swift to Stevenson', *Nineteenth-Century Fiction*, vol. 28 (1973–4) p. 304. Subsequent references are given in the text, preceded by the initials *NH*.

23. Martin J. Wiener, *English Culture and the Decline of the Industrial Spirit* (Cambridge: Cambridge University Press, 1981) p. 82.
24. Gavin Browning, 'Scientism in Science Fiction', *Foundation*, vol. 33 (Spring 1985) p. 24. Subsequent references are given in the text, preceded by the initials *SSF*.
25. Consider the following book-titles: H. G. Wells, *Mankind in the Making* (London: Chapman and Hall, 1903); J. B. S. Haldane, *The Inequality of Man and Other Essays* (1932; Harmondsworth, Middx.: Penguin Books, 1937); Bertrand Russell, *Has Man a Future?* (Harmondsworth, Middx.: Penguin Books, 1961); not to mention famous titles by T. H. Huxley and Charles Darwin.
26. Gregory Benford, *Timescape* (London: Gollancz, 1980).
27. Istvan Csissery-Ronay, 'The Book is the Alien', *Science-Fiction Studies*, vol. 12 (1985) p. 6.
28. Johann Wolfgang von Goethe, 'Der Zauberlehrling' (1797), in *Poems of Goethe: A Selection*, ed. Ronald Gray (Cambridge: Cambridge University Press, 1966) pp. 140–3.
29. Asimov stops short of exploring his contradictions, and this accounts for the thinness of his extremely popular stories. Heinlein is more complex.
30. Julian Huxley, 'The Tissue-Culture King' (1927), rept. in *The Road to Science Fiction*, vol. 2, ed. James Gunn (New York: Mentor, 1979) pp. 145–66.
31. J. B. S. Haldane, *Daedalus: or Science and the Future* (London: Kegan Paul, 1923) pp. 44, 92–3.
32. David Porush, *The Soft Machine: Cybernetic Fiction* (New York and London: Methuen, 1985) p. 186.
33. It is significant that, in the twenty-first century world of William Gibson's *Neuromancer* (London: Gollancz, 1984), the name of Alan Turing, the pioneer of artificial intelligence, is perpetuated in the repressive 'Turing Police'.

6

The World as Code and Labyrinth: Stanislaw Lem's *Memoirs Found in a Bathtub*

JERZY JARZĘBSKI

In *Memoirs Found in a Bathtub*, written in 1960 and published in 1961, we find – as in *Solaris* which dates from the same time – the *world as metaphor* and a blending of inner and outer experience;[1] we also find the methodological directives of *The Investigation* (1959),[2] only now they are applied to an attempt to solve the mysteries of one's existence (or that of the hero), rather than the mystery of the disappearances of corpses from a mortuary, as in this metaphysical quasi-mystery novel, a conventional police investigation that offers also an alternative statistical solution in addition to the tried stereotypes of such a case.

In the introduction, written in the 32nd century, we learn that the *Memoirs* are a precious relic discovered in the ruins of the Third Pentagon where once the military and espionage services of a crumbling United States had found their last refuge (*MB*, p. 11). Cut off from the world in the Rocky Mountains, the 'Building' degenerates into a totally closed institution, whose activities exhaust themselves in ceaseless inner reorganisations, which consist of nothing more than an exchange of personal roles within the system, whereas there are no changes in the under-lying structure of the 'Building', the basic system of masks or functions.

A newly recruited agent – the narrator – traverses the endless corridors of the 'Building' in an attempt to discover its *essence*, the meaning of his mission, which is shrouded in mystery from the beginning. The novel is constructed upon the same principle as a nightmare: every few moments the hope arises that the hero has arrived at the core, the 'authentic' state, but again and again it turns out that this was just another test, a provocation, a set-up game. Gradually we arrive at the conviction that there is no single

79

'*truth*' about the 'Building'; or rather, that its mere existence and nothing more is 'the truth'.

The idea would, of course, be absurd that the general pattern of a strict political satire could support meanings of this kind. The author enters smilingly into a secret agreement with the reader when he gives him to understand that the 'Hyberiad Gnostors . . . consider the first twelve pages apocryphal, an addition of later years' (*MB*, p. 12). That is exactly the number of pages of the introduction. In a world of total make-believe the text of *The Memoirs* too can only be a code, or, to put it exactly, a many-levelled code, like the fragment of *Romeo and Juliet* that is 'cracked' in several ways by the decoding machines.

Therefore *The Memoirs* are a satire on the bureaucratic apparatus of modern espionage on the surface only; the author confesses that he got the idea for his book after he had read the memoirs of espionage agents: 'I discovered that a spy who habitually works for both of two inimical sides, after he has worked in this manner for a number of years, cannot himself know any more to whom he causes harm and for whom he is useful; the difference between the patriotic and the traitorous activities is then simply a statistical difference (it is the result of to whom he has done more harm by the information he has provided, and to whom he has done less harm or helped more or less, respectively).[3]

Of such a spy it could be said that his whole life becomes a code that permits of two interpretations. The *meaning* of the acts of the spy can be gauged only if we know both purposes which he serves at the same time. If we are in possession of a single key, we will subtract anything from his behaviour that as a result seem to be mere 'noise', and concentrate our attention on those of his actions which are of importance from the standpoint of that mission. If we take the other mission as the key, then something else will now, of course, appear to be the 'noise', and something else the coded signal. In his *Memoirs* Lem has extrapolated this situation to the point of absurdity, in that he has the whole 'Building' crawl with agents who not only serve two, but three, four, five or more missions simultaneously. In this situation every human being that one encounters proves to be a palimpsest, a many-layered structure of text-masks, which only the initiated can rip off one after another. This applies even for more complex interactions between characters, such as the drinking session with the 'professors', for which the priest Orfini provides the hero with many interpretations. Generally it can be said that in the novel *The Investigation*, and in the short story 'Inwazja' ('The Invasion', 1959), we encounter phenomena which give the impression of intentionality;[4] but these works end with the discovery that they mean nothing and serve *nobody*, whilst in *Memoirs* Lem leads us into a world in which, on the contrary, *everything* has some hidden meaning and in which reality is semantically so overloaded with meaning that it becomes impossible to find a single consistent interpretation for it.

'The Building' is a kind of labyrinth, in which the centre – the protected holy place – is simultaneously nowhere and everywhere. The hero succeeds without difficulty in penetrating to the most holy place – the office of the supreme commander – but he doesn't discover there anything that would deserve any attention, nothing that would explain the essence of the *'Building'*.[5] The motif of the labyrinth plays a key role in Lem's work and appears in manifold ways: as the intestines of a cosmic monster ('Szczur w labiryncie' ['The Rat in the Labyrinth'], 1957), as weird cities on alien planets (*Astronauci* ['The Astronauts'], 1951; *Eden*, 1959), as a gigantic Gla (*Obłok Magellana* ['The Magellan Nebula'], 1955), as airports in *Return from the Stars* (1961) and *The Chain of Chance* (1976), as the city of London in *The Investigation* (1959), and finally in the threatening vision of a mind-labyrinth in the mechanical King Gnuff ('The Tale of King Gnuff', 1964) who grows to the dimensions of a whole city.[6] In European cultures, indeed in the civilisations of the world, the symbol of the labyrinth carries many different meanings: it forms the structure of heaven but also that of the human soul, it may hide the divine and the satanic; for some it is only a maze of misleading ways, for others an image of the burdensome path of life, the search for knowledge and holiness.[7] Practically all of the meanings mentioned apply to Lem's 'Building', if only because paradoxically all the elements of these pairs of opposites co-exist. In the introduction the hypothesis is briefly touched upon, 'that the building was raised purely in the minds and hearts of the faithful' (*MB*, p. 9), and although we are then given to understand that the physical ruins of the building had been discovered, the meaning of this hypothesis is basically not devalued, since *nothing* in the building is simply truth or lie, for it strives after perfection through the realisation of all possible states of being. The 'Building' therefore may be understood as a certain psychic structure as well as a cosmos, and this view is supported in the novel itself:

In fact, I had suspected for some time now that the Cosmic Command, obviously no longer able to supervise every assignment on an individual basis when there were literally trillions of matters in its charge, had switched over to a random system. The assumption would be that every document, circulating endlessly from desk to desk, must eventually hit upon the right one. A time-consuming procedure, perhaps, but one that would never fail. The Universe itself operated on the same principle. And for an institution as everlasting as the Universe – certainly our Building was such an institution – the speed at which these meanderings and perturbations took place was of no consequence.   (*MB*, p. 16)

The question whether such a cosmos is of a satanic or a divine essence appears to be meaningless, since in it 'good' and 'evil' are created by chance and the observer can at every moment look upon the structure of facts and interpretations as they emerge in each case to form the face of the Devil or of God. The world-building projected by Lem is therefore a *text*, a text however that can be interpreted with the help of a million different codes. Moreover, every single one of those codes is 'true', since it creates some meaningful import when applied to the text.

In interpreting Borges's literary parables Lem finds that the *Memoirs* are comparable to those of them which see the world as a structure which remains immutable as a system of processes and roles, regardless of how one interprets its essence, and independent from the interchangeable agents who execute ready-made patterns or actions.[8] It would also be possible to discover a similarity of concept in other texts of Borges which Lem discusses without mentioning his own novel, especially with 'The Library of Babel', in which the world is seen as a library with an immeasurable number of volumes which exhaust all the permutations of graphic signs possible in the usual volume.[9] It is easy to see that such a library would contain all possible discoveries of the past and the future, in so far as they can be expressed in language at all, but also works of inspiration and perversion, the true descriptions of planets of which we do not know, and the telephone books of any city on Earth; unfortunately, it would also contain an ocean of nonsense and utter hogwash, and all of this would be created by the tiresome but also absolutely infallible method of combining a certain set of letters, numbers and punctuation marks.[10]

The universe thus conceived is an attempt to reconcile two apparently contradictory qualities: total chaos and total order, utmost thoughtlessness and the most refined intention. It is easy to see that Lem's 'Building' is based on similar principles (it is no accident, by the way, that it not only *functions* in its own right, but also *collects* books and the objects accumulated in museums), and its senile rottenness by no means impairs its functioning, for impeccable perfection of action must in any case be realised somewhere in it – accidentally.

Memoirs Found in a Bathtub, a plan of a universe and at the same time an allegory of the life of the individual under the most different aspects (of cognition, the striving after values, service for society and the state, individual self-realisation and so on) may be seen in relationship to various works by other authors. A far-removed source of inspiration is certainly the – similarly 'labyrinthic' – *Saragossa Manuscript* by Jan Potocki;[11] the existential allegory, the entanglement of the individual in the institution, connect it with Kafka's *The Castle* and Genet's *The Balcony*;[12] the category of the 'interpersonal' as an antidote against the extravagance of the contents and the potentional meanings of the universe with Gombrowicz's *Cosmos*;[13] the topical political metaphor with Tadeusz Breza's *Urzạd* ('The Office').[14] Examples could be multiplied. All of these (and other, similar) texts must be contained potentially in the meaning of the 'Building', just as in it (the 'Building') is also hidden in the text of the *Memoirs* itself, which falls into the hands of the hero for a moment.[15]

At the beginning of this essay we attributed the message of Lem's book to the 'methodological' stream which is represented by 'The Invasion' and *The Investigation*, as well as the anthropological-philosophic in which *Solaris* precedes *The Memoirs* most closely. The world-view which we know from the first two works has been stood on its head, as has already been noted. But this only seems to be the case: a world in which *everything* is intentional, *everything* meaningful, and in which at the same time any element and any occurrence is buried under a hill of (contradictory) meanings, is just as inaccessible for the simple procedures of an investigation as is the reality of the 'anti-mystery', *The Investigation*. After a certain threshold of complexity, the intentional apparatus of the 'Building' can hardly be distinguished from a nature that works without aim. For we recognise that the hero, in asking what the meaning of his secret mission may be, is basically asking about the meaning of his own life, and that the Building which is at the same time the universe, answers him evasively and ambiguously, as if it were nature itself, for which the question of 'meaning' is in itself meaningless. It is not the 'essential' nature of the subtext that is of decisive importance for the cognitive processes, but the informational complexity of the research subject itself. The 'methodological instructions' remain unchanged.

Much more interesting than this is an attempt to interpret the anthropological–philosophical contents of *Memoirs*. Its hero is unmistakably an allegory of Everyman, and the cognitive-axiological labours that await him in the Building may now be mastered by instructions derived from cognitive theory. They are totally unpalatable for the individual, who has somehow to make the best of life in the labyrinth. Is it really so astonishing that the hero should try to find out what the nature of his mission may be? Perhaps he should accept that its meaning may be, after centuries, accidentally divulged to one of his successors. From the standpoint of the individual, such stoicism would hardly appear to be likely, to say the least. Therefore the hero sticks to the thread of his mission, for this is all that he has, and this will lead him, as he believes, through all the labyrinthine byways of the Building and help him to arrive at the centre, the essence, the structure of the universe-building. The strange old man he meets hastens to assure him that there is an infinite number of *authentic* patterns of the labyrinth, and afterwards he learns that there exists no text that could be decoded without leaving some residue, and that the mission is merely a roundabout way of pursuing desperate attempts to understand one's own fate.

But if the Building is a poor imitation of the universe, it can also be called a paraody of the perfectly self-serving leviathan state. In this sense the question: to what purpose do I live?, which the hero asks nature and its hypothetical creator, can also be put to the rulers of organised society. The hero then would not only be a 'human being' but also a 'citizen', in respect to whom the state is so superior and powerful that the individual can neither understand its actions in their totality nor even find a meaningful place in its structure. This leviathan cares in a special way for its citizens, that is to say, it takes notice of them, but only as statistical persons without any individual qualities. In the actions of the state towards the individual it is difficult to decide what is intentional and what unintentional, what arises from a caring and what from a repressive attitude. It should be added here that both are equally an insult to the dignity and the sovereignty of the individual. The 'Building' is furthermore a parody on the police state which is based on the total supervision of all of its citizens. However, this model has been, if one may call it that, 'thought through' to its consequences: the state is informed about every step of every citizen, not because it incessantly spies after him or her, but because it knows from the beginning *everything* that can be known, even including that which will occur to the hero only a moment, an hour, a month or a year in the future. For this reason the 'Building' appears to any person lost in it now also as an institution that completely ignores his/her existence, and now as a reality built for him/her alone. Out of the chaos of random steps of the 'agent' there finally emerges a consistent thread, and the colleague from the Secret Service unfailingly predicts imminent events. But even these two diametrically opposed hypotheses can be reconciled.

To live authentically, to do good or evil spontaneously, is impossible in the 'Building', for every conceivable human act is already contained in it and has been foreseen; you cannot strive after anything save for the 'exit', which is the same as death (but even death is at the end of the novel subject to the suspicion of falsification and make-believe). In this situation the hero, who has exhausted all attempts to mislead nemesis, enters into a 'conspiracy' with the priest Orfini, a 'conspiracy' in which everything proceeds according to the scenario which is preset by the structure of the Building. The secret organisation is exposed immediately, for the traitorous accomplice sacrifices the hero with cold intent. But this treason has no larger significance. Both conspirators have from the beginning agreed to the price which they have to pay for their endeavour, and they consider the whole ritual frame of their plot as something of no consequence. The important thing is only the 'inner agreement' that they share over this new game – it alone remains to them as something of their own in a desert of ubiquitous pretence. This private, interpersonal 'reality' proves to be their only redoubt in a world infested with total distrust.

Memoirs Found in a Bathtub had not much luck with the critics. Often the reviewers could not read anything but a surface level; they wrote of a 'satire on the secret service' and held forth on the grotesque humour of the hero's adventures. I see now that I myself have fallen into the opposite extreme: from the remarks above it can hardly be gauged how witty the book is. However, the humour of *Memoirs* is bitter, for it is a philosophic humour. It is all too easy for us to laugh about the poverty of the characters' existence, for instead of faces they only present masks, they have – like the mannikins of Bruno Schulz – only the one side which they show in public. Even the main protagonist has neither a biography nor a clear psychological individuality. The comic aspects of a mind that overreaches its logical categories to grasp the world with their help appear in a different light, whether seen from the viewpoint of somebody who struggles with a problem or from the viewpoint of an observer who isn't involved in the events of the plot. Sometimes the reader sees the undergrowth of problems through the eyes of the hero from such a proximity that it is as if he himself must worry about them, and in other cases the literary characters appear to him like ridiculous puppets who are wholly caught up in their conventional world. If the one reading experience causes feelings of metaphysical awe and shudder, the other causes frenetic explosions of mirth, and yet both can be traced, as happens often with Lem, to one and the same philosophical dilemma.

Lem's work could be arranged along an axis connecting a point in which the viewpoint of a hypothetical recipient is partly identical with that of the hero (or heroes) and partly with a point at which these perspectives are separated by the utmost distance. In such a representation of Lem's narrative strategies, *Memoirs Found in a Bathtub* would thus occupy a place right in the middle of the axis between the point of 'identification' and the point of 'distancing'.

Translated by Franz Rottensteiner.

NOTES

1. Stanislaw Lem, *Memoirs Found in a Bathtub*, trans. M. Kandel and C. Rose (New York: Harcourt Brace Jovanovich, 1986); Stanislaw Lem, *Solaris*, trans. J. Kilmartin and S. Cox (London: Faber and Faber, 1971). Future references to the former will appear in the text, preceded by the initials *MB*.
2. Stanislaw Lem, *The Investigation*, trans. Adele Milch (New York: Harcourt Brace Jovanovich, 1986).
3. Stanislaw Lem, *Fantastyka i Futurologia* (Krakow: Wydawnictwo Literackie, 1970) vol. II, p. 289.
4. Stanislaw Lem, 'Inwazja', in *Inwazja z Aldebarana* (Krakow: Wydawnictwo Literackie, 1959).

5. On the motif of the labyrinth in Lem's writing, see Piotr Kuncewitz, 'Dezdroza otkurtnej niekończoności', *Współczesność* no. 13 (1982).

6. Stanislaw Lem, 'Szczur w labiryncie', in *Dzienniki Gwiazdowe* (Warsaw: Iskry, 1958); *Astronauci* (Warsaw: Czytelnik, 1951); *Eden* (Warsaw: Iskry, 1959); *Obłok Magellana* (Warsaw: Iskry, 1955); *Return from the Stars*, trans. B. Marszal and F. Simpson (London: Secker and Warburg, 1980); *The Chain of Chance*, trans. L. Iribarne (London: Secker and Warburg, 1978); 'The Tale of King Gnuff', in *Mortal Engines*, trans. M. Kandel (New York: Seabury Press, 1977).

7. Compare J. E. Cirlot, *A Dictionary of Symbols*, trans. from the Spanish by J. Sage (London: Routledge and Kegan Paul, 1971) entry: 'Labyrinth'; P. Santarcangeli, *Il Libro dei Labirinti: Storia di un mito e ti un simboli* (Florence: Vallecchi Editore, 1967).

8. Lem, *Fantastyka i Futurologia*, pp. 288ff.

9. Jorge Luis Borges, 'The Library of Babel', trans. D. A. Yates and J. E. Irby, in *Labyrinths* (New York: New Directions, 1962).

10. Lem uses a similar method in his 'The Sixth Sally, or How Trurl and Klapaucius Created a Demon of the Second Kind to Defeat the Pirate Pugg', in *The Cyberiad*, trans. M. Kandel (New York: Seabury Press, 1974).

11. Jan Potocki, *The Sargossa Manuscript*, trans. E. Abbott (London: Cassell, 1962).

12. Franz Kafka, *The Castle*, trans. W. Muir and E. Muir (London: Secker and Warburg, 1930); Jean Genet, *The Balcony*, trans. B. Frechtman (London: Faber and Faber, 1966).

13. Witold Gombrowicz, *Cosmos*, trans. E. Mosbacher (London: MacGibbon and Kee, 1967).

14. Tadeusz Breza, *Urząd* (Warsaw: Panstwowy Instytut Wydawniczy, 1960).

15. This text is not identical with the one which we have to hand; the quotations are not totally identical. It is rather an analogous structure of meaning, one of the countless versions of standardised history.

7

The Neglected Fiction of John Wyndham: 'Consider Her Ways', *Trouble with Lichen* and *Web*

THOMAS D. CLARESON and ALICE S. CLARESON

Because the name of John Wyndham is widely known in Britain and because Michael Joseph and Penguin have kept his works in print, the manner in which both British and American critics have dealt with his fiction comes as a surprise. In a two-page commentary Brian Aldiss, while acknowledging the 'magic' in *The Day of the Triffids* (1951), labels *Triffids* and *The Kraken Wakes* (1953) 'cosy disasters', declaring that both books are 'totally devoid of ideas but read smoothly'.[1] He covers the other three novels of the 1950s in a sentence for each. The American John Scarborough relies heavily on Aldiss, even to the 'magic' in *Triffids*, although he names *The Chrysalids* (1955) as Wyndham's finest book but remains uncertain as to Wyndham's stance regarding the mutations so necessary to the story.[2] He finds Wyndham 'deeply committed to comfort and reliability in existence', a man who 'speaks clearly about a desired complacency . . . a widespread desire to return to the "good old days"'.[3] The academic use of his books continues 'because they are quite clean [sexually] and generally free of controversy'.[4] In a brief overview in Peter Nicholls's *Encyclopedia*, John Clute notes that Wyndham gave an 'eloquently middle-class English response to the theme of DISASTER' and wrote for a specific market at a specific time.[5] Perhaps the critic who gives a reader the greatest help is Julius Kagarlitski, who names Wyndham the 'truest disciple of H. G. Wells in English literature'.[6]

Given the political temper of the last twenty years or so, one can readily accept these judgements as far as they go. What remains troublesome is what the critics omit. In fact, with the exception of Clute, they tease the reader. For example, Kagarlitski asserts that '*Trouble with Lichen* is the least interesting of Wyndham's novels' and refers to Shaw's *Back to Methuselah*.[7] 'By contrast' to *Triffids* and *Kraken*, Aldiss believes ' "Consider Her Ways" and *Trouble with Lichen* are rich in speculation',[8] while Scarborough suggests that 'Only *Trouble with Lichen* would rise to *Chrysalids'* level'.[9] Similarly an earlier checklist of science fiction novels with a strong woman protagonist, Neil Barron's *Anatomy of Wonder*, summarises *Trouble with Lichen* only in terms of extending life 'virtually indefinitely' and of the need to mass-produce the lichen.[10] Despite the publication of these basic reference books – Nicholls's *Encyclopedia* excepted – in the 1980s, none so much as mentions Wyndham's posthumous novel, *Web* (1979).[11]

From the early 1950s onward one of the chief characteristics setting John Wyndham's fiction apart from that of his contemporaries is his introduction of strong women characters. Increasingly essential to the development of his story-lines and themes, they provide a woman's perspective of the action and emerge as Wyndham's chief critics of society. In *The Day of the Triffids*, originally written for the American market, Josella Playton soon becomes more than a damsel-in-distress and, particularly in the late stages of the narrative, serves as a critical voice (only in one sequence during her separation from William Masen, the first-person narrator, does Wyndham take her off-stage in order to give Masen a chance to see a variety of communities set up by survivors of the disaster as he searches for Josella). Phyllis Watson, a writer of documentary radio scripts, is clearly brighter and more concerned than her husband, the narrator of *The Kraken Wakes*; at several crucial points her observations anticipate subsequent feminist criticism. The young mutant Sophie Wender precipitates the action of *The Chrysalids*; the telepaths Petra (six years old) and Rosalind (early adolescence) join her to develop the plot and themes, while the woman from Sealand (New Zealand) effects the rescue of the mutant children. After the initial sequence of *The Midwich Cuckoos* (1957) Wyndham does arbitrarily take the colourful Janet Gaylord out of the action, just as he allows her husband, the first-person narrator, to spend eight years in Canada in order to gain a convenient time lapse during which the alien children grow up.[12] However, Anthea Zellaby – who is pregnant by her husband instead of the aliens – gains as much importance as her husband Gordon, the author of 'While We Last'. Not only does she warn him about the nature of the alien children, but she both teaches and consoles the women of Midwich during their pregnancies.

Significantly, only in *The Outward Urge* (1959), the one narrative in which Wyndham dealt with man's conquest of space, are women unimportant, though not entirely absent.[13] During the 1950s his most provocative achievement occurred when he created Jane Waterleigh, the first-person narrator whose letter makes up the body of 'Consider Her Ways' in 1956. The importance of that date cannot be emphasised too much. Despite the concern of such writers as Philip José Farmer and Theodore Sturgeon with sexuality in their early fiction, and except for Philip Wylie's *The Disappearance* (1951),[14] John Wyndham was the first postwar writer to focus on the problems of gender as they have been explored in more recent decades. Certainly he is the first major mid-century writer to portray a feminist Utopia/dystopia.

A Bachelor of Medicine and recently bereaved widow, Jane Waterleigh volunteers to be the first human to test the effects of the drug chuinjutain. Its use brings about a 'personality transfer' projecting her almost a century into the future to a world in which only women survive. At least a lifetime earlier a plague had exterminated men. (Like all of Wyndham's plagues, this one was man-made: a Dr Perrigan sought to find a virus to eliminate the brown rat; somehow his experiments went astray.) Momentarily amnesiac, Jane Waterleigh regains consciousness in the 'elephan-tine' body of Mother Orchis, a woman who has recently given birth to her third set of four babies. The amnesia is a skilful touch; not only does it heighten her bewilderment, her sense of estrangement, but it also permits her to view the world with pristine eyes as she is moved from the Centre to her home. She surprises her companions by suggesting that she would like to read a book, and then she horrifies them by proposing that there are two sexes. Almost at once, even before she regains her memory, Jane decides that she suffers from hallucinations, for she cannot accept as reality the world around her.

Centring on Jane Waterleigh's immediate perceptions, Wyndham gives the narrative a rich texture. Jane (and the reader) experiences the future society before its structure is explained by a woman nearly 80 years old, an historian who asks to be called simply Laura. But Jane is no passive onlooker overawed by Utopia; Wyndham was too skilled a craftsman and too knowledgeable of the literary flaws of Utopian fiction to permit that. Confronted by an authoritarian state made up of four classes – the Doctorate, professional women who also govern; the oversized Mothers, who breed; the muscled Amazons, who work; and the 'miniature'

Servitors, who care for the Mothers and the Doctorate – Jane refuses to assume the role of Mother Orchis in that world. This attitude first brings the threat of arrest and then the interview with Laura.

As the little parlourmaid offers Jane wine, Jane changes the tone of the narrative with a single question when she suggests that the wine should be Madeira (*CW*, p. 44). Gone is the sense of estrangement; the two women settle into a discussion dominated by the historian's analysis of the historical process. Jane does not accept unquestioningly the thesis that the plight of twentieth-century women arose from the manner in which commerce and cinema glamorised the Romantic ideal originating in eleventh-century France; women, indoctrinated to be '"consumers"' and '"spenders of money"', became an '"exploited class"' (*CW*, pp. 48, 54). Although Jane does not deny this premise in principle, she protests that it distorts her time, her personal experience. In short, she tries to argue. While Laura insists that Jane is a conditioned product of twentieth-century society, Jane asserts that there is an essential and necessary place for romantic love. Laura replies that such love was a mere '"convention"' of a small, protected segment of humanity (*CW*, p. 60). She introduces a theme increasingly common to Wyndham's fiction: the will of a species to survive. She explains that the '"Will to power"' motivates humanity at all ages and that survival is the end-all (*CW*, p. 54). To achieve survival, the designers of the future society took the anthill as their model.

One can perhaps fault Wyndham for not coming down explicitly on Laura's side. Indeed, read in the 1980s, Jane's protestations regarding the role of/need for romantic love may well seem, at best, perfunctory and dated. What is of greater importance, however, is that in the mid-1950s Wyndham initiated in science fiction a discussion which has not yet been completed. Although some contemporary feminists might regard Laura and Jane's debate as too simplistic, Wyndham nevertheless anticipated some important issues a decade before the Women's Movement found its voice. In addition, through the use of an open ending, he gave 'Consider Her Ways' a dystopian tone absent from his earlier novels. By shifting abruptly to a third-person dialogue, Wyndham dramatises the reaction of a solicitor and Dr Hellyer, for whom she worked, to Jane's manuscript. They read her letter after she has killed Dr Perrigan. They agree that her experience with chuinjutain has led to hallucinations, but they regard the letter as a figment of her distorted imagination. Its existence, hopefully, will strengthen a legal defence admitting her temporary insanity. After reading Jane's manuscript/letter, they muse over the fact that parthenogenesis is not '"*impossible*"' (*CW*, p. 72); thus the premise itself is '"faintly disturbing"' to them both (ibid.). The solicitor would also feel a '"bit easier"' in mind if Jane had been '"more thorough in her inquiries"' (p. 73); Dr Parringer has a son who promises to continue his father's research. This punchline, with its implications of the futility of Jane's efforts and of impending catastrophe, anticipates the ending of the posthumous *Web*.

From Josella Playton of *The Day of the Triffids* onward, Wyndham gave more and more of his attention to complex women who increasingly broke away from traditionally feminine roles. If Jane Waterleigh – his first woman narrator in a major work – voiced his awareness of problems which would shape the ensuing decades, then Diana Brackley, the protagonist of *Trouble with Lichen*, became his activist – the first full portrait of a conscious female activist in science fiction. To dramatise her story most effectively, Wyndham changed several of his basic narrative strategies. In his novels his usual narrator is a man who serves more as an observer than as an actor who brings about whatever resolution is possible. It is as though Wyndham sought to achieve a neutrality or an aesthetic distancing resulting in an objectivity. (Much happens to the youthful narrator of *The Chrysalids*, but he himself does not effect the resolution. Though he is obviously not neutral, he is another of Wyndham's reporters.) In *Trouble with Lichen* Wyndham switches to the omniscient third person. Whether or not they present an account of events which happened sometime in the past, his narrators unfold the action chronologically in a single sequence from the beginning – one is tempted to say from first encounter – to the end. Not so *Trouble with Lichen*: it opens with the funeral of Diana Brackley, which is compared to the funeral of Emily Wilding Davison, the Suffragette who was fatally injured when she threw herself in front of the King's horse at the Derby in 1913. Immediately one understands that whatever the action of the novel, its theme will elaborate on the 'unfinished work' of Diana Brackley.

Having thus served notice, Wyndham deftly sketches the early career of his protagonist, beginning just after she has received a scholarship to Cambridge. Her initial conversation with several of her teachers sets her apart from her mother who has been '"awfully sweet"' about the scholarship and Diana's plans to read chemistry:

> She tries. . . . Why is it that mothers still think it so much more respectable to be bedworthy than brainy? . . . I mean, you'd expect it to be the other way round. . . . Well, being just a woman and nothing else does strike me as one of the dead-end jobs. . . . I mean you can't get any promotion in it, can you? – well, not unless you take it up as a courtesan, or something. (*TL*, pp. 12, 14)

Wyndham carefully shows the differences in expectations between Diana and her mother, who repeatedly suggests that marriage, child-bearing and a home are what a young woman '"ought"' to cherish and desire; '"she's happier that way"' (*TL*, p. 41). Earlier, she has compared Diana to her own Aunt Annie, a Suffragette arrested several times just before the First World War, of whom her family was ashamed. In her mind 'neither Diana nor Annie is '"just an ordinary person"'; Diana's father, however, does not '"give a hoot"' what his daughter has inherited from '"a militant great-aunt"'; he believes that she is a remarkable young woman (*TL*, pp. 15–16).[15] Diana knows of her great-aunt and speaks of '"male privilege"' and women's '"readiness to be conditioned"' (pp. 43, 44). Soon after she inherits £40,000 on her 25th birthday, thereby gaining a financial independence unknown to her parents, she admonishes her mother: '"I know, darling. A sensible girl would go out and buy herself a husband"' (p. 41). Repeatedly everyone around her remarks how unfortunate it is that she possesses both intelligence and physical beauty; after she goes to work for Darr House Developments, Dr Francis Saxover, who heads the institute, says to his wife:

> I'm beginning to get reactionary. Wondering whether young women above a certain level of plainness should be allowed to squander the time of higher educationists at all. It's become one of the expensive items in our economy of waste. (*TL*, p. 28)

Perhaps no contemporary writer has stated the dilemma of twentieth-century women more cogently than does Wyndham in the first section of the novel. Yet it is Diana's mother who, unwittingly, first enunciates an awareness of the problem which will motivate

Diana's subsequent actions: '"A woman is always up against time, and it doesn't do to forget it"' (p. 41).

Initially, while Wyndham lays the groundwork of his theme, he keeps the storyline simple. At Cambridge after hearing Dr Francis Saxover lecture, Diana decides to read biochemistry; after graduation, still having '"a schoolgirl crush"', she goes to work for him at Darr House (*TL*, p. 36). By chance (and separately because of a misunderstanding) they both investigate a lichen which grows only in a limited area of Manchuria. As an omniscient author Wyndham repeatedly allows her to reflect 'years later' on the early stages of her research (p. 39). She understood even then that she/they had discovered one of the 'cardinal . . . explosive' secrets of the world (p. 39), but she also believed that her idol, Dr Saxover, did not know what to do with it. Troubled, she made a decision only after one of her frequent conversations with Saxover's daughter, Zephanie. The young woman reports that her history teacher agrees '"about the change from forcing women to do things to simply diddling them"' into roles as '"squaws and second-class citizens"' (p. 44). But the teacher echoes Diana's mother when she remarks that because of the cycle of child-bearing and raising and because '"life is so short"', women do not have enough '"time to spare"' to correct the injustices of the world (p. 44). The next morning Diana resigns to undertake her new 'career' (p. 44). Despite such implications Wyndham does not yet reveal the nature of the secret.

Just as eight years were skipped over in *The Midwich Cuckoos*, so fourteen years elapse before Saxover tells Zephanie and her brother that the lichen was the source of an 'antigerone' which retards ageing. Treated with 'lichenin' since their childhood, the two may expect a lifespan of some 220 years. He tells them only because he has just learned that Diana has the secret and expects publicity because of a lawsuit. In London during the intervening years Diana has supplied the antigerone to the patrons of her beauty salon, Nefertiti. Not surprisingly, throughout the remainder of the narrative Saxover remains hesistant/indecisive, always waiting for the proper time to reveal his research, while Diana takes action. The novel gains a sharp edge of satire as Wyndham shows the ways in which corporations and individuals alike attempt to gain control of the lichen; his wit and anger intensify as he focuses increasingly on the news media, especially the papers, each with its own 'angle'.

As controversial rumours build, one of Diana's patrons, Lady Janet Tewley, informs her that '"the jig is very nearly up"'; her husband, the friend of a director of Sandworth Chemical Products Limited, has been making enquiries. (Lady Tewley comes from the same mould as Diana. She '"did do four years of medicine"' and three years earlier became convinced that her beauty treatments somehow involved an age retardation factor.) Diana at once releases the letters she has prepared for her patrons and members of the press and calls for a news conference. As Wyndham's vignettes scathingly but humorously scan the reactions of various segments of society, both public and private (a part of the religious establishment invokes God's will that man live for three-score and ten years, while the *Evening Flag* desires that the first to receive the antigerone be the Queen), Lady Tewley becomes instrumental in forming the League for the New Life (LNL). As critics organise a demonstration to be held in Trafalgar Square, Diana requests time on BBC–TV to tell all about the antigerone. At one point she goes to Darr House, where Saxover asks her:

> Do you see yourself marching at the head of a monstrous regiment of women? Addressing mass rallies? . . . Is it power you want?   (*TL*, p. 144)

Diana wants no personal power. She denounces the '"nugatory, piffling sort of lives that most women live"' (ibid.). Undoubtedly there is something of Wyndham personally – and of George Bernard Shaw – in her succinct assertion of the novel's theme and modern society's central dilemma:

> All my life I've been watching potentially brilliant women let their brains, and their talents, rot away. I could weep for the waste of it; . . . But give them two hundred, three hundred years, and they'll either have to employ those talents to keep themselves sane – or commit suicide out of boredom.   (*TL*, p. 145)

She wants *Homo diuturnus* to be '"born somehow"', even if it '"takes a caesarian to give him a start"' (ibid.). In this way Wyndham ties *Trouble with Lichen* to that vision within science ficton going back into the nineteenth century which sees the emergence of a species superior to *Homo sapiens* as the next step in the development of humanity.

On the way to the BBC broadcast Diana is shot down; the Home Service announces her death. The demonstration by those opposed to the antigerone in Trafalgar Square is broken up by its supporters. After Diana's funeral the LNL itself demonstrates in Trafalgar Square and marches to Parliament Square. Because he is impressed and because China has turned the small part of Manchuria where the lichen grows into a collective farm, the Prime Minister allocates £10 million for research – after a conversation with his wife Lydia provides him with insight into the problems his government faces as a result of the 'disappearance' of the expected antigerone (*TL*, p. 185).

Particularly in view of the dénouement, however, some may suggest that Wyndham gave the novel too tidy an ending. They may well forget that immortality itself was not the main issue for Wyndham as it was for a number of his contemporaries in science fiction. He used the single premiss of an extended lifespan as a means to satirise the nature of mid-century British society and to raise basic questions about the role of women in modern society, questions which have shaped much of the thinking of the English-speaking world during the last two decades.

Early in *Trouble with Lichen* Diana's 'maths' teacher reflects that the faculty of St Merryn's High not only tries to educate the young women at the school but conducts 'a kind of jungle warfare' on their behalf – 'and the better-looking the child, the more slender, generally speaking, are her chances for survival, for the partisans of ignorance enfilade [the teacher's] route in greater numbers' (*TL*, p. 10). *The Midwich Cuckoos* ends with Gordon Zellaby's note to his wife Anthea: 'We have lived so long in the garden that we have all but forgotten the true face of Nature. . . . If you wish to keep alive in the jungle, you must live as the jungle does.'[16] Appropriately, Wyndham used the jungle – the isolated island of Tanakuatua in the Western Pacific (9°N, 170°W) – as the setting for the main action of his last novel, the posthumous *Web* (1979).

Despite continuing interests in giantism (monstrosities), psionics and encounters with extraterrestrial aliens, Wyndham's mid-century contemporaries concentrated on engineering and technology to create their science fiction worlds. As late as the 1950s, even when dealing with some catastrophe, most science fiction grew out of the American infatuation with the machine. With very few exceptions – the dogs in Clifford D. Simak's *City* (1951) come to mind – genetic engineering was presented as a matter of faith rather than an area to be explored closely.[17] In contrast, throughout Wyndham's fiction, as in H. G. Wells's romances of the 1890s, the heart of Wyndham's speculations lie in biology. Especially when coupled with statements regarding the will of a species to survive, as in 'Consider Her Ways', his references to the jungle lead to associations with Charles Darwin as readily as to Wells. At one point in *Web*, for example, another of his noteworthy women, the biologist Camilla Cogent, tells his narrator – who becomes increasingly disillusioned with the premises behind the vision of Utopia – that the concept of the balance of nature ' "could only have arisen in a comfortable, well-fed society which has forgotten what it is to struggle for existence" ':

> Nature is not motherly, she is red in tooth and claw, she ravens for food – and she has no favourites. . . . The same laws that operate for every species that outbreeds its food supply will operate for us.   (*W*, p. 84)

Such assertions must be carefully read, however, for one must not too easily judge Wyndham as a backward-looking conservative who believes in the outdated concept of the survival of the fittest. In like manner, to speak of his relationship to Wells primarily or solely in terms of their mutual concern for catastrophe – *The War of the Worlds* is most frequently referred to – misreads his greater indebtedness to the dark side of Wells's vision. They both worry about the ability of humanity and its civilisation to endure; both are aware that in the never-ending flow of change humanity is only one more transient species. From the turn of the century onward, Wells promoted the idea of Utopia. Wyndham never did. For a time, like the early Wells, he suggested that humanity might rebuild – *The Day of the Triffids*, *The Kraken Wakes* and *The Chrysalids*. After those three novels of the 1950s such hope disappeared. His posthumous novel *Web* stands as the most thoroughly dystopian statement of his growing disenchantment with the premisses of his own society and the future of humanity.

Internal evidence indicates that he wrote that novel during the last years of his life; he may well have been revising it at the time of his death. It seems idle to speculate here as to why it was not published until 1979. Although one may call its narrative structure cumbersome because two essentially expository chapters make up the first third of the novel, thereby postponing any account of the central dramatic action, those chapters remain essential to the development of Wyndham's themes.

To read 'the spider book' – as Wyndham himself apparently called *Web* – as just another tale of disaster ignores his complex interweaving of these themes.[18] Perhaps more than any other novel – at least in English literature – it chronicles the failure of a conscious and deliberate attempt to found a Utopia, '"a new society liberated from superstition, purged of blind faiths and ignorant beliefs, freed at last from the cruelty, misery, and frustration that these things have plagued mankind with from time immemorial"' (*W*, pp. 22–3).

Not only does the reader know immediately of that failure, but from the outset the narrator, Arnold Delgrange, '"the dreamer"'(*W*, p. 26), reveals his attitude toward the venture. Whenever asked how he became involved in such a '"crazy affair"' he suggests that his '"undiscriminating enthusiasm"' resulted from his being '"a little off-balance"' after the deaths of his wife and daughter in an automobile accident (pp. 5–6). Later on he reflects that once the journey to the remote Pacific got underway, he made '"the disconcerting discovery [that] I seemed in my earlier, or lyric, phase to have been thinking with all the naïvety of an early socialist that all [men] must love the highest rationality when they saw it"' p. 53). He asserts that as his judgement reawakened, '"as if from hibernation"', he had realised that the plans and intentions of the would-be Utopians were '"very general, not to say sketchy"' (pp. 68–9).

Delgrange's performance marks the most skilled use that Wyndham made of the first-person narrator, for he does more than merely observe/report the downfall of the 'Project'. In his disillusionment, he judges. While some element of satire colours most of his reflections, he does allow Frederick, First Baron of Foxfield, 'a man in search of a memorial' (*W*, p. 7), to speak for himself. This is essential, for the reader in the present, unromantic age must hear the enthusiastic, confident voice which infused so much of Western speculation from the Enlightenment through the '"Wonderful Century"' (p. 37) to, at least, the immediate postwar period. On the eve of the departure of the group whom he has financed, at a time when '"the State, now so pervasive, tends to abrogate to itself even the function of benefactor"' (p. 8), Lord

Foxfield addresses the would-be founders of the 'Enlightened State' (p. 12) at a hotel in Bloomsbury:

'. . . since man's image is God's, God must have intended man to become like God. . . .
'We have long been aware that man is the mightiest species in the creation. . . . Even now his domination of much of his environment is godlike: and his potentialities are unguessable. . . .
'We have now acquired the knowledge and the means to construct for ourselves a rational and mentally healthy form of society. . . . We have reached a stage where we can and must, if we are to survive – stop living with the fecklessness of animals, and take charge of our own destiny. If we are afraid to become men like gods – then we shall perish. . . .' (*W*, pp. 21–2)

Such is his clarion call to the voyagers. As Delgrange reminisces over a picture of the group assembled the next day on the deck of the *Susannah Dingley*, he acknowledges that, '"after all, given a fair chance, we might have made it – some of us"' (p. 23). And so they sailed for Tanakuatua; Lord Foxfield did not accompany them.

The second chapter records the history of Tanakuatua from its discovery in the last decade of the eighteenth century to the 1960s. It is undoubtedly intrusive, but through the narrator's reflections it permits Wyndham not only to comment on the ways of imperialism but also to emphasise that the once romantically idealised actions of heroic native migrations (and warfare) from island to island are gestures of an outmoded past, as well as pointing out that Tanakuatua became a site for a possible Utopia only because postwar nuclear tests forced Her Majesty's government to remove the native population. Lord Foxfield bought it from the government; not until much later did the natives – long interned on another island – learn of the sale.

At this point *Web* becomes essentially a dialogue between Delgrange and Camilla Cogent as they encounter the infestation of spiders. On the other hand, as a biologist she provides both information and insight about the spiders; on the other, she repeatedly questions the concept of 'man like god' – one should not forget how thoroughly that idea has been associated with Wells's Utopian speculations – and argues that the concept of the balance of nature is a '"myth. . . . An offshoot of the desire for stability – of the attempt to reduce the world to a tidy, static, and therefore comprehensible and predictable place"':

> It is part of the conception of a divinely appointed order in which everything had its place and purpose – and every man had *his* place and task.   (*W*, p. 82)

She concludes that the ' "search for stability is the most constant – and the most fruitless, quest of all"':

> [for] Nature is a process, not a state – a continuous process. . . . No species has a *right* to exist; it simply has the ability, or the inability.   (*W*, p. 83)

While reducing humanity to just another species, Camilla adds to her grim assertion when she asserts that ' "Mind is only a phenomenon which distinguishes the present dominant species"':

> The rest of creation gets along all right without it. But there are powers other than the mind. Again I refer you to the termites and the bees. . . . Mind, for all we know, is just a flash in the pan, interesting as a phenomenon, but unnecessary. Dominate today, gone tomorrow.   (*W*, pp. 132–3)

Although her views initially shock Delgrange, he acknowledges that society must change because, for example, ' "Nationalism is becoming too narrow, too restrictive. . . . but unification must come in one way or another – or else destruction"' (p. 86). One point that they readily agree on is that humanity will not survive into the future unless the problem of overpopulation is solved.

Camilla also gives the first warning that something is wrong on the island when she repeatedly wonders at the absence of the myriad of birds one would expect to see on a tropical island. They have been, of course, among the early victims, for the spiders have stripped much of the island of all animal life. Camilla infers that soon they will have to hunt for fish. She notices, too, that threads of their web carry 'millions of baby spiders' aloft on thermal currents (p. 118); the spiders are not irrevocably confined to Tanakuatua. Once begun, the action moves rapidly as members of the Utopian party are killed. When Camilla and Delgrange scout the periphery of the spiders' domain – networks of web in the trees and bushes, so bulky that they are visible from a distance, enclose the 'conquered and settled' territory of the spiders (p. 113) – the two are captured by three natives. On his chest their leader wears 'a childlike representation' of a spider painted in yellow so that Delgrange thinks it is '"like a crude heraldic emblem"' (pp. 145–6). He is the son of Nokiki, the witch doctor who resisted authority at the time of the nuclear tests and subsequently invoked a tabu forbidding any human to use the island. The three are militant activists seeking vengeance for the improper sale of Tanakuatua. Their leader denounces the effects of European civilisation on the natives and rejects the idea of Utopia 'free from outside interference' because '"There is no place in the world like that. No more"' (*W*, p. 157). He and his companions wish to help the spiders, their 'Little Sisters', whom the god Nakaa caused to spring from the corpse of Nokiki, the witch doctor (p. 157). They have destroyed the radio, thus isolating the Utopians, and finally they throw bags of spiders into the Europeans' camp to kill the remaining members of the party. Camilla and Delgrange regain the camp and, for a week until they are rescued, they remain in the state of siege. They cannot convey to their rescuers or the authorities in Britain 'the scale of the infestation' (pp. 181–2).

As he had done in such earlier works as *The Day of the Triffids*, Wyndham reveals that what happened is not the result of a freak natural accident nor of primitive magic; modern civilisation must take the responsibility. The spiders mutated because of '"radio-active contamination"' from the nuclear tests after the Second World War (p. 185). Momentarily, through Delgrange's report, he seemingly obviates any further problem by announcing that volcanic eruption left Tanakuatua 'devoid of all signs of life' (p. 186); but in Camilla's latest communication from 'somewhere in Peru', Delgrange receives 'a bottle of spirit' containing a specimen he recognises as a 'Little Sister' (p. 187). As in 'Consider Her Ways' the novel ends with a threatening uncertainty – far worse than a future in which only women survive, because in *Web* proud, militant man has destroyed humanity.

A close examination of these neglected works enhances John Wyndham's already prestigious reputation. To evaluate his place in twentieth-century letters soundly, one must look at all his fiction from 1931 on. Whatever the quality of his early work, he became far more than an entertaining storyteller. To speak of Wyndham's 'conservatism, his antihistorical stance, and his blunt anti-intellectual values', as John Scarborough has,[19] gives more insight into the critic than into Wyndham. Caught between the 'space opera' of the 1930s and the 'new wave' of the 1960s, Wyndham used the popular field of science fiction to explore the tensions within modern society. Drawing upon historical events in the British past, he dramatised the plight of women in the twentieth century at least a decade before that theme gained widespread favour. It is not an overstatement to say that he asked for a revolution in contemporary thinking. If nothing else, his portrayal of women makes his fiction unique at mid-century. But in *Web* he did even more. Disciple of H. G. Wells that he was, he nevertheless attacked – and allowed a woman to be his speaker – the single concept which, since the Renaissance and Enlightenment, has led humanity into a terrible cul-de-sac: the concept of 'men like gods'. Since it is his last novel, one must infer that he knew increasing disillusionment and despair. Although there is at present no textual evidence to provide support, one hopes that, like the narrator of *The Time Machine*, he was able to say – at least to himself:

He [the Time Traveller] . . . saw in the growing pile of civilisation only a foolish heaping that must inevitably fall back upon and destroy its makers in the end. If that is so, it remains for us to live as though it were not so.[20]

NOTES

1. John Wyndham, *The Day of the Triffids* (London: Michael Joseph, 1951); John Wyndham, *The Kraken Wakes* (London: Michael Joseph, 1953); Brian Aldiss, *Trillion Year Spree* (London: Victor Gollancz, 1986) p. 254: a briefer form of this chapter was presented at the annual meeting of the Society for Utopian Studies, 'Bellamy's *Looking Backward* and Other Utopias', held at Emerson College, Boston, Mass., 29 September–2 October 1988.
2. John Wyndham, *The Chrysalids* (London: Michael Joseph, 1955); John Scarborough, 'John Wyndham', E. F. Bleiler (ed.), *Science-Fiction Writers* (New York: Charles Scribner's Sons, 1981) pp. 219–24, esp. p. 221.
3. Scarborough, 'John Wyndham', pp. 222, 223.
4. Ibid., p. 223.
5. John Clute, 'John Wyndham', in Peter Nicholls (ed.), *The Science Fiction Encyclopaedia* (Garden City, NY: Doubleday, 1979) p. 667.
6. Julius Kagarlitski, 'John Wyndham', in Curtis C. Smith (ed.), *Twentieth-Century Science-Fiction Writers* (New York: St Martin's Press, 1981) pp. 602–3, esp. p. 602.

7. Kagarlitski, 'John Wyndham', p. 603.

8. Aldiss, *Trillion Year Spree*, p. 254.

9. Scarborough, 'John Wyndham', p. 221; John Wyndham, 'Consider Her Ways' (1956), in *Consider Her Ways and Other Stories* (London: Michael Joseph, 1965), pp. 7–73; John Wyndham, *Trouble with Lichen* (London: Michael Joseph, 1960). Future references to the latter two works will appear in the text, preceded by the initials *CW* and *TL* respectively.

10. Neil Barron and Neil Barron (eds), *Anatomy of Wonder: Science Fiction* (New York: Bowker, 1976) p. 190.

11. John Wyndham, *Web* (London: Michael Joseph, 1979). Future references will appear in the text, preceded by the initial *W*.

12. John Wyndham, *The Midwich Cuckoos* (London: Michael Joseph, 1957).

13. John Wyndham and Lucas Parkes, *The Outward Urge* (London: Michael Joseph, 1959).

14. Philip Wylie, *The Disappearance* (New York: Rinehart, 1951).

15. The Ballantine American paperback edition of *Trouble with Lichen* (New York: Ballantine, 1963) cuts the text to 160 pages from 190 (Michael Joseph) and 204 (Harmondsworth: Penguin, 1965). At least half of the cutting occurs in the first section of the novel. Her mother is largely eliminated, most of the remarks about brains and beauty are deleted, and the account of her great-aunt is omitted. But Wyndham's basic theme is left intact. The British editions suggest the date of composition, for, recalling 'Consider Her Ways', Francis Saxover has produced a virus which causes sterility in the male locust.

16. Wyndham, *The Midwich Cuckoos*, p. 239.

17. Clifford D. Simak, *City* (New York: Gnome Press, 1951).

18. During separate interviews in the spring of 1987 with Thomas D. Clareson both Brian W. Aldiss and Leslie Flood said that Wyndham had referred to *Web* as 'the spider book' during the 1960s.

19. Scarborough, 'John Wyndham', p. 223.

20. H. G. Wells, *The Time Machine* (1895, rpt. London: Pan Books, 1953) p. 101.

8

Frank Herbert's *Dune* and the Discourse of Apocalyptic Ecologism in the United States

R. J. ELLIS

The novel *Dune* is plainly concerned with issues of ecology. It takes its title not from its hero, Paul Muad'Dib, but from the planet Arrakis, colloquially known as Dune in response to its dominant topographical characteristic. It is dedicated to 'the dry-land ecologists, wherever they may be',[1] and, tantalisingly, in this same dedication, the novel is described as a 'prediction', presumably inviting us to go on to read into it an account of a possible ecological fate for the planet Earth. The contents page tells us that a whole appendix is devoted to 'The Ecology of Dune', and the appendix itself focuses on the fictional career of an ecologist – Pardot Kynes. The novel then commences with a map of Dune and some 'Cartographic Notes', thus underlining its concern with Dune's environmental features (*D*, pp. 8–10). Yet, despite all this preparation, the novel's opening chapters in fact place stress on Paul Muad'Dib's youthful development, and take as their setting not Dune, but Paul's home planet, Caladan. The novel's efforts to promote Dune's significance, which even include placing, at the head of the first chapter, one of Princess Irulan's epigrams asserting that, though Paul was born and raised on Caladan, 'Arrakis, the planet known as Dune, is forever his place' (*D*, p. 13), are therefore not sustained by the narrative opening. This instead leads the reader to focus on Paul as hero, enduring the painful and traumatic gom jabbar test of his 'human-ness' at the hands of the Bene Gesserit Reverend Mother. A structural tension exists, then, in this two-faced focus, and it is accompanied by a complementary tension, as the narrative unfolds, in the novel's ambiguous treatment of Paul Muad'Dib, who, by the end of the book, has assumed the role of both hero and demagogue (albeit the latter reluctantly). It is my contention that these tensions are interdependent, constitutive and revelatory, and to substantiate this, my paper proposes to explore some key contextual correlatives.

It is, in fact, quite possible to read *Dune* as crucially concerned with advancing an ecological message concerning the need to adopt a holistic viewpoint on the environment, by regarding it on a planetary scale and from an ecological perspective. Early on, one of the most charismatic characters in the novel is the Imperial planetary ecologist assigned to Dune, Liet Kynes, son of the Pardot Kynes commemorated in both the Appendix and the opening 'Cartographic Notes'. Indeed, when Paul's father is killed early on, Liet seems set fair to become his mentor, until Liet in turn dies whilst resisting the evil Harkonnen enemies of Paul's House Atreides. Liet, it seems, has secretly, visionarily, in furthering his father's project, been working on a series of planetary ecological measures, such as moisture traps and underground reservoirs, which, given the opportunity, could transform Dune from a wilderness into a garden 'Eden' (*D*, p. 136). As Paul matures on Arrakis under the protection and the tutelage of the native Arrakian Fremen, he undergoes an evolving instruction about Dune as an environment, begun by Liet, and grows progressively in understanding (a development which could be said to stretch through the whole *Dune* trilogy); he comes, in effect, to assume Liet's mantle of planetary ecologist. It is, however, the special status conferred by the combination of Paul's intellectual training as a 'mentat', his genetic breeding and upbringing, engineered by the Bene Gesserit, and his insight, enhanced by both the drug melange and a type of fifth-sense secured by his genes, that enables him to envision how Arrakis can be transformed into a paradise within a very short period, using the resulting holistic viewpoint that parallels his gestalt capabilities in the field of perception. Thus, the time-scale of ecological intervention is rendered down till it assumes a human, rather than epochal, scale: Pardot Kynes's original estimate of 'three hundred to five hundred years' (*D*, p. 568) is dramatically revised.

The results of this representation of the potential imminence of ecological change at the end of the book are profound. Ecological balance is effectively represented as a precarious state, and its fundamental adjustment as humanly available, so long as the approach is comprehensively holistic. The future of the planet Dune is literally at stake and, as a consequence, the political theme contained within the book assumes a necessarily apocalyptic tone, and this in turn affects the whole representation of power and its exercise. Paul's history can in this light, therefore, be read as one that bears within it, as he comes to power, the future of Dune as an environment; the problem is that Paul's parallel and predominant, if uneasy, representation as a hero fundamentally compromises the coherence of the book's treatment of power as a theme.

Before exploring the dimensions of this compromise, we therefore need first to consider in what ways the apocalyptic representation of ecological balance set up in the book is one that is constrained from coherence by its narrative reproduction of the discursive formulations of the science of ecology in mid-century America, or, more specifically, in the early 1960s, and these discourses' instabilities. In fact, Herbert's own background knowledge suggest a *modus operandi* for undertaking such an exploration, since we know that he was aware of, and influenced by, both Rachel Carson and, particularly, Paul Bigelow Sears.[2]

Carson's *Silent Spring* was published in 1962, the year preceding *Dune*'s completion (though *Dune* was not published until 1965),[3] and Herbert certainly read her work, as his references to the North American Carsonites in his *The Green Brain* make clear.[4] Carson's apocalyptic representation of the impact of modern pesticides upon North America's ecology became a *cause célèbre* with best-seller status;[5] however, I am concerned here neither with presenting *Silent Spring* as a direct influence on *Dune* (I can detect little internal evidence for such a speculation, though we can note that Paul's and his mother's Bene Gesserit training enables them, like Carson's chemists, to manipulate the structure of complex organic molecules – *D*, pp. 409ff.), nor with presenting *Silent Spring* as constitutive, but rather as symptomatic, in its discursive formations, of key features of late 1950s and early 1960s ecological representations of America's environmental status.

In this respect, it seems to me significant that Carson recurrently makes analogous reference to the impact of radiation's deadly effects when describing graphically the potential destructiveness of modern pesticides.[6] The impact of the introduction of atomic warfare, the revelations from Hiroshima as to its long-term effects, and the consequent debate about fall-out, culminating in the 1963 test-ban treaty, were clearly beginning to grip early 1960s' ecologists' representations of humanity's environmental future. The sentence, 'radiation is now the unnatural creation of man's tampering with the atom', with its overtly evaluative language, is coupled by Carson to her argument concerning the potential dangers of synthetic molecular compounds in chemical pesticides as a quite natural means of buttressing her opposition to the latter (*SS*, p. 24). Herbert, in his science fiction future, envisages a universe in which atomics have become obsolete as weaponry, thus setting aside this particular potential source of ecological disaster, but he replicates the note of Apocalypse that Carson carries in her book. More crucial is the way that Carson bases her argument upon an appeal to the traditional agrarian discourse of a rural Eden. This occurs in the opening paragraph of the book, where 'A Fable for Tomorrow', disconcertingly told in the past tense, imagines 'a town in the heart of America' which, quite suddenly, is transformed from being 'in harmony with its surroundings' into the victim and part-propagator of a 'strange blight' (the pseudo-Biblical language is indicative), an 'evil spell' that 'silenced the rebirth of new life in this stricken world' (*SS*, pp. 21–2). As the redundancy in this phrase indicates, Carson is not at her best when writing what amounts to dystopic science fiction. For my purposes, however, it exemplifies well enough the Apocalyptic cast brought to her examination of the damage wrought upon the United States's ecology by modern chlorinated hydrocarbon and alkyl phosphate insecticides and, particularly, their indiscriminate use or over-use.

Carson's book can be seen clearly to be based upon substantial research, and reveals the increasingly orchestrated concern of a wide variety of ecological commentators about such insecticides, and their potentially catastrophic consequences. Carson plainly sets out to widen the lobby by generating anxiety about the presence of carcinogens in these pesticides, and by depicting their potentially devastating effects upon hunting, shooting and fishing (*SS*, pp. 101ff.), but above all she situates her project within an appeal to the agrarian reflexes present in the discursive representations of America's past and its evolution up to the early 1960s. This, in turn, is relatable to the vigorous period of growth that America's economy, particularly its industrial and commercial economy, was going through in the aftermath of the Second World War, with the consequent increase in urbanisation, typified by spreading suburban development. The United States' population, by the start of the 1960s, was predominantly metropolitan with ever-spreading suburbs; between 1950 and 1960 over thirteen million homes were constructed in the USA, and eleven million of those were built in the suburbs.[7] Attendant upon this was the decisive emergence of what has been called the 'wilderness cult' in the postwar period, which has tempted at least one commentator to speak of a 'wilderness explosion'.[8] One statistic will serve here: in 1952 a total of nineteen people travelled through the Grand Canyon on the Colorado River; by 1962 that figure had risen to 372; by 1972 to 16, 428.[9]

Quite obviously, in this respect, then, Carson's narrative account of the threat posed by chemical insecticides links up with a contemporary accentuation of a very familiar discursive representation of America's evolution, which can readily be traced back to the early nineteenth century, and without much difficulty into the eighteenth century as well: writers can be found recurrently expressing concern about 'the ravages of the axe' throughout this period.[10] *Dune*, in turn, potentially at least, conforms to this mode of representation, as man-made changes threaten to disrupt completely *Dune's* ecological characteristics and even, in later *Dune* volumes, threaten its main non-human life-form, the sandworm, with extinction. Indeed, *Dune's* portrait of Arrakis as a wilderness threatened by apocalyptic change, can be viewed as mapping fictionally the discursive modes within which the ecological debate about America's future was being conducted.

When one comes to relate *Dune* to the writings of Paul Bigelow Sears, these correlations become even more pressing, and now perhaps unavoidably suggestive of a clear influence – as more than one commentator has proposed.[11] This debt, however, is more comprehensive than previously observed, and this can be preliminarily indicated by the fact that, where Herbert writes of 'pattern' as an ecological universal, so Sears repeatedly makes detailed reference to such 'pattern', from *Deserts on the March*, first published in 1935, in which one chapter is entitled 'The Great Pattern', through to *The Biology of the Living Landscape* in 1962.[12] Herbert's clear debt to Sear's 1960 text, *Where There Is Life*, has been well, if rather too peremptorily, noted.[13] Just as fundamental, and from my point of view, more informative, is his debt to Sear's *Deserts on the March*, which, though first published in 1935, was republished in revised form in 1947 and was still in print when *Dune* was completed.

Sears, like Carson, was a populariser of ecological issues, seeking to promote ecological awareness in accessible texts which recurrently assume an almost anecdotal narrative structure. One example of this is the use, at the start of *The Biology of the Living Landscape*, of an exemplary tale concerning the dramatic ecological effects of a barbed wire fence first written about almost three decades earlier, in *Deserts on the March*.[14] This last text is a seductive, though superficial, Cook's tour through the history of civilisation from an ecological perspective. As such, it raises broader issues than Sears's more purely ecological texts, and accordingly renders itself more available to use in Herbert's epical project. This accounts for the repeated borrowing. Herbert's use of Sear's insistence on ecological pattern has already been noted; he also takes up the idea of 'balance' proposed by Sears at the very start of *Deserts*: 'nature . . . maintains a balance which will permit the briefest time to elapse between burial and renewal. The turnover of material for new generations to use is steady and regular' (*DM*, p. 3). Sears's text goes on to refer frequently to this concept of 'balance', and Herbert, too, gives it comparable priority; he introduces it in Princess Irulan's very first epigram (*D*, p. 13), and makes recurrent mention thereafter, noteworthily when Liet Kynes is left to die by the Harkonnens in the desert, and deliriously launches into a monologue about the need to create 'ecological literacy' in which, more than incidentally, the reader is introduced to some basic ecological concepts (*D*, pp. 313–20, esp. p. 317). The theme in Herbert, entirely predictably, climaxes in the appendix on Dune's ecology: '"There's an internally recognised beauty of motion and balance on any man-healthy [as opposed to man-sick] planet" . . . This was Pardot Kynes lecturing' (*D*, p. 566). Unsurprisingly, further borrowing stems from the fact that both *Deserts* and *Dune* are, as their titles suggest, concerned with problems of precipitation shortage, and consequently, where *Deserts* speaks of how 'The water pattern . . . controls the pattern of human activity directly, as well as indirectly, through its influence on plants' (*DM*, p. 61), so in *Dune*, Liet Kynes explains that 'The newcomer to Arrakis frequently underestimates the importance of water here. You are dealing with the Law of the Minimum' (*D*, p. 165). In fact, the 'Law of the Minimum' nominated here is a borrowing from *Where There Is Life*,[15] and all the concepts so far detailed are recurrent in Sears's *œuvre*.

Deserts on the March emerges more as a seminal influence in terms of the sheer pervasiveness of its echoes within *Dune*. Thus, where *Dune* presents grass as performing a central role in converting Arrakis from a vast desert into a green world and in the development of agriculture – held to be the 'source of civilisation' (*D*, pp. 314–16), so Chapter X, 'Leaves of Grass', in *Deserts* describes how 'grasses . . . elevat[e] mankind from the beasts . . . and . . . are the strategic buffer between civilization and the desert' (*DM*, p. 86). Similarly, *Dune*'s scepticism about the desirability of growth ('remember that *growth* itself can produce unfavourable conditions unless treated with extreme care' – *D*, p. 165), is predicted by the debate in Chapter VIII of *Deserts*, which interrogates the benefits of uncontrolled growth (*DM*, pp. 68ff.). More precisely, the representation in *Dune* of how Fremen culture is constructed around preserving all water on Arrakis, even the body water of corpses, in turn reminds us of Sear's contention that 'In a state of nature . . . the utmost benefit is received from whatever moisture happens to be available' (*DM*, p. 64). The most seminal link of all, however, is offered by Sear's reflections, in *Deserts on the March*, on the problem of arriving at political solutions to the ecological crisis that he describes, now that the 'magic girdle' is 'broken': 'Thus have come the deserts . . . to break their bonds . . . the girdle of green has been forced to give way' through human mismanagement (*DM*, pp. 66–7). This may sound speciously apocalyptic, until one recalls that Sears first published *Deserts* in 1935 and actually, he tells us, commenced writing it when 'Dust storms obscuring the sun for days at a time were raging', at a time when the US was facing the 'menace of drought' (*DM*, p. 164). What has to be done is to restore 'the balance', Sears tells us on the same page, having carefully established humankind's responsibility for the march of the deserts in the preceding chapters. In fact, in the closing sections of *Deserts*, Sears does now seek to undertake a sustained consideration of the political context for his ecological concerns; he raises, but conspicuously fails to answer, some fundamental questions.

In the main body of the book, Sears had appeared to be drifting, at least by implication, towards an endorsement of government intervention. When, in its main body, the book does address political action, this drift seems to be amply confirmed: 'Robert Marshall . . . not only attacks the abuses of private ownership, but the institution itself so far as applied to forests, and suggests a policy of alienation of them into government hands' (*DM*, p. 81). Yet when in its final chapters the book addresses these political dimensions concertedly, a quite different thrust emerges from that of Marshall, which, with the advantage of hindsight, one sees

Sears not to have explicitly supported. But Sears is not guiltless of contradiction: less than twenty pages before the final chapters commence, whilst contemplating the crisis in the Dust Bowl, we find him writing: 'government is the only agency that can supply the assistance in any practical way' (*DM*, p. 122). This could be regarded as straightforward enough support for the New Deal; but things are almost immediately rendered more complicated, when, on page 146, we read: 'we have a philosophy of individual initiative and freedom confused by emphasis on equality'. This turns out to be the prologue to a consistently confused reflection on the relationship between State and individual. Sears cannot simply dismiss the fact that the Dust Bowl was the product of private-sector market financing; his defence of *laissez-faire* individualism is consequently strained: 'Is it not possible that the trouble has been not with private ownership as such, buy with the fact that it has not seriously and consistently been the rule in this country?' (*DM*, p. 147). Sears is struggling towards advocacy of a programme which would seek to maximise personal stewardship of personal property, rather than tenancy of rented estates, and the rearing of 'a new generation trained in the efficient stewardship of private property' (*DM*, p. 152). What Sears does not confront is the fact that this programme must be promulgated upon a substantial amount of initial, quite lengthy, State intervention.

The inherent contradictions in this position are nicely laid bare by an unintended ambiguity a little later on: 'One fact certainly must be granted. It is human nature for a man to take better care of his own property than of another's, if he has been trained to do so' (*DM*, p. 149). In context, one would be reasonably sure that what is meant is that a man, because of human nature, will look after his own property better than another's; but this interpretation is destabilised by the seemingly antithetical addition of the phrase 'if . . . trained': presumably what is meant is that training is needed to bring out this hypothesised facet of human nature, but an alternative, and by no means completely excluded, meaning is that it is human nature to accept training, and, if trained to do so, man will look after his own property better than he will another's. We move here, either way, within the terrain of ideological interpellation. The discourse in fact strives to obliterate its own instability with its introductory sentence, 'One fact certainly must be granted'. It is tempting, and quite possibly correct, in the light of this cliché, to take up a Machereyan position here, and regard the textual lapse that follows as symptomatic of ideology's revelatory incompleteness in attempting to conceal a real social contradiction: the 'absent sun' around which ideology fixedly revolves, drawing the text's discourse into 'disarray' at this point of intersection.[16] Any hesitation that I feel concerning such a subscription focuses on the over-emphasis placed by most contemporary interpreters on the tendency of Macherey's approach to render up the author as passive; in fact, I would maintain, Macherey allows for the author's project to be interrogative but lays stress on the instructive significance of points of formal breakdown in any such attempted interrogation.[17] Certanly, one must account for the extraordinary transparency of the conflicts apparent when, for example, Sears writes: 'The unrestricted mergers of great industries, which form a perfect precondition for state socialism, were arranged under conservative recent administrations, as were those breaches of corporate trust which have inflamed the popular mind' (*DM*, pp. 146–7).

Sears's essential conservatism has become at points so discursively etiolated by the dilemmas posed by the Depression as to resemble a species of romanticised individualism bordering on anarchy; nevertheless, his political thrust is at other points clear (and crude) enough:

> We are on the eve of a determined movement to increase the property held and administered by government. . . . It is reasonable to expect that the burden of these . . . costly government enterprises . . . will fall most heavily upon the middle classes, already reeling from the successive blows of war and depression. It is axiomatic that political and social stability rests with the middle classes. There is . . . the serious question as to how much this group can bear. . . . If it becomes impossible for people of good capacity to prosper in our system, it is too much to hope that their talents will not be lent to help destroy that system.   (*DM*, pp. 148–9)

As he trenchantly puts it a few lines further on: 'We shall have to make the choice' (p. 149). Beware the middle class, indeed. It is unfortunately too simplistic to attempt to depict the instabilities of Sears's political position as the product of the double chronology of his text: first published in 1935, revised in 1947. In fact, the bulk of Sears's reflections on the political ramifications of an ecological perspective were almost entirely penned in the 1930s, during the emergence of the New Deal's policies of limited intervention, amounting to a tentative exploration of a recasting of the relationship of State, citizen and capital. *Deserts'* 1947 revisions and added final chapter were written in a quite different political climate, soon to enable McCarthyism, when disaffection with government intervention had again taken clear consensual hold and when, in a sense, Sears's 'choice' *was* made; now, in the late 1940s, Sears fails conspicuously to readdress his original political uncertainties about the potential benefits of State intervention into ecological crises. And this textual paralysis is, I would suggest, precisely a significant silence and one which, for Sears, noteworthily persisted: in his *The Biology of the Living Landscape*, published in 1962, this virtual silence continues. At most we are offered platitudes about 'Responsible citizenship'.[18]

Silent Spring, also published in 1962, is equally unsatisfactory in this arena. Carson recruits her readers to the cause of ecology by the unsubtly polemical technique of nominating herself and her putative readers as an implicit 'us', against a just as frequently implicit 'them' which fluidly, and duplicitously, shifts identities – representing, variously, different government agencies, town halls, farmers. The essential vagueness is formally secured by the recurrent resort to indirect speech:

> These sprays, dusts and aerosols are now applied almost universally to farms, gardens, forests and homes – non-selective chemicals that have the power to kill every insect, the 'good' and the 'bad', to still the song of birds and the leaping of fish in the streams. . . . Can anyone believe it is possible to lay down such a barrage of poisons on the surface of the earth without making it unfit for all life? (*SS*, p. 25)

But this formal device is not sustained uniformly. Carson's holistic view, like that of Sears, endangers such rhetorical compartmentalisations; 'we' are, after all, often gardeners and, potentially, voters, and side by side with passages such as the above we find: 'To adjust to these chemicals would require . . . the life of generations. And even this were it possible, would be futile, for the new chemicals come from *our* laboratories in an endless stream' (*SS*, p. 24; my emphasis). Like Sears's 1960s text, *Silent Spring* makes no concerted attempt to explore these political ramifications of ecological crisis: the more pronounced tone of Apocalypse brought to its subject sharpens, however, the horns of the dilemma created by its discursive evasions.

The residual political discourse deserves sifting out, therefore, and, as with Sears, a profound uncertainty emerges: on the one hand a clear attack on government gains momentum, feeding off conservative populism: 'For the most part . . . blanket spraying continues to thrive, to exact its heavy annual cost for the tax-payer. . . . When taxpayers understand that the bill for spraying should come due only once a generation instead of once a year, they will surely rise up' (*SS*, p. 79). The parallel with Sears's vision of middle-class insurgence is plain enough, as are the monetary motives proposed. Alongside such assaults on wastefully inefficient government, however, runs a counter-current which relentlessly pushes the reader towards a sense that chemical company profits play a part. This drift reaches a climax on page 225, where chemical companies' research programmes are indicted, though the motives for their shortcomings are unexplored. This perspective is fleetingly proposed early on: 'This is an era dominated by industry, in which the right to make a dollar at whatever cost is seldom challenged' (*SS*, p. 29). Again, *Deserts on the March* will be recalled, with its reference to breaches of corporate trust, and as Carson proceeds to describe what appears in her account to be an inexplicable, near-genocidal reluctance on the part of the US government to enact restrictive legislation, a comparable politically incoherent formal disarray develops, though now located, in the early 1960s, at a more implied level than the eventually extensive discussion found in the 1935 *Deserts*.

These examinations of the politics of ecology in Sears and Carson have been deliberately detailed, as they establish a discursive frame of popularising ecological narratives within which to set Herbert's fictional rehearsal of these self-same dilemmas. Crucially, however, I want to distinguish between the artistic project of Herbert and the documentary and educational parameters delimiting the narratives of Carson and Sears. Their texts are instructive in purpose, and actively seek a consensual position. To an extent, this can be held to be true of Herbert's *Dune* as well. However, his narrative's self-conscious location within the epic sub-genre of science fiction (edged, but only edged, arguably, with fantasy) deploys a quite discrete set of generic expectations that, I want to further propose, enable him far more freely to explore in a fictional narrative the political implications of what I shall henceforth, in short-hand, refer to as apocalyptic ecologism. As we have seen, this proposes imminent disaster and a dystopic future if no action is forthcoming; what it fails significantly to do is to articulate comprehensibly a political programme for such action. The popularising accounts of Sears and Carson, we have seen, lose coherence and fall almost silent.

Centrally, of course, what is at issue is the distribution of political power within this doomsday scenario. In this terrain, discursive elaboration is vestigial indeed. Sear's more extensive and overt political discussion in the 1930s in *Deserts on the March* does result in his confronting the existence of alternative political programmes: we find him on page 130 describing 'the really vital contribution' to planned economy which can be made by the science of climate and weather', but, within fifteen pages, despite the direction suggested by the phrase 'planned economy', he firmly sets aside Communism, bracketed with Fascism, as 'contain[ing] the canker of its own destruction, for each involves the suppression of individual personality by means of individual force of leadership' (*DM*, p. 144). Here, in obviously deformed, apparently idiosyncratic form, his narrative finally engages with a question of power; but his equation of Communism and Fascism elides both, leaving unanswered the question of how to enact a planned economy, and his narrative reverts to a maimed representation of the need to overcome present 'exploitation and waste', the product of 'our general lawlessness', by tempering 'freedom' with 'a strong code of responsibility' (*DM*, pp. 142, 145). Carson's engagement with the issue of political power is even more truncated, its occasion an anguished anaphora about the effects of insecticides: 'Who has made the decision. . . ? Who has decided – who has the right to decide. . . ? The decision is that of the authoritarian temporarily entrusted with power' (*SS*, p. 121). From quite different angles of attack, Sears's and Carson's narratives both arraign authoritarianism, in characterisations that betray their discursive formation as one of individualism: control is equated quite simply with tyranny, and their analyses of political power, such as they are, are consequently disabled.

This surely provides us with a perspective from which to view the narrative formation of Herbert's *Dune*. Commentators explicating Herbert have recurrently experienced some difficulty in reconciling his engagement with ecology on the one hand,

and his extensive exploration of the dilemmas confronting Paul Muad'Dib on the other.[19] These last centre on Paul's fears that his assumption of control of the future of Dune and its inhabitants will render him up as tyrannous. Herbert, within the generic conventions of the science fiction epic, is thus able to set up an extended reflection on the relationship of power, control, responsibility and foresight. The dilemmas are now rehearsed fictionally with relative clarity. They still operate within the discursive formation of individualism, but, whilst full coherence is not obtained, active interrogation plainly does occur. One needs here not to be sidetracked, as Timothy O'Reilly was, by the retrospective comment of Herbert in 1977 that 'I had this theory that superheroes were disastrous for humans'.[20] Plainly this theme does emerge in Paul's constant agonising about the processes by which he is becoming elevated to the status of Messiah by his sense of 'terrible purpose' (*D*, p. 55): 'he remembered the vision of fanatic legions following the green and black banner of the Atreides, pillaging and burning across the universe in the name of their prophet Muad'Dib. / *That must not happen*, he told himself' (*D*, p. 354). Paul here fears that his Mentat intellectual training, Bene Gesserit breeding and upbringing, and evolving, *mélange*-enhanced prescience will cause him, despite himself, to promote a holy war, a *jihad* across the universe: 'The imperfect vision plagued him. The more he resisted his terrible purpose and fought against the coming of the *jihad*, the greater the turmoil that wove through his prescience' (*D*, p. 447). We can, of course, read this account of Paul's agonising about power, a 'two-edged sword' as his mother describes it (p. 185), within the conventional reading strategies of realist illusionism,[21] which is what, I take it, O'Reilly does. By doing this one reduces *Dune* to the status of 'a costume drama . . . of considerable banality',[22] which is perhaps a fate to which the whole *Dune* cycle consigns itself, as the ecological theme becomes almost wholly subordinate to the portrayals of cosmic conflict. It is, however, my contention that the first volume's concerted engagement with the politics of Apocalyptic ecologism rescues it from such banality. This rescue hinges on the reader's recognition of the implicit parallel between the history of Arrakis and the history of the United States, a recognition accessible enough to the habitués of science fiction, and which is enabled by the strategy of establishing that this is the story of clashes of various descendants of planet Earth, now dispersed across the universe. Constant residual traces of terrestrial human culture thus occur within the text of *Dune* to establish this metaphor.

The depiction of the Fremen is central to this process: in part based on the tribes of the Kalahari, in part on the nomads of the Arabian Peninsula, their most fundamental social and cultural analogies are with the North American Indians, and specifically the Apaches.[23] Paul, his parents and their Atreides following arrive from another planet, displace an existing Imperial power, the Harkonnens; and then Paul, evicted from his citadel, is forced to confront Dune's wilderness, learn from the Fremen, before returning to finally take over and reform his world. It is, I think, relatively easy in this broad summary to detect a mythologised resumé of the impact of the Frontier (in its Rousseauvian guise), regarded, within this myth, as 'the most rapid and effective line of Americanisation'.[24] This myth is characteristically articulated as a Romantic quest based within an anarchic yearning after a lost Edenic past – lost, since the myth achieves its full, modern articulation in the period after the frontier had been declared 'closed'.[25] Within this articulation the American undergoes a transcendent refiguration on the Frontier: at first 'The wilderness masters the colonist', who adopts the ways of the Indian, then 'step by step' he 'transforms the wilderness', but in this process 'a steady growth of independence on American lines' occurs.[26] *Dune*'s deep-rooted respect for the transformative value of primitive wilderness conditions operates fully within this myth discourse, and here the narrative plainly elects Paul to the role of proto-typical American Frontier hero. This is, after all, a species of environmental determinism, and the strand of Social Darwinism in it is deep-seatedly pervasive. Such a fundamental debt to Darwinist environmentalism, transposed to the social sphere, is facilitated by the strong trace of Darwinism in the Apocalyptic ecologism that we have been examining: both Sears and Carson demonstrate explicitly Darwinist predilections, and Sears himself published a book on Darwin in 1950.[27] The tendency of all three – Herbert, Sears and Carson – to exhibit such traces of Social Darwinist determinism in their writings inevitably hinders the coherence of their respective searches for political solutions to the ecological problems they present; unless, that is, such explorations are formulated within the dominant discursive practices that legitimate *laissez-faire* individualism.

In tandem with this, however, *Dune* develops an accentuating note of tragic destiny, as Paul leads the Fremen, whether he will or no, towards their destructive *jihad*. Paul's increasing capacity for control as he rises to leadership can bring ecological transformation of Dune's man-made desert conditions, causing the planet to bloom again, in a romantic regeneration, but such absolute control also has a destructive potential for tragic disaster apparently out of Paul's hands. Indeed, Paul's leadership is represented very much in the same terms as those used in Sear's instructively idiosyncratic political model in *Deserts on the March*, which presents both Communism and Fascism as systems necessarily suppressing individualism by way of 'individual force of leadership' (*DM*, p. 144). Crucially, however, Herbert portrays in Paul someone who regards this process as simultaneously unavoidable and negative (an analysis adopted in turn by Paul's son in later *Dune* volumes). Indeed, whilst Paul holds to the opinion that 'A leader . . . is one of the things that distinguishes a mob from a people. He maintains the level of individuals. Too few individuals, and a people reverts to a mob' (*D*, p. 338), this same quotation also makes clear that his rise to charismatic leadership invests him with an increasingly absolute dictatorial power that, ironically, he deeply mistrusts himself, and, crucially, cannot control. The paradoxes in this position defy resolution, and the text is clearly fractured. The remaining political residues are unwholesome, and the implications of the word 'maintains' take the reader back to Paul's father's ominous words: 'To hold Arrakis . . . one is faced with decisions that may cost one his self respect' (*D*, p. 127).

Dune, though only the first volume of the *Dune* series, makes these tensions plain enough. What I am proposing is that the resulting dialectic functions as a critique of Apocalyptic ecologism's lack of any political analysis of power. Herbert's deployment of the Frontier myth, confronted with the contradictory tensions that result from this incompleteness, is conventional enough – indeed, Lévi-Strauss tells us that myths are deployed precisely 'to contain a contradiction',[28] but here the tactic is unsuccessful: the despoliation of America enabled by the ideological values enshrined within the myth cannot sustain its deployment in any 1960s ecological text taking a holistic view. There is, literally, no adequate ideological representation of the crisis to hand within the established discursive representations of America's environmental state, and incoherence results. At one point in Herbert's *Dune*, as with Carson and Sears, we encounter a tentative allusion to a collective solution: 'The Duke felt in this moment that his own dearest dream was to end all class distinctions' (*D*, p. 97), but once more, as the narrative here even goes so far as to warn us, this is only momentary. The deflection secured by the qualificatory 'in this moment' can again be regarded as a Machereyan disarray, but this does not exclude the sense that Herbert's thrust is interrogative. It is, I feel, indicative that Herbert's test to destruction of the romanticised Frontier myth in Paul's epic story, in an effort to contain the countervailing sense of the inevitable potential for tragic abuse of dictatorial power, is accompanied by a representation of myth as an ideological mode of social control, disseminated by the Bene Gesserit as part of their sinister genetic programme: 'The wisdom of seeding the known universe with a prophecy pattern for the protection of B[ene] G[esserit] personnel has long been appreciated' (*D*, p. 62).

Significantly, Paul, the text's potential romantic Frontier hero, is instead very much a victim of their myths, which propel him towards the status of Mahdi and blight his attempts to bring ecological deliverance to Arrakis. But to say this is not to portray the text as fully coherent in its interrogation of the discursive restrictions it discovers. If, for example, we accept Barthes's invitation to take up the free play of meaning within a text's signification patterns,[29] then we could focus on the CHOAM-sponsored harvesting on the surface of Dune of the spice *mélange* – itself a by-product of the 'makers' or sand-worms which keep Dune a desert through the activities of their juveniles, the 'little makers' whose moisture-control prevents Dune from becoming once again a flourishing green planet (*D*, pp. 316ff.). Herbert's text lays considerable stress on the profits to be made from the spice because of its geriatric and prescient qualities, and it is but a small step to portray the climatological blight upon Dune as being the product of this profit-taking by the multi-national, or rather multi-planetary corporation, CHOAM, which is encouraged to preserve Dune as a barren desert, since it is there the spice is found. However, and here exists the Machereyan lapse, the text in no way privileges or enables this reading, though it can be imposed upon the text by virtue of the latter's formal disarrays in its representation of the exercise of power as the privilege of élite individuals, despite its endeavours to establish a holistic viewpoint on planetary ecology.

It is in this interplay between discursive disarray and textual interrogation that the breadth of *Dune*'s popularity in the decade following its publication perhaps resides. In 1974 Jack

Williamson's survey of science-fiction courses confirmed that its best-seller status was the product of more than just *aficionado* appeal, for *Dune* proved to be the fifth most popular text for study on such courses.[30] It is possible, I would claim, that in *Dune*'s discursive dialectical tension is enacted Michel Foucault's thesis that 'discourse can be both an instrument and an effect of power, but also a hindrance, a stumbling-block, a point of resistance and a starting-point for an opposing strategy. Discourse transmits power; it reinforces it, but also undermines and exposes it, renders it fragile and makes it possible to thwart it'.[31] *Dune* precisely, despite its eventual surrender to the conventions of science-fiction epic, exposes within its tensions these possibilities. However, this exposé is limited by *Dune*'s mode of discursive interrogation; the Frontier myth is distinctly male, explicitly patriarchal in form. When Turner tells the story of Daniel Boone's heroic quest, the female Boones are reduced to a reproductive function,[32] and *Dune* in turn conventionally consigns its females to comparably subordinated positions. In the early 1960s, such a discursive formulation was, arguably, given the postwar strengthening of patriarchalism in representations of American familial life,[33] more compelling than would be true after the late 1960s – particularly in the light of attempts to reconstitute ecological discourse: as eco-feminism, as social ecology, as 'deep ecology', or even as (at present usually fraught) endeavours to develop an interface between aspects of the three.[34] Such differences in historical context I would hold to be crucial, though *Dune*'s macho excesses are still difficult for 1980s readers to come to terms with.

The problem, I would maintain, is very much a product of *Dune*'s location within the discursive framework of apocalyptic ecologism's popularising polemics. As Herbert himself puts it: 'I wrote in the mid Sixties what I hoped would be an environmental awareness handbook . . . called *Dune*, a title chosen with the deliberate intent that it echo the sound of "doom"'.[35] This sense of urgency in the early 1960s fundamentally disabled any approach by Apocalyptic ecologism's discursive formations to a coherent analysis of political power, by generating a sense of distress which propels commentators like Sears and Carson into at best silence, or else into a half-stated adherence to conventional representations of political power distributions. *Dune* interrogates this disablement, but from inside such formulations, where the novel is limited to the institution of unresolved tensions within the character of Paul, whose policy of intervention is purchased at what for him is the unacceptable cost of individual tyranny. Significantly, as the novel moves towards closure, the accent is placed more and more emphatically on this being Paul's doom, for all his control, and the fractured state of the novel's discourse is emphatically underscored: 'Paul saw how futile were any efforts of his to change any smallest bit of this' (D, p. 554). What remains unresolved is the consequent tension within Paul: 'He had thought to oppose the *jihad* within himself, but the *jihad* would be . . . / A sense of failure pervaded him' (ibid.), and this constitutes the interrogation the novel sustains (and which the *Dune* cycle will go on to reiterate, and again fail to resolve). If we take Herbert's word for it, and read *Dune* as an environmental-awareness handbook, we are forced to conclude that the only answer to the unavoidable political questions raised by its holistic viewpoint is, quite literally, a holy 'green' war against the existing order. If the text had not reduced this message to a debate about Paul's now problematic character as a heroic descendant of the Frontier tradition, all-powerful yet powerless in the hands of fate, and had instead emphasised more the *jihad*'s collective nature, the text would be truly subversive. Instead, the text is constantly deflected into a conventional representation of Paul as a Frontier hero, confronting and defeating the evil Harkonnen Empire, and, ironically, in terms of the ecological theme, establishing his own House Atreides' Imperium. Herbert's textual project is thus finally compromised by its individualisation of the political debate about the environment within the extra-ordinary Paul Muad'Dib – a wholly conventional strategy in terms of the USA's modes of ideological representation. But in *Dune*'s science-fiction universe the unreconciled, and unreconcilable, contradictions within that strategy can also be established. Discourse can indeed transmit and reinforce power and yet expose it and render it fragile; it is indeed a terrain of struggle. Thus, *Dune* can offer an extensive, if disablingly individualised, exploration of the question of power that interrogatively exposes the bases for this question's relative neglect in early 1960s American ecologists' representations of imminent Apocalypse. The problems Herbert encounters in groping towards a coherent political resolution to his novel's ecological dilemmas, and which, despite itself, finds the text investing Paul Muad'Dib with increasingly autocratic powers, is, I would further suggest, itself an indicator as to why extensive discursive engagement with ecological issues in fiction are characteristically encountered not in realist writing, but in the imagined futures of the science fiction genre.

NOTES

1. Frank Herbert, *Dune* (1965; rpt. London: New English Library, 1968) p. 5. Future references will appear in the text, preceded by the initial *D*.
2. See Timothy O'Reilly, *Frank Herbert* (New York: Frederick Ungar, 1981) pp. 55ff., 99.
3. Ibid., p. 61.
4. Frank Herbert, *The Green Brain* (New York: Ace Books, 1966) *passim*.
5. For an account of *Silent Spring*'s impact see Jean L. Latham, *Rachel Carson: Who Loved the Sea* (New York: Garrard, 1973) *passim*. At the time of writing this chapter, Patricia Hynes's new, feminist study of Carson, *The Recurrent Spring* (Oxford: Pergamon Press, 1989), had not yet been published. Godfrey Hodgson, in *In Our Time: America from World War Two to Nixon* (London: Macmillan, 1972) offers a very brief summary: 'After the publication of Rachel Carson's *Silent Spring* in 1962 forty states . . . pass[ed] legislation restricting pesticides within two years' (p. 402).
6. Rachel Carson, *Silent Spring* (1962; rpt. Harmondsworth: Penguin, 1965) pp. 24ff. and *passim*. Future references to *Silent Spring* will appear in the text, preceded by the initials *SS*.
7. For an account of the post-war growth of urbanisation, suburbia and mobility, see William W. Chafe, *The Unfinished Journey: America Since World War II* (New York: Oxford University Press, 1986) pp. 111ff.; Howard Zinn, *Postwar America, 1945–1971* (New York: Bobbs Merrill, 1973) pp. 89ff. The statistics are taken from Chafe, *The Unfinished Journey*, p. 117.
8. Roderick Nash, *Wilderness and the American Mind* (New Haven, Conn.: Yale University Press, 1973) pp. 263ff.
9. Ibid. p. 263.
10. The phrase is Thomas Cole's in his 'Essay on American Scenery' published in 1835, and reprinted in John W. McCoubrey, *American Art, 1700–1960* (Englewood Cliffs, N.J.: Prentice-Hall, 1965) pp. 98–110. For an account of the persistence of this discursive representation of America's development in a tragic mode, see Nash, *Wilderness and the American Mind*, *passim*.
11. Leonard M. Scigaj, in his '*Prana* and the Presbyterian Fixation: Ecology and Technology in Frank Herbert's *Dune* Trilogy', *Extrapolation*, vol. 24, no. 4 (Winter 1983), makes reference to Herbert's borrowing from Sears (pp. 348ff.); O'Reilly, too, makes similar reference to Sears (*Frank Herbert*, pp. 55ff.).
12. Herbert, *Dune*, pp. 178, 438, 566; Paul B. Sears, *Deserts on the March* (1935; revised edn 1947; rpt. London: Routledge and Kegan Paul, 1949) p. 60; Paul B. Sears, *The Biology of the Living Landscape* (1962; rpt. London: George Allen and Unwin, 1964) p. 112. Future reference to *Deserts* will appear in the text, preceded by the initials *DM*.
13. Scigaj, '*Prana* and the Presbyterian Fixation'; O'Reilly, *Frank Herbert*; Paul B. Sears, *Where There Is Life* (New York: Dell, 1960).
14. Sears, *Biology of the Living Landscape*, pp. 9ff.; Sears, *Deserts on the March*, p. 133.

15. Sears, *Where There Is Life*, p. 60.
16. Pierre Macherey, *A Theory of Literary Production* (1966), trans. G. Wall (London: Routledge and Kegan Paul, 1978) pp. 132, 155. For one outline of the concept of interpellation, see Louis Althusser, 'Ideology and the Ideological State Apparatuses' (1969), rpt. in *Lenin and Philosophy and Other Essays*, trans. B. Brewster (London: Monthly Review Press, 1971) pp. 127–86.
17. Macherey, *Theory of Literary Production* pp. 132ff. For a reasonably representative portrait of the way in which Macherey allegedly renders the author as over-passive, see Ann Jefferson and David Robey, *Modern Literary Theory*, 2nd edn (London: Batsford, 1986) pp. 177–83.
18. Sears, *The Biology of the Living Landscape*, p. 170.
19. For one extensive example, see O'Reilly, *Frank Herbert*, pp. 8ff. and *passim*.
20. Frank Herbert [liner notes], '*Dune*: the Banquet Scene, Read by the Author' (New York: Cædmon Records, 1977) quoted in O'Reilly, *Frank Herbert*, p. 5.
21. See Catherine Belsey, *Critical Practice* (London: Methuen, 1980) pp. 103ff.
22. Patrick Parrinder, *Science Fiction: Its Criticism and Teaching* (London: Methuen, 1980) p. 93.
23. O'Reilly, *Frank Herbert*, pp. 41ff.
24. Frederick Jackson Turner, 'The Significance of the Frontier in American History' (1893), in *Frontier and Section*, ed. R. A. Billington (Englewood Cliffs, N.J.: Prentice-Hall, 1961) p. 39.
25. Ibid., p. 62. For an analysis of the narrative structure of the modern Frontier myth, see R. J. Ellis and Alun Munslow, 'Narrative, Myth and the Turner Thesis', *Journal of American Culture*, vol. 9, no. 2 (Summer 1986) pp. 9–16.
26. Turner, 'The Significance of the Frontier in American History', p. 39.
27. Sears, *The Biology of the Living Landscape*, pp. 58ff.; Carson, *Silent Spring*, p. 25; Paul B. Sears, *Charles Darwin* (New York: Charles Scribner's Sons, 1950).
28. Claude Lévi-Strauss, *Structural Anthropology* (1958), rpt. trans. C. Jacobsen and B. G. Schoepf (London: Allen Lane, 1968) p. 229.
29. Roland Barthes, *The Pleasure of the Text* (1973), rpt. in part in *Barthes: Selected Writings* (1982, rpt. London: Fontana, 1983) pp. 404–14; Roland Barthes, 'Theory of the Text' (1973), rpt. in Robert Young (ed.), *Untying the Text: A Post-Structuralist Reader* (London: Routledge and Kegan Paul, 1981) pp. 32–45.
30. Jack Williamson, 'Science Fiction in the Classroom', in W. E. McNelly (ed.), *Science Fiction: The Academic Awakening* (1974), quoted in Parrinder, *Science Fiction*, p. 139.
31. Michel Foucault, *La Volonté de savoir* [The History of Sexuality, vol. 1: An Introduction] (1976), trans. R. Hurley (London: Allen Lane, 1979) pp. 100–1.
32. Turner, 'The Significance of the Frontier in American History', pp. 48–9.
33. See Chafe, *The Unfinished Journey*, pp. 123ff.

34. Such conjoining of ecofeminism, deep ecology and social ecology is being vigorously debated, and can best be described as contentious, not least because of the strongly 'macho' strand extant in some, but not all, of deep ecologists' writings. See Kirkpatrick Sale, 'The Cutting Edge: Eco-feminism – a New Perspective', *The Nation*, vol. 245, no. 9 (26 Sept. 1987) pp. 302–5; Ynestra King, 'What Is Ecofeminism?', *The Nation*, vol. 245, no. 20 (12 Dec. 1987) pp. 702, 730–1; Janet Biehl, 'Deep Ignorance', *Green Line*, no. 59 (Feb. 1988) pp. 12–14; Kirkpatrick Sale, 'Deep Ecology and its Critics', *The Nation*, vol. 246, no. 19 (14 May, 1988) pp. 670–9; Andree Collard (with Joyce Contrucci), *Rape of the Wild* (London: Woman's Press, 1988). The debate between the three areas is in danger of becoming too vituperative to be productive. Sale's first article provides a useful list of texts on ecofeminism, and his articles seek to build bridges; he is probably by now regretting that enterprise.
35. Frank Herbert, 'Introduction', in *New World or No World*, edited with commentary by Frank Herbert (New York: Ace Books, 1970) p. 5.

9

Ursula Le Guin and Time's Dispossession

ROBERT M. PHILMUS

> We shall not cease from exploration
> And the end of all our exploring
> Will be to arrive where we started
> And know the place for the first time.
> T. S. Eliot, 'Little Gidding', v. 26—9[1]

The Dispossessed, like Eliot's *Four Quartets*, problematically centres on the human meaning of time. Taking as its focal consciousness – and conscience – the point of view of a 'temporal physicist' and telling of his quest (as he finally regards it) to redeem his past and the future, the book is above all else a science-fictional *Bildungsroman*. But the uncertainties attending that quest make for a *Bildungsroman* whose *Bildung* remains in doubt almost to the very end. Oscillating meanwhile between seemingly antithetical worlds, *The Dispossessed* describes 'the waste sad time / Stretching before and after' Shevek leaves Anarres for Urras (T. S. Eliot, 'Burnt Norton', v. 174–5).

I

The two worlds are polar opposites in a strictly – which is not to say merely – nominal sense. Indeed, *Anarres* initially acquires its precise, honorific meaning only when understood as the negative form of *Urras*. Thought of in that way, and not simply as deriving from *anarchy*, the name points to Odo's original (that is, an-archic) intent rather than to the chaotic state of affairs actually prevailing on Shevek's home planet at the moment he boards the *Mindful*. Furthermore, *Anarres* in the same manner establishes – or educes – the significance of *Urras*. The latter in itself evokes the Cold War model for the fictional world on which two mutually hostile powers precariously co-exist and over which each seeks exclusive hegemony. Yet the name of that world, in its semantic opposition to *Anarres*,[2] appears not as a kind of anagrammatic compound of USA and USSR but as an amalgam of the two.[3] After all, A-Io and Thu, despite the enmity that they have for one another and whatever differences in thinking may underlie it, agree in regarding Anarres as an ideological threat, and this policy joins them together as an 'I-You' confronting the Anarresti 'Them'.[4]

For their part, the Anarresti in general reciprocate that animosity. Not only do they make no distinction between A-Io and Thu as embodiments of a 'propertarianism' they despise and of the 'statism' consequent from it, they by and large look upon all Urrasti as an undifferentiated 'Them' inimical to an Anarresti 'Us'. In doing so, however, they perforce ignore the Odonian dissidents still on Urras and thus in effect absolutise and implicitly sanction the status quo there. Nor is brotherhood the only Odonian tenet they subtly betray by assuming a stance which simply reverses that of official Urras. They also subvert another – and perhaps the most fundamental – of Odo's principles with respect to Anarres itself. Their community as Odo conceived it was one whose anarchism would serve the maximising of individual freedom. But her putative ideological descendants, defining themselves in terms of what they are against, have dialectically involved the identity of Anarres with that of Urras as they perceive it. They have thereby done worse than lose sight of their essential Odonian purpose. Though in theory they continue to repudiate property and the political control that goes with it, they have put into practice a principle of social cohesion which at once undermines their community's ideal basis and perverts its distinct *raison d'être*. What at present unites them is not the socio-political objective that Odo had in mind, but 'fear of the stranger' – and of whatever they regard as strange, alien or new.[5]

Their xenophobia, while it logically binds them to the object on which they primarily fix it, also prompts the Anarresti to cut themselves off from that world. Their resolve, however, does not extend to breaking the compact whereby the Urrasti leave them alone in return for the mineral riches of Anarres. Their attempt to dissociate themselves from Urras is therefore hypocritical, and not just by ordinary standards but also on the peculiarly Odonian grounds of collectively violating 'the ethical imperative of brotherhood', the injunction against 'keeping [one]self to [one]self' (*D*, p. 126).

Yet beyond its hypocrisy, their locking out of Urras amounts to an act of mass self-deception. The measures which the Anarresti suppose insulate them against that exploitative world are not merely ineffectual for disconnecting them from it; they threaten to ensure that they will repeat its oppressive example. Without disrupting an ongoing, if unacknowledged, complicity with the 'profiteers' of that planet, they otherwise impose on Anarres itself a closure which would exclude the kind of 'permanent revolution . . . [that] begins in the thinking mind' (*D*, p. 267; see also *D*, p. 142). Hence the metaphoric wall which the Anarresti erect to immure themselves from Urras and from the past which it represents instead separates them from their own – their Odonian – past and thereby jeopardises their (Odonian) future. A barrier to the very ideas which Odo intended Anarres to stand for, it serves at the same time as the foundation for the increasingly despotic power of the council for Production and Distribution Coordination (or PDC).

The danger of bureaucratic tyranny is all the greater because most Anarresti on principle do not and can not recognise it. Indeed, that sense in which it is both 'unadmitted' and 'inadmissible' explains how it can be that a 'government . . . rules . . . [their] society by stifling the individual mind' (*D*, p. 134). Their Odonian assurance of the impossibility of such a government on Anarres has allowed this creature of their misoneism and their 'fear of the stranger' to make its way imperceptibly into their world, where its tenure depends upon their refusal to see it for what it is. So long as they remain blind to it, what is happening to their community – the changes which the Sabuls of the PDC are inadvertently bringing about – cannot be something for them to decide on.

Against a prospect which is far from Utopian their Odonian past can give the Anarresti some ground for hope. Nevertheless, their past cannot secure them from such a prospect; for that past itself is at stake in their future, which by reason of 'causal reversibility' (cf. *D*, p. 222; also p. 37) presides over the past. Nor does a world as 'dry' and 'inimical' (p. 95) as the Arrakis of Frank Herbert's *Dune* (1965) guarantee their Odonian vocation.[6] 'It is true that the climate and geography of Anarres at first seem to exact co-operation as the price for human survival. But the events ensuing from '[t]he longest drought in . . . forty years' (p. 190) – and especially those incidents that Shevek witnesses en route to Southrising (pp. 205–6) or hears about from the driver who takes him to Chakar (pp. 250–1) – prove that an ecologically privative world is as conducive to 'mutual aggression' as it is to 'mutual aid' (p. 167).[7] Then again, non-propertarianism appears to be inevitable on a planet which offers no thing that anyone would desire to appropriate. Yet this same consideration which makes propertylessness a matter of natural necessity rather than ethical principle nullifies it as an Odonian virtue.[8] Besides, the nature of Anarres exempts it only from a propertarianism of the form operative on Urras. Even there, however, material possessions have importance chiefly as signs of the power to possess them – and hence of power in the abstract. Logically considered, the Urrasti system therefore requires things solely for the symbolic value they are invested with – an investment which, as it idealises its object, is all the more readily transferrable to what the Anarresti do not lack: ideas. That, of course, is exactly what Sabul and his ilk are in the process of doing: they are establishing a 'power structure' (p. 134) based upon the possessive control of ideas.

The Anarresti thus seem doomed to become the 'dispossessed' in every pejorative sense. For that word, as it signifies ongoing economic fact and past historical circumstance, their desert-planet inherently warrants no synonyms except material poverty and eviction. To be sure, dispossession, even as their world immediately confers negative value on it, still indicates the distance between their community and Urras. But any positive meaning that that distance can have must come from an Odonian inheritance which the Anarresti are in imminent peril of losing forever. Indeed, the past tense which *dispossessed* implicitly retains suggests that they may have already and irrevocably forfeited their Odonian ideals.

To the extent that that seems true, their literal and figurative wasteland points to Utopia not as a receding horizon but in terms of what it is not. Even so, it is Anarres far more than Urras which points toward Utopian possibilities, and especially those of a socio-political order, and that is a paradox well worth inquiring into. What makes for the paradox are certain undeniable facts about Anarres as Le Guin has imagined it. The inhospitability of its environment, the open social strife provoked by food shortages consequent upon persistent drought, the struggles for power tending towards oppressive bureaucratisation, the hypocritical collusion with Urrasti 'profiteers' and the self-deceptive blindness to it, the treatment of dissidents like Tirin (reminiscent of horror-stories about Soviet psychiatric prisons) – all of these are features which ought to qualify, if not overdetermine, Anarres as a dystopia. Yet, easy as an account of that sort would be to construct, all readers of *The Dispossessed* except the most obtuse and obdurate right-wing ideologues must be uneasy with it, recognising it as the kind of part-truth which is tantamount to falsehood. And they have good reason for their uneasiness; for the Anarres which thus appears as the negation of Utopian possibilities also – indeed, by the same movement – identifies them. They do not reside in some etherial and extraneous Nowhere, having a dubious connection with the text and an even more uncertain relation to the – or rather, any other – empirical world.[9] Instead, they enter into *The Dispossessed* from the Elsewhere that is the historical or legendary past of Anarres itself, and they do so in significant part through an Anarres which in its denial of them brings them into definition. That is chiefly why Utopian possibilities, particularly of a socio-political kind, are immanent in *The Dispossessed* and not some figment hovering outside the text in need of fleshing out according to the subjective inclination of any given reader: because they are the very possibilities which Sabul's Anarres (let us call it) seems to deny. In fact, it is that denial which enables the fiction to figure and articulate such possibilities persuasively and precisely – and in terms of precisely the principles which are failing to operate in Anarresti actuality. Those principles, furthermore, do not appear merely as a species of palpable absence; like the *Analogy* (their fictively-given source), they also have a real presence as they inform Shevek's – and with him, the reader's – judgemental perception. Hence, the *inherent* standards by which we gauge the Anarresti social order, the standards that *authorise* us to see it as dystopian (or, more accurately, as anti-Utopian)[10] prove to be Odo's – that is, the very ones holding Anarres' Utopian promise.

II

It is the burden of *The Dispossessed* to redeem that promise, and to do so in and through the person of Shevek. By the same token, however, this is a burden properly speaking, a burden in the philosophical as well as in an honorific sense, and one belonging to the narrative as much as to its focal character. It does not fall to Shevek automatically or from the outset and it is no foregone conclusion that he can or will assume it; and correlatively, it is not something which Le Guin posits by mere authorial fiat or asks her readers to take for granted, but rather what her fiction must demonstrate. In other words, it is a responsibility which Shevek must earn – and be shown to earn – through certain painful realisations about his Anarresti past and his present life on Urras.

His process of realisation is both problematic and dialectical. He ultimately comes to look upon his native planet as a locus of Utopian hope, but only by way of perceptions which represent Anarres as the antithesis and betrayal of such hope, as they indicate how precarious and imperilled Odo's legacy is there. Moreover, the Anarres which gradually appears as the negation of its original heritage emerges as such through a narrative which adheres rather rigorously not only to Shevek's point of view, but also to the terms of his own experience – terms which duplicate on a personal level the selfsame dialectical and problematic movement operative in regard to the could-be Utopian status of the Anarresti social order.

This is to say that Shevek's future, and with it his past, are as parlous as those of Anarres itself; indeed, that they are made ambiguous by similar factors. He arrives in A-Io literally empty-handed, to be welcomed as the alien and ambassador that in time he conceives himself to be. Yet in the course of the unfolding, in alternating narrative sequences, of his Anarresti past and his Urrasti present, the full irony of his being thought of – and thinking himself – a representative of his home planet slowly becomes evident. For one thing, the circumstances of his departure for Urras (beginning, in the narratological order of events, with the rock-throwing send-off that some of his compatriots give him) leave the motive for that undertaking radically uncertain in a way that makes his exodus a kind of mirror-image recreation of Odonian history. Whether he is fleeing into exile or being driven out makes little difference, and not only because both exclude pure or gratuitous choice, but also because he is therefore apparently recapitulating – *mutatis mutandis* in his own person – the collective past of the escape or eviction from Urras of Odo's followers over 150 years earlier.

Nor is that the only respect in which the Shevek who disembarks in the land of his biological and would-be spiritual ancestors does so as a representative of all the ambiguities of Anarres that threaten to disable and nullify its Utopian vocation. He comes to Urras, he thinks, as the proverbial Anarresti 'Beggarman' (*D*, p. 56); but in this he is self-deceived in a manner similar to his fellow Anarresti when they imagine they have no truck with Urrasti profiteering. Though he arrives on Urras with virtually nothing by way of material possessions, he in time discovers that in part he owes his existence there to the rather large sum of money accruing to him as Seo Oen Prize Laureate. His sponsors, of course, have given him leisure to pursue his work because they intend to appropriate his theory, exploit its practical application and thereby get a considerable return on their investment in him. In fact, their expectations in this regard are great enough for the Ioti Establishment to have risked importing a man who could prove to be a rallying point for the Odonian revolutionaries on Urras. And if they have reckoned the degree of that risk on the basis of Shevek's being an exemplar of Anarresti attitudes towards and ignorance of Urras, their calculation by no means instantly appears to have been wrong. Shevek, after all, largely keeps to himself for most of his sojourn; and it is a long while before he sees that he has unwittingly been playing into the hands of those who would exploit him: that he has been isolating himself from the Odonians indigenous to A-Io and thus co-operated with profiteers – just as the Anarresti have collectively been doing by immuring themselves against Urras.

So, too, Shevek stands in for the Anarresti generally in what he brings with him to Urras. Although he goes there a man dispossessed of his country and literally empty-handed, he is also a man possessed. It is appropriate that he makes his journey aboard a spacecraft called *Mindful*, for he departs with much to think about, and most of it painful. An exile from a planet of exile, he brings with him his virtually lifelong obsession with an idea and a personal past that continues to haunt him. These ghosts, moreover, are the personal correlatives of those looming over the Anarres that he has left behind, the Anarres which aggregatively seems to be failing the very foundational principles which absorb it.

That Anarres is one of the things on Shevek's mind; indeed, as it is his own life which chiefly supplies the terms for revealing Anarres's problems – the negative ambiguities attaching to it – so his public and personal concerns intersect. And like the Anarres reflected in his experience of it, his own promise seems very much in jeopardy. His seemingly enforced exit has meant his having to

abandon Takver and his daughters; but the exigencies of the
Anarresti drought had already placed Takver and him at antipodes
to one another (she remains at a fisheries laboratory in the North
east while he is posted to Southrising and then volunteers to
work in the Dust of the South west). And that may be somewhat
the case between them not merely in a literal, geographic sense
and for the moment; for the ostracism that his theoretical work
has brought him is clearly putting a strain on their marriage, not
only by reason of the guilt he feels for the social hostility that
Takver and their eldest child, Sadik, are being subjected to on his
account, but also because those same pressures (in the person of
Sabul) have frustrated his work in temporal physics to the point
of putting an end to it.[11] External constraints, however, are not
the sole factors incapacitating his professional endeavours. He is
blocked as well by his own inability to conceive how the temporal
synthesis that preoccupies him might be worked out and demonstrated. In short, he goes to Urras with his life in a near-total
shambles, on every side confronting a wall that would cut him off
from his past and bar the way to any emotional and intellectual
fulfilment.

The youthful hopes that circumstances seem to force him to
detach from Anarres he projects on to Urras. To be sure, he has
long known that the latter world leaves much to be desired in its
socio-political arrangements. But his knowledge of such matters
has been in the abstract, not the result of first-hand experience;
and it does not begin to trouble him seriously until Chifoilisk,
himself a spy from Thu, causes Shevek to have the paranoiac shock
of recognition that Ioti secret police and their informers have been
clandestinely monitoring his activities. Concurrently, Shevek is
also in the process of discovering that even the Urras he has
thought of and witnessed to be an ecological Utopia has ambiguities
as such in the same pejorative sense which applies to Anarres.
Long before his interview with the ambassador from Terra makes
him aware that that devastated planet may forewarn of the future
that Urras itself is in for (if the profiteers have their way),[12] he
starts to realise that another deathly Ego presides over the would-
be Urrasti Arcadia. He comes to see that the pleasures this Arcadia
offers – the sensual gratification he first experiences from the
accoutrements of the *Mindful* – are extricable from a sensate culture
which is every bit as debilitating to his lifework as its Anarresti
antithesis has proved to be.

In this regard, it is no accident that he becomes fully conscious of the perils of Urras's seductive luxury while he is still in the throes of the profound self-doubt that near as he is to the General Temporal Theory the Ioti want him for, he 'had not achieved it and might never do so,' either because the 'goal' may be 'illusory' or because 'he was not the man to do the job' (*D*, p. 165). Wandering alone through Nio Esseia to escape such thoughts, and feeling for perhaps the first time the danger of a society 'where the basic moral assumption was . . . mutual aggression' (p. 167), he suddenly espies Vea sitting next to a pool (of the kind having a purely ornamental civic purpose). His reaction, however, is not what would be expected under the circumstances. Instead of being relieved at the sight of a familiar face, he perceives her as the embodiment of the subliminated sexuality inhering in all the artefacts that the Ioti 'haves' surround themselves with. The image conveying this to him – 'He saw Vea across the broad, bright circle of water' (p. 171) – seems to prepare for an epiphany of an altogether different sort; but as she is instantly revealed to him as a 'body profiteer', he recognises the reflected sunlight as a mirage and both she and it as figures of Urras's false promise. And at the same moment, his connection with Vea – now appearing as a travesty of a true bond, the sort he has had with Takver – typifies the speciousness of the contact he has so far made with Vea's world, and especially of his human ties there.

Shevek thus confronts two worlds which, for all their mutual antagonism, converge in subverting his deepest impulses and aspirations. The events on Anarres leading up to his departure tend towards realising the long-standing anxiety that he first becomes conscious of in late adolescence, that 'I'm cut off' (*D*, p. 40); and this also seems to be the direction that his life is taking on Urras. By such an account, his story on the one essentially repeats that on the other: both are stories of alienation, particularly from the human environment but above all from his seemingly past self and what he ideally might have been. And this is the case as well for the worlds with which his life is interfused: theirs, too, appears as a story of lost hope, of broken promises.

Even so, hope and promise abide, and not simply as a measure of personal and social failure, but in the very telling of the story of failure, especially as it relates to Anarres. After all, the flashbacks to Shevek's life there amount to more than the usual device for filling the reader in about his past; they also re-present that past, and hence make it as accessible to change as the future is. But the latter statement is something of an equivocation. Not only can we take it to mean that the future is as unalterable as the past; we are logically obliged to do so in reading Shevek's as a story of 'waste sad time', of irrecoverably lost promise. That change is possible is not at issue here. Le Guin grants – what we readily assume to be true from historical experience since early on in the First Industrial Revolution – that the objective world is changing. Nor does she cast doubt on the introspectively-based conviction that we can change our minds about it and ourselves. Indeed, it is in view of Shevek's rethinking of his life *vis-à-vis* an Anarres heading away from its Odonian ideals that *The Dispossessed* poses its central problem, the urgency of which appears all the greater by reason of the fact that the changes Shevek undergoes or bears witness to seem to be for the worse, if not the worst.

Put one way, the question Le Guin addresses is whether this course of events is reversible. The hope that it is comes out of Shevek's despair; for in revaluing his identity and that of an Anarres forgetful of Odo's dream, he instances the future's altering of the past. This last notion, however, is hopeful only when we recognise it as the paradox which it must strike us as being to the extent that we suppose, with the Orwell of 'Looking Back on the Spanish War' (1942), that history is an absolute, a concatenation of immutable facts.[13] Otherwise, we can easily reconcile ourselves to the idea of temporal malleability by taking it to bear solely on human psychology, not on the material universe. Yet the disjunction implicitly appealed to, to empty the corollary to metanoia and historical change of its paradoxical content, is exactly of the kind making for the problem Le Guin faces, and faces up to – a problem which we can now articulate in terms of the connection(s) between the objective and subjective realms.

Their obvious connection is not in itself problematic. What makes it so is its fictive illustration. External factors, as they impinge on Shevek's thinking and even appear as determining his scientific pursuits,[14] contribute substantially to the wrecking of his life and hence to the poignancy of *The Dispossessed*'s real question: Can we intentionally influence our environment so as to have some control over the course of our lives? The evidence for the reciprocity of influence – especially of the kind fictionally exemplified by a Terra whose ecological desolation is humanly made – does not suggest an easy and affirmative answer. On the contrary, it serves only to sharpen the question as applying to the chances of our avoiding or undoing our destructive impact. Indeed, given the disastrous effects of human activity on the natural (as well as the human) world, we have all the more reason to wonder if our actions are – or can be – the result of deliberative choice, of the weighing of consequences.

That phrasing emphasises the political aspect of a question which centrally involves our responsibility also to ourselves as individuals. Furthermore, responsibility as the ethical imperative that Shevek conceives it to be will not countenance any disjunction of the political from the personal. Yet by the same token, and also because it extends to the past along with the future, responsibility in his normative sense offers itself as a(nother) way into, not out of, the problem that Le Guin raises; and it does so for practical as well as theoretical reasons. Willing as we may be in principle to join Shevek in his insistence that we hold ourselves accountable, individually and collectively, for both the private and the historical course of events, we may well be reluctant in practice to deem ourselves entirely responsible for our own lives (let alone any wider sphere) even if we are not encountering setbacks as chronic and extensive as those which Shevek experiences. More often than not when the alternative entails considering an unhappy outcome to be our own doing, we automatically incline towards laying blame on others or on impersonal circumstances – this according to a motive whose strength is directly proportional to the degree of failure, and which is almost irresistible where the failure is of the magnitude Shevek contemplates. Nor is it difficult to rationalise our actual behaviour in this regard by appealing to traditional tenets of moral philosophy. As these would have it, it is tautologically true to say that we are exempt from responsibility for whatever is not of our doing or could not have been otherwise. The problem with this line of self-justification as it tacitly enters into *The Dispossessed* is not that it is logically circular so much as that in theory it excludes ethical responsibility altogether and thereby puts our personal and collective destiny beyond our control. That is so from a Sequentialist as well as a Simultaneist perspective on time. Whether the present and future be perceived as having the same status as what has already happened or as proceeding from a past gone forever, and thus forever unalterable, comes down to a meaningless difference between history's never having been liable and its no longer being susceptible to free human choice.

Responsibility as Shevek understands it does not admit of exceptionable instances, in the rationalising of which we in effect evacuate the concept of its real function by forfeiting real choice completely. To his mind, we become responsible beings, capable of 'mak[ing] a pulley, or a promise' and accountable for the consequences of our actions, the moment we can see 'the difference between *now* and *not now*' (*D*, p. 181). Yet if responsibility as the globally operative principle Shevek would have it be depends on nothing more than '[s]eeing th[at] difference', it likewise depends on nothing less than the validation of such a difference as real – depends, in other words, on the theoretical proof which Shevek has still to arrive at. His predicament, then, parallels and reproduces in apparently fictive terms the one we get ourselves into as soon as we appeal to responsibility in any sense which would allow it to designate a solution to the problem of whether we can shape and alter the future (or the past) in accordance with our ideals. Indeed, the question-begging here has to do with our direct positing of what is implicitly entailed in Shevek's 'seeing the difference': the sort of free and intentional act whose possibility is at stake.

In Shevek's case, the logical circle seems inescapable. He comes to recognise that any hope for redeeming his life rests with his taking responsibility for what has happened to him. But he also realises that responsibility in the sense required is theoretically impossible without the temporal synthesis to which he has devoted his life, whose course appears to have put such a synthesis beyond his reach. He thus finds himself in the bind of not being able to recuperate his life's promise unless he first or simultaneously fulfills it.

III

By putting the question in fundamentally temporal terms, Le Guin does not alleviate its burden on Shevek or ease her own way towards disposing of it. On the contrary, she makes it appear all the more intractable by reason of its circularity. Those same abstract terms, however, allow us to remove ourselves from the problem and doubt its urgency. We can have some understanding of Shevek's intellectual struggle with the competing notions of time imaged, for example, by the river and the circle, and still not be troubled that each entails its own unacceptable paradox, the outcome of which Shevek summarises by the instance of 'throwing a rock at a tree': 'if you are a Simultanist the rock has already hit the tree, and if you are a Sequentist it never can' (*D*, p. 182). Even conceding that such objections are fatal to Sequentist and Simultanist thinking alike for their not admitting of human causality, we may remain untroubled, secure in our conviction of Sequentiality; and this may be the case despite our awareness that the paradoxes of Zeno the Eleatic which Shevek rehearses constitute an ineluctable *reductio ad absurdum* for any concept of time as an infinitesimally divisible composite of discrete moments.[15] On similar grounds we may also dismiss the ethical concomitant of this logical absurdity: that the Sequentist 'now', receding from us at the speed of light, allows no time to reflect upon our actions, past or future. This objection, too, we may regard as merely theoretical inasmuch as it contradicts what we know from experience.

Yet our very reasons for not taking such arguments seriously reinstate Shevek's problem in both its specific and its general form. The same commonsense which assures us that the universe as we objectively perceive it unfolds sequentially also lends equal weight to our introspectively-derived belief that through 'memory and intention' (*D*, p. 149) or forethought we can hold the past and the future together in our minds. Simultaneism, then, is as much a truth of and about our common experience as is Sequentiality.[16] This, in fact, is the basis for Shevek's chronosophical dilemma in regard to the apparent incompatibility of Sequentialism and Simultaneity: that the one allows the flow of events to be open to our direction but no time for us to think about what choices we have, while the other affords an eternity for such cogitations but to no real purpose whatsoever. If we attempt to sweep away the dilemma as being only theoretical, we in effect – *and thereby* – restate the problem in somewhat broader terms: those of the disparity between theory and practice, the ideal and the actual, the *vita contemplativa* and the *vita activa*.

Shevek's, in other words, is a chronosophical version of a problem perennial in Western philosophy since the age of the Pre-Socratics at least. There is, however, this difference: that his version, as it ramifies analogically to take in his entire life, loses the abstractness of traditional formulations. Le Guin does not require that we be chronosophers to empathise with his difficulties; nor does she demand that we conceive of them by reference to any purely intellectual dichotomies. To appreciate what he is up against, we need only identify with his frustration, and perhaps with the despair that accompanies it, as he looks helplessly on his life and his world moving ever further away from their original promise.

Following Shevek out of frustration and despair is another matter. To do that, we must have some mental grasp of their logical source: in a series of oppositions typified by the alternative of Simultaneism or Sequentiality. These Le Guin makes intellectually available to us through their instantial embodiment in Shevek's story as he reflects upon his past, his present and his future. It is his 'spiritual suffering' over 'seeing' his and others' 'talent, . . . work, . . . lives wasted' (*D*, p. 135) that brings home the human meaning of abstractions such as 'is' versus 'ought', memory versus desire. Nor does Le Guin permit us to understand them otherwise, as pure ideas unconnected with the world of our daily experience; for to do so necessarily involves ratifying the kind of discrepancy from which, by her analysis, our personal and political malaise arises. And acknowledging this, we also become aware that Shevek's project for reconciling temporal opposites stands as both the precondition and the paradigm of what we must realise to have any hope of ministering to our disease.

The bare possibility of such a reconciliation is doubly inscribed in *The Dispossessed* as a narrative of broken promises. As Anarres, seen through Shevek's eyes, appears heading in the socio-political direction of Urras, so Urras is gradually approaching the Anarres he has found to be 'a place of disaffection' (T. S. Eliot, 'Burnt Norton', III. 1). This converging of antithetical worlds is not in itself hopeful, of course; but, as it comes about irrespective of human intention, it contributes to defining the reconciliation of opposites that Shevek is seeking: one which human beings deliberatively bring about. Furthermore, in reflecting upon his existence, Shevek becomes conscious not only of the fact that *as he enters into it* the actual rapprochement of Urras and Anarres constitutes a *via negativa* pointing to the kind of synthesis he is after, but also that it instances the universal operation of a principle of radical instability, which is the necessary condition for his enterprise to have any ameliorative impact. Recognising that he has all along been mediating between mutually hostile worlds that are fundamentally changeable, he decides to bring them together in a positive sense by throwing his lot in with that of the Ioti rebels. He thus deliberately assumes the role which the Ioti popular press had assigned him in advance, a role which has, as it were, been waiting for him from the moment of his arrival in A-Io: he incarnates the 'myth' of the 'Forerunner', 'the one who comes before the millennium – "a stranger, an outcast, an exile, bearing in empty hands the time to come"' (*D*, p. 186). By joining the General Strike, then, he takes a step towards making his, but also its, promise in regard to Urras a reality: the promise of a revolution which would refashion that world according to Odonian precepts.

Certain though the prospect of revolution may be, its success is as open to doubt as is that of the afforestation project by which Anarres would verge towards the Utopian promise located in (and by) Urras. Yet whatever the outcome, Shevek's remains a redemptive act, and not only for him. When he tells the enormous gathering in Nio Esseia's Capitol Square, 'It is our suffering that brings us together', he is speaking 'out of his own isolation, out of the center of his own being' (*D*, p. 241) and from the self-realisation that suffering has supplied the bond between his own life on Anarres and on Urras. Representing this emotional concomitant of his alienation as the basis for human solidarity, he breaches the wall separating individual from collective existence. But beyond that, and as the occasion makes clear, the (speech-)act by which he does so involves the sort of revaluation of time that lets in 'causative reversibility' (p. 37).[17] He had gone to Urras, Anarres's historical past, thinking that it was his future and that he had put Anarres, his personal past, behind him along with its shattered dreams. Yet the Odonian sentiments he gives voice to in Capitol Square presuppose that he has come to believe otherwise. Indeed, he expressly identifies the promise that he is there to deliver – 'You have nothing. You possess nothing. You are free. All you have is what you are, and what you give' – as the one 'made two hundred years ago' and 'kept . . . on Anarres' (p. 241). By this apparent change of mind, this reversal, he restores his homeland to its original place in relation to Urras – as the future – and not only through his words and in his own mind, but by a gesture which itself promises that Anarres may yet become what it always was.

Both the paradox and the promise derive from the discoveries that Shevek has been making about time. In this regard, it is no accident that he learns of the events behind the planned mass protest in Capitol Square from one of the 'birdseed papers', so called because they are written 'in the verbal mode of the Nioti, past and future rammed into one highly charged present tense' (p. 162). This last phrase applies to the self-understanding he has reached as much as to his sense of what is going on in consequence of the Ioti government's move to intervene against the rebels in far away Benbili. Furthermore, these two areas of his awareness are intimately related in their bearing on his revolutionary gesture. Viewing the situation as 'highly charged' because it is a moment in which the oppressive past converges on and reinforces the possibility of an Odonian future for Urras, he judges that some such gesture would be timely and appropriate; but in its particulars, that gesture is possible only because he is already conscious of a similar convergence of his own past and future. In other words, he is able to speak as he does – is able to articulate A-Io's Odonian prospects and in that way enter into them as a catalyst – because he has seen how the fragments of his own life fit together, because he has already made the temporal connections informing the details of his verbal public act.

The circumstances preceding that act compel the same conclusion. His commitment to an Odonian revolution on Urras immediately follows a moment of insight in which he sees his way towards the temporal synthesis he has long been searching for. Just before that, however, his thoughts were of how to escape. Believing that 'to do the work he was individually called to do' meant 'serv[ing] . . . the [Ioti] State', he thinks that he 'had made a mistake in coming to Urras', that by doing so he has 'locked himself in jail'; and this leads him to ask, 'how might [I] act as a free man?' (*D*, p. 219). In context, the question is surely desperate in its expression of his desire to disengage himself from A-Io. It can therefore not be a fallacious case of *post hoc, ergo propter hoc* that he determines upon the opposite course right after his instant of chronosophical illumination.

That instant, as it apparently supplies the answer to his question about freeing himself, is also apparently the turning point of his life. But how it indicates the way out of the prison he has got himself into is no more obvious than why it should prove pivotal, and for the same reason: the seeming privacy of Shevek's moment of illumination. We are told that '[h]e had seen the foundations of the universe and they were solid' (p. 226); and these words, as they call to mind one of the most famous of 'Ainsetain's' obiter dicta,[18] also imply that Shevek's glimpse into the 'unity' of 'successivity and presence' (p. 225) has something of the character of a supernatural revelation. Yet the experience which in its effect on Shevek appears as mystical may seem from the details we are given about it to be merely mystifying. We may incline to look upon such statements as 'The coexistence of succession could be handled by a Saeban transformation series' (ibid.) as so much mumbo-jumbo intended to obscure the fact that Le Guin understands the whole subject or simul-sequentiality no more than we do. We may thereupon either condemn her for not delivering on a promise or excuse ourselves for not troubling our brains any further as to what all the palaver about time might signify. This, to judge by what has been written about *The Dispossessed*, would appear to be the alternative for a good many readers: that of tacitly dismissing all temporal matters from consideration or of in effect seizing upon Shevek's assertion of 'the unprovability of the hypothesis of real coexistence' (ibid.) as meaning that no demonstration whatever is given of the point.

Nevertheless, there is something highly implausible about supposing that Le Guin would shirk the onus of proving 'real coexistence' while making it clear that the life of her central character centres upon its validity, in his envisioning of which he sees 'the way home, the light' – 'The wall was down' (ibid.). Nor need we look far for why this is so. The answer lies, somehow, with the reality of temporal coexistence; and the demonstration of that reality is in front of us. But it does not enter into the fiction in the form of mathematical equations involving 'Saeba variables' (p. 224) or 'the lovely geometries of relativity' (p. 225) – abstractions of the kind which, as we have seen, make for the problem confronting us through Shevek. And the demonstration does not otherwise figure in a manner that would permit its detachment from (the rest of) his story: although the signs of its presence are everywhere, and perhaps have their greatest concentration in the very paragraph persuading some readers that Le Guin has given over the attempt, it is not contained in (or by) that passage describing Shevek's moment of inspiration or any other single narrative instance. Still, it is literally – and always – before our eyes: right where Le Guin, through Shevek, has in effect told us to look for it.

Speaking to Dearri, but also clarifying his thoughts about time for himself (and us), he says:

we think that time 'passes,' flows past us, but what if it is we who move forward, from past to future, always discovering the new? It would be a little like reading a book, you see. The book is all there, all at once, between its covers. But if you want to read the story and understand it, you must begin with the first page, and go forward, always in order. (*D*, p. 178)

The point of this version of the time-honoured analogy between the book and 'the universe' (ibid.) holds for any text whose narrative or logical cohesiveness exacts an incremental understanding. Such a text, from the standpoint of its having already been read (or written), corresponds to the Simultaneist idea of time as 'presence', to the idea that past and future are forever 'now' and eternally unalterable; but in the reading (and writing) of it, that same text is the correlate of Sequentiality, of the idea that time is synonymous with perpetual change, perpetual movement away from the no-longer and towards the yet-to-be. Furthermore, we have no warrant for supposing that one or the other of these seemingly antithetical notions of time is merely a matter of appearances: both, in the terms of the analogy, are equally real. What those terms do allow, however, is the conclusion that, in regard to both time and books, the Simultaneous understanding we finally reach supersedes and obliterates our Sequentist understanding.

It is this imbalance, and the problem for real coexistence which goes with it, that Le Guin designs *The Dispossessed* to obviate. With the moment on which the fiction opens as our point of reference, we can look upon Shevek's life as emerging in two sequences: one taking him up to the instant of his departure for Urras from his earliest recollection of childhood, and hence moving from the past to the present; the other unfolding from that present moment into the future as the series of events leading to his decision to go back to Anarres. From this same account, however, it is evident that the two sequences which separately appear as exactly that, as sequential, together constitute a circle imaging Simultaneity, and not just by reason of their converging on the same geographical point, the spaceport at Abennay. After all, the circularity of Shevek's spatial voyage is the objective correlative of the mental process by which he recuperates his original ideals, both for himself and for Anarres, and thus returns figuratively to his Odonian beginning place. Yet the Sequentist reading which thereby eventuates and subsumes itself in Simultaneity ignores a textual fact so obvious that we can easily overlook it: namely, that no such continuity objectively exists in this book. What Le Guin gives us instead are discrete moments from Shevek's past and future made even more fragmentary by their mutual interruption as the scene regularly shifts back and forth from Anarres to Urras.

This is not to say that *The Dispossessed* flatly denies the very connections which it thus calls upon us to make and by which we arrive at the Simultaneist understanding of '*true voyage is return*' (*D*, p. 68): 'that the end precedes the beginning. / And the end and the beginning were always there / Before the beginning and after the end' (T. S. Eliot, 'Burnt Norton', v. 10–12). Rather the purpose of the discontinuity is to make us aware of the insufficiency of such a reading. We cannot take Shevek's narrative as an exclusive affirmation of Simultaneity without disregarding the disconnectedness built into his story and hence misrepresenting both the text and its universe. Nor is that the only respect in which our purchase on certainty comes at the expense of meaning; for as the text compels us to supply the connections which necessarily entail the Simultaneist position, it allows us to be absolutely secure in a Simultaneist truth that is merely tautological. And our cognate assurance that Shevek is destined to return to his point of origin, that the ending of the narrative is indelibly inscribed in its beginning, likewise comes down to the empty proposition that any outcome is inevitable after the fact.

A rigorously Sequentist reading, on the other hand, while it does justice to Shevek's as a voyage into perpetual possibility, does not allow for the coherence of the (narrative) universe. In its faithfulness to the physical text, so to speak, such an understanding emphasises the truth of contingency by isolating every moment in Shevek's life as a potential turning point, an end and a beginning. But by the same process, it at once denies meaning to those instants and distorts our reading experience of them in its refusal to admit not only their connection, but also the consciousness that goes into and comes out of the connections which we actually make. A strictly Sequentist perspective, then, opens on the prospect of radical indeterminacy: it would have events totally evitable, but solely inasmuch as they be totally arbitrary; and it permits our going anywhere (figuratively speaking), but not to any purpose or with any destination in mind.

The consequence is essentially similar when we moderate the rigour of Sequentism by introducing 'the concept of interval' (*D*,

p. 225). We can thereupon proceed to re-form the discrete narrative instants into two series. But if we would preserve the dichotomy between Sequence and Presence, we cannot go so far as to link the series leading Shevek to the Anarresti Dust and terminating in his exile with the one eventuating in the suppressed rebellion on Urras. We thus give Shevek's life a direction which, as it takes him to dead ends, is hardly preferable to none at all.

All of this brings us back to Shevek's chronosophical dilemma, but now with the perception that it involves and is involved in *The Dispossessed* as a whole. Moreover, the manner of its involvement answers to the need that the dilemma in itself indicates: the need for reconciling temporal opposites. The answer abides in the fiction; and it does so because LeGuin has constructed a text which we cannot properly construe so long as we hold to the alternative of Sequency or Presence. Any reading that sides with the one against the other must falsify the narrative in respect either to the real continuity of Shevek's life or to its real disruption. So, too, we cannot endorse Sequentialism or Simultaneity as the sole truth without sacrificing either our sense of Shevek's Being, that 'What might have been and what has been / Point to one end, which is always present', or our sense of his Becoming, that 'What might have been' is *not* 'an abstraction / Remaining a perpetual possibility / Only in a world of speculation' (T. S. Eliot, 'Burnt Norton', ı. 9–10, 6–8).

Nor can we understand the text as alternately validating those ideas of time, and with them those versions of Shevek's life. This should be evident in regard to the aphorism epitomising his story: 'You *can* go home again . . . so long as you understand that home is a place where you have never been' (*D*, p. 68). That statement does not express the Sequential and the Simultaneist points of view serially any more than it presents them as an alternative. Its meaning is not compound or dichotomous, but complex: not only does it assert the reality of permanence and change, it recognises them as aspects of one another.

This is likewise true for the entire fiction. Its 'static and dynamic aspect[s]' (*D*, p. 225) are as indissociable as are those of the universe it models. That is why the text is so resistant to paraphrase, with its inherent tendency to hypostatise a course of events which in this case is radically unstable, forever changing direction. Indeed, any kind of analysis focusing singly on each fictional moment – on, say, that of Sabul's ascendancy – must point us away from 'home' in its aphoristic sense, even – or rather, especially – if the analysis then takes account of that instant's momentum.

To arrive at the conclusion that Shevek has always been coming 'home', we must therefore follow him on a journey that he ultimately sees as one of continuous self-discovery. In doing so, however, we are making a voyage which is as fundamentally simul-sequentist as his own. We return to his and our starting point, but with the understanding of Heraclitus's dictum, 'You shall not go down twice to the same river'.[19] In fact, any conviction we have that it is Shevek's destiny to go back to Anarres finally depends on the inner necessity which compels him to return to the locus of his Odonian ideals; and that ethical compulsion derives from the simul-sequentist truth about his life: his *discovery* that he has never lost his ideal self. This truth, his sudden awareness of which comes out of prolonged reflection on his temporal existence, coincides with the General Temporal Theory he has been looking for because it carries with it the perception that Being and Becoming, Presence and Process, Permanence and Flux, are indispensable to defining Shevek's identity and hence to one another. Their complementarity, moreover, is not simply an idea; it is a 'functional' idea, in the Odonian sense of the word, by reason of its pointing to what neither Simultaneity nor Sequency by itself allows: the possibility that seemingly broken promises can be kept.

This is the possibility that Shevek brings back to Anarres in his empty hands. Yet even though his prospective return to Anarresti soil implies that his compatriots are now willing to break '[t]he Terms of Closure of the[ir] Settlement' (*D*, p. 287),[20] the only guarantee we have that their xenophobia and their misoneism lie behind them is Shevek himself. Still, the very fact that their renewal of Anarres' Odonian promise is, by his example,[21] an open possibility is sufficient for transforming the Simultaneist eternal cycle into the ongoing Circle of Life.

Such a transformation perhaps figures its simul-sequentist significance most clearly as it applies to a boyhood nightmare of Shevek's. He dreams that walking along a road, he sees 'a line' which, on closer inspection, turns out to be 'a wall' stretching 'from horizon to horizon across the barren land' (*D*, p. 26). He knows that '[h]e had to go on or he could never come home again', but the wall blocks the way (p. 27). What he ultimately recognises, not at the moment but long afterwards – what enables him to perceive the unity of Sequence and Presence which means coming 'home' – is that the wall *is* the way. As an image of Sequential experience, the wall of Shevek's nightmare is like the 'glittering rails' that he rides to Chakar (p. 247) or the 'metalled ways' of the Underground in 'Burnt Norton' (III. 37): it takes him to spiritual death. But as it extends 'from horizon to horizon', it also extrapolatively images Simultaneity and thus becomes instead the road 'home'. So, too, it figures what would otherwise be a mere abstraction: that the way to time's dispossession, to redeeming the past, goes 'Only through time' (ibid., II. 43) – indeed, runs concurrent with it.

As Shevek himself bears witness to this transformation, he also stands as its 'undemonstrable proof' (*D*, p. 287). The sense in which this is true takes us from an obvious fact about our real-life experience to an obvious fact about our reading experience: from the fact that he cannot appear before us in the flesh to the fact that within the confines of the book to which he wholly owes his existence, his temporal (self-)discovery is nowhere plainly and fully spelled out. This last, self-imposed, limitation, however, finally appears to be as inescapable as the first, the external constraint, which thereupon becomes as much a dictate of artistic necessity as Le Guin's withholding an overt explanation of simul-sequential-ism. Why this should be so she hints at in Shevek's words about his *Principles of Simultaneity*: 'I am that book' (p. 194). Through its context, the statement applies even more emphatically to *The Dispossessed* as the expression of the redeeming synthesis of which his *Principles* is only a small part. For that reason, the self-discovery which is his synthesis must, at least as much as Odo's precepts, remain prominent in and by virtue of its absence. It cannot appear in *The Dispossessed*, cannot be merely a moment in the book which holds his identity; it must *be* that book, coextensive with it, just as he is. And, as we have in effect been seeing, his 'holorganismic' discovery (p. 132) is coextensive with the book, not only in the *Bildung* the narrative leads to, but in *The Dispossessed*'s very structure, as it demonstrably incorporates the promise that through time a redemptive dispossession of time is possible.

NOTES

1. The phrase quoted comes from Section v of 'Little Gidding'. This and subsequent citations follow the text of T. S. Eliot's *The Complete Poems*

and Plays, 1909–1950 (New York: Harcourt, Brace and World, 1952) pp. 117–48. Since (as far as I am aware) no complete edition of *Four Quartets* exists with enumerated lines, I identify quotations from it by section and line(s) within that section. Such references will appear in the text.

My implicit point, as my epigraph is meant to indicate preliminarily, is that *The Dispossessed* constitutes a reworking of the argument of *Four Quartets*, whose Eliotic meaning Le Guin secularises and gives a decidedly 'political' application to (in the broadest sense of *political*). This, she has privately communicated to me, is neither the result of conscious intention on her part nor an accident (that is, an arbitrary connection of mine).

2. By 'semantic opposition' I mean to suggest not only that Anarres at first defines itself as the syntagmatic negation of Urras, but also that its name is to be thought of as the phonemic negative of *Urras* – that is, as *Un-Urras*. This notion is consistent with other proposals about the derivation of the name of Shevek's home planet, at least if they be regarded as negational forms (of *archy* and *res*). It should be stressed, however, that any such understanding of *Anarres* must give way to another by the time Shevek returns: that the name finally takes on a positive meaning all of its own, correlative to that of *dispossessed* in the sense he redeems. By that transvaluation, moreover, the syntagmatic dependency of *Anarres* and *Urras* reverses: *Anarres* appears as the primary signifier, with *Urras* the *Ur*-form that according to Odonian (but not Shevek's) history it has been all along.

3. Thinking of *Urras* as a compound of USA and USSR becomes more plausible when we remember that the French initials for the latter are URSS (see my next note). On the other hand, the presence of Terra in the fiction serves to point to some of the respects in which Urras is not (simply identifiable as) Earth.

4. Recalling that Le Guin at Radcliffe was a student of Romance languages specialising in French and Italian literature, we can take the 'Io' of A-Io as the Italian first-person singular pronoun and Thu, pronounced 'tu', as the familiar form of 'you' in French (but also the French term for the [Martin] Buberian 'Thou'). In this connection, see the passage in *The Left Hand of Darkness* (1969) in which Genly Ai and Estraven between them establish the 'duality' of 'I and Thou' as 'essential' (New York: Ace Books, 1969, p. 222); and consider also Donald Theall's gloss on that passage: 'This duality of "myself and the other" or "I and Thou" is naturally at the heart of human communication' ('The Art of Social-Science Fiction: the Ambiguous Utopian Dialectics of Ursula K. Le Guin', *Science-Fiction Studies*, vol. 2 (1975) p. 260).

It should be added that the 'Thu' which we sound as (if it were) a Vietnamese–French name points to the fact that *The Dispossessed* is as much a product of the American War in Indochina as is *The Word for World is Forest* (1972). (The difference between them is that the latter is situated in a fictional equivalent of Vietnam, so to speak, while *The Dispossessed* – as becomes evident from events towards the end of Shevek's stay on Urras – emanates from the United States of the era of anti-war protest and as seemed at the time, its promise that radical change in the direction of America's foundational ideals might be possible.) In this connection, 'A-Io' should also be deciphered as 'A-One-o', a sardonic acknowledgement of America's pretensions to world hegemony.

5. Ursula K. Le Guin, *The Dispossessed* (New York: Avon, 1974) p. 292. Future references will appear in the text, preceded by the initial *D*.

6. Frank Herbert, *Dune* (New York: Chilton Books, 1965).

7. Whether by authorial intention or not, the episode concerning the Dust proleptically militates against the widely held view that Anarres is a privative Utopia, a place where 'the valued social . . . interdependence of the propertyless' is 'environmentally coerced' (John Fekete, '*The Dispossessed* and *Triton*: Act and System in Utopian Science Fiction', *Science-Fiction Studies*, vol. 6 (1979) p. 133); this same assumption governs Raymond Williams's account of *The Dispossessed* in his 'Utopia and Science Fiction'. *Science-Fiction Studies* vol. 5 (1978) pp. 213–14, and it underlies Nadia Khouri's contention that 'the economic entropy of Anarres becomes the necessary condition for [its] virtuous . . . superiority . . . over Urras' ('The Dialectics of Power: Utopia in the Science Fiction of Le Guin, Jeury, and Piercy', *Science-Fiction Studies*, vol. 7 (1980) p. 52).

   'Mutual aid' is a recurrent phrase bringing to mind P. A. Kropotkin and his best-known treatise on anarchism. For a compelling discussion of his and other anarchist thinkers' influence on the conception of Anarres, see Victor Urbanowicz's 'Personal and Political in Le Guin's *The Dispossessed*', *Science-Fiction Studies*, vol. 5 (1978) pp. 110–17.

8. 'What', Shevek rhetorically asks Chifoilisk, 'is idealistic about social cooperation, mutual aid, when it is the only means of staying alive?' (*D*, p. 109).

9. For reasons that I try to make clear in section III of this chapter, the meaning of *The Dispossessed* is predicated on the truth that the text, through our reading of it, is as much a matter of our experience as is what we usually think of as 'the empirical world'.

10. According to the distinction I have in mind, 'anti-Utopian' is immanently and continually (if not continuously) engaged in a dialogue with 'Utopian' fiction, whereas the 'dystopian' occupies the already-evacuated space formerly held by Utopian ideas / ideals, which figure (if at all) only as a vacancy. On this understanding of the three terms, 'Utopian' and 'dystopian' fictions are more or less monological. Compare John Huntington's discussion in Chapter 7 of *The Logic of Fantasy: H. G. Wells and Science Fiction* (New York: Columbia University Press, 1982), and see also Robert Philmus, 'The Language of Utopia', *Studies in the Literary Imagination*, vol. 6, no. 2 (Fall 1973) pp. 61–78.

11. This point is borne out by the following passage, which (moreover) indicates that the estrangement between Shevek and Takver has been mutual:

   He had withdrawn from Takver since the winter, since the decision about the book [i.e., Sabul's decision not to publish Shevek's

Principles of Simultaneity]. She had been increasingly quiet, passive, patient. He understood that passivity now: it was preparation for her death. It was she who had withdrawn from him, and he had not tried to follow her. He had looked only at his bitterness of heart, and never at her fear, or courage. He had let her alone because he wanted to be let alone, and so she had gone on, gone far, too far, would go on alone forever.   (*D*, p. 195)

That this last thought of his proves not to be the case is largely owing to the process of reflection in which it is situated. ('*Looking back on the last four years*, Shevek saw them not as wasted, but as part of the edifice that he and Takver were building with their lives' – *D*, p. 269; my emphasis.)

12. Against the possibility that Urras will repeat the self-desolation of Terra stands the fictive given that A-Io 'had led the world for centuries . . . in ecological control and the husbanding of natural resources' (*D*, p. 66). In the face of universal instability and the 'profiteering' impulse, however, there is no guarantee that this will always be the case.

13. For Orwell's expression of dismay 'that the very concept of objective truth is fading out of the world', see 'Looking Back on the Spanish War', in Sonia Orwell and Ian Angus (eds), *The Collected Essays, Journalism and Letters of George Orwell* (London: Secker and Warburg, 1968) vol. 2, pp. 258–9. This same idea, of course, figures in its absence in *Nineteen Eighty-Four*.

14. See E. E. Nunan and David Homer's 'Science, Science Fiction, and a Radical Science Education', *Science-Fiction Studies*, vol. 8 (1981) pp. 311–12, 324–6, for a consideration of *The Dispossessed*'s bearing on the debate between 'the traditional "internalist" view of science as a totally self-regulated activity and their "externalist" opponents, who emphasize outside forces as determining the rate, direction, and form of knowledge production' (p. 311). Their essay, however, hardly exhausts what the fiction has to tell us about such matters as the impact of socio-politics and ideology on scientific pursuits.

15. One version of Zeno's paradoxical *reductio ad absurdum* of Sequentist time (cum space) appears (unattributed to him) at *D*, p. 23. See also Jorge Luis Borges, 'Avatars of the Tortoise', in *Other Inquisitions*, trans. Ruth L. C. Simms (New York: Washington Square Press, 1966) pp. 114–20.

16. Our common supposition that Sequence is a feature of the external world and Presence merely a fact of human psychology is directly inverted in Shevek's remark (to Dearri): 'Within the strict terms of Simultaneity Theory, succession is not considered as a physically objective phenomenon, but as a subjective one' (*D*, p. 178).

17. On the concept of 'speech-act' in relation to Le Guin, see Victoria Myers, 'Conversational Technique in Ursula Le Guin: a Speech-Act Analysis [of *The Left Hand of Darkness*]'. *Science-Fiction Studies*, vol. 10 (1983) pp. 306–16.

18. 'God does not play dice with the world.' Einstein in effect explains the meaning of this favourite saying of his in his 1941 additions to

'Science and Religion', where he writes: 'The more a man is imbued with the ordered regularity of all events the firmer becomes his conviction that there is no room left by the side of this ordered regularity for causes of a different nature' (quoted from *Out of My Later Years* (New York: Philosophical Library, 1950) p. 28). It is worth remarking that Einstein, by reason of his political concerns as well as his professional stature, clearly stands as a real-life model for Shevek.

19. Heraclitus's apothegm is quoted (but not attributed to him) at *D*, p. 68. Borges's gloss is pertinent to Le Guin's meaning here: 'I admire [Heraclitus's] dialectic skill, because the facility with which we accept the first meaning ("the river is different") clandestinely imposes the second one ("I am different")' ('A New Refutation of Time', in *Other Inquisitions*, p. 187).

20. Shevek in fact doubly breaks those Terms of Closure, which would prohibit not only his return, but his bringing with him the Hainishman Ketho.

21. According to my reading, the burden of *The Dispossessed*'s argument about time entails a valorising of Shevek as the bearer of socio-political change, whose very possibility inheres in his capacity as subject for self-alteration through temporal self-discovery. Khouri, when she implicitly objects to the élitism of the book (in her essay cited in note 6), in effect ignores the point of Le Guin's demonstration, which validates the Shevekian 'I' as the paradigmatic premise of societal transformation rather than its unique *sine qua non*.

Part Three
Some Branches: Contemporary Feminist Responses

10

Men in Feminist Science Fiction: Marge Piercy, Thomas Berger and the End of Masculinity

MARLEEN BARR

Literary gender war is not new. Jane Tompkins describes the battle between women's nineteenth-century domestic novels and men's Westerns:

> This point for point contrast between a major popular form of the twentieth century and the major popular form of the nineteenth is not accidental. The Western *answers* the domestic novel. . . . And so, just as the women's novels which captured the literary marketplace at mid-century had privileged the female realm of spiritual power, inward struggle, homosociality, and sacramental household ritual, Westerns, in a reaction that looks very much like a literary gender war, privilege the male realm of public power, physical ordeal, homosociality, and the rituals of the duel.[1]

The war Tompkins describes rages on in science fiction. Feminist Utopias answer male-authored sex-role-reversal novels – and discussions of men in feminist theory can contribute to this bellicose conversation. In 'Amor Vincit Foeminam: the Battle of the Sexes in Science Fiction', Joanna Russ responds to men's sex-role-reversal fictions by declaring postmodern generic gender war. Russ's article and Alice Jardine's and Paul Smith's *Men In Feminism* proclaim an announcement pertinent to both feminist science fiction and feminist theory: The men are coming! The men are coming![2]

Jardine's and Smith's acquiescent tone is not at all a part of Russ's response, however. She is combative and dismissive towards male-authored sex-role-reversal fictions, the works she calls 'flasher novels': 'The male ignorance betrayed by such fictions is appalling; the male wishes embodied in them are little short of soul-killing.

153

But consider the title I almost used. . . .: *The Triumph of the Flasher*.'³ After considering Russ's comments in the light of Paul Smith's and Stephen Heath's contributions to *Men In Feminism*, I conclude that Russ too hastily chastises flasher novels.⁴ These novels can be read as men's attempts at flashes of feminist insight rather than as ignorant invasions of feminist science fiction's territory. In other words, when Smith states that men's involvement with feminism 'is often looked upon with suspicion: it can be understood as yet another interruption, a more or less illegal act of breaking and entering . . . for which these men must finally be held to account', he addresses Russ's response to flasher novels. He also suggests an alternative for Russ's hostility: 'Perhaps the question that needs to be asked . . . is to what extent their interruption [men's presence in feminist discourse] (penetration and interruption) is justified? is it of any political use to feminism? to what extent is it wanted?'⁵

I pose similar questions through a reading of a flasher novel, Thomas Berger's *Regiment of Women*, in terms of a feminist Utopia, Marge Piercy's *Woman on the Edge of Time*. Although much inferior to *Woman on the Edge*, *Regiment* shares a great deal in common with this feminist Utopia and is really not all that negative. A point by point contrast between the two novels reveals that a female feminist author and a male author (a male who would not exist in some feminist Utopias) both use science fiction to explore the real world's gender-related cultural problems. I argue that rather than being viewed as the despised penetrators of science fiction's feminist sanctum, Berger and his fellow creators of flasher novels might be welcomed by science fiction feminists.

After all, the science fiction flashers do follow Smith's suggestions for men who wish to engage with feminism: they 'undertake to write and speak as if they were women . . . [and] mime the feminist theoretical effort of undermining the male economy'.⁶ Men who use the science fiction sex-role-reversal convention necessarily view the world from female perspectives and confront questions, raised by feminist science fiction and feminist theory. Men in feminist science fiction are useful; the genre's female and male feminists both posit alternatives to patriarchy – the end of masculinity.

I A FLASH BACK TO THE GENERIC BATTLE GROUND

Science fiction's gender war is being waged between individual tales as well as between the tales' individual characters. On one side of the OK Corral stands the subject of Russ's article, the sex-role-reversal stories about powerless men. Feminist Utopias stand on the other side as they form a rebuttal to male flashers' powerful – but inept – women and downtrodden men who always win in the end.[7] For example, Suzy McKee Charnas's *Motherlines* (1978), Joanna Russ's *The Female Man* (1975), and James Tiptree's (Alice Sheldon's) 'Houston, Houston Do You Read?' (1976) present feminist Utopian worlds which exclude men.[8] Although these feminist works are, of course, much more complex than the flasher sex-role-reversal tales, they fail to answer a question important to women who are not separatists: how do men and women live together with dignity and equality? In fact, some feminists may find that the all-female Utopias have little to say to them.[9]

Although the all-female feminist Utopias certainly are useful, in order to interest readers who insist upon reality their creators may have to move a little closer to Earth. Marge Piercy is one writer who has done so. Instead of eradicating men, *Woman on the Edge* changes them. Men in Mattapoisett – like men in Berger's Manhattan – have bodies and attitudes which differ from those of real contemporary men. In Mattapoisett, men mother babies who have been gestated within machines; in Berger's Manhattan, men assume the social constructions reserved for women and become new-gendered beings. Piercy and Berger change human biology (and these are possible changes) by attaching breasts to men and embryos to machines. Piercy's feminist Utopia does not exclude men; Berger's flasher novel does not exclude feminism. Georgie Cornell, Berger's protagonist, is a feminist who could be at home in Mattapoisett.

Both novels articulate 'the real point at which change must come . . . the end of "masculinity" – which, of course, is the end of "woman" too'.[10] The male mothers in *Woman on the Edge* and the male feminists in *Regiment* reflect changes signalling the end of gender roles – the end of the marginalised woman and the end of masculinity.

II REPRODUCTION ON THE EDGE OF CHANGE

When Berger creates Georgie's world, he adheres to Heath's criteria regarding the most any man can do to engage feminism. *Regiment* reveals its author's desire 'to learn and so to try to write or talk or act in response to feminism, and so to try not in any way to be anti-feminist, supportive of the old oppressive structures'.[11] Although *Regiment* is far from a flawlessly feminist work, the gender role reversals Berger imagines certainly show his mastery of what Heath suggests men learn from feminism: '[O]ne of the things men learn from feminism is that women have had enough of being marginal, marginalized: patriarchal society is about margi- nalization, keeping women out or on the edges of its economy, its institutions, its decisions'.[12] Berger is sensitive to the marginal woman's plight; Georgie has certainly had enough of being margi- nalised.

Georgie experiences the marginalised position usually reserved for women because he, like male residents of Mattapoisett, inhabits a society characterised by the end of men's masculinity. In Piercy's and Berger's novels, women no longer have to give birth and, if they so desire, men can burn their bras. Georgie acquires silicone breast implants because they are fashionable. Like some real women, he spends money and experiences pain to please the opposite sex: 'Not only had the silicone injections cost him a pretty penny; the operation had been much more painful than promised; surely taking them [silicone breasts] off would be even less pleasant'.[13] His breasts, which do not have a natural function, are degrading fashion accessories. Stanley, a male liberation movement member, explains this degradation to Georgie while they are both in the Manhattan movement headquarters: 'When women produced young, the mammary glands were functional, secreting milk. Is it not degrading, now that tits are useless, that we are the sex who wears them?' (*RW*, pp. 128–9). Men's male breast implants exemplify how the novel's fantastic role reversals emphasise real sexist attitudes.

In contrast to Georgie's useless breasts, men in Mattapoisett have breasts which are quite functional. Connie Ramos, Piercy's protagonist, is appalled when she learns about male nursing mothers:

He [Barbarossa] had breasts. . . . Then with his red beard, his

face of a sunburnt forty-five-year-old man . . . he began to nurse.
    She felt angry. Yes, how dare any man share that pleasure.
These women thought they had won, but they had abandoned
to men the last refuge of women . . . they had let men steal from
them the last remnants of ancient power, those sealed in blood
and in milk. . . . She could almost hate him in the peaceful joy
to which he had no natural right; she could almost like him as
he opened like a daisy to the baby's sucking mouth.[14]

Despite Connie's – and our own – immediately adverse reaction
to a nursing male, Barbarossa's ability is a possible future alternative
to present sex roles. The end of masculinity has been constructed
in Mattapoisett; the end of masculinity is a potentially constructive
aspect of our reality.
    Georgie is also 'milked'. But his version of the end of masculinity
is not positive and his 'milk' is not extracted from his breasts. Men
in his Manhattan, a society which labels 'normal' heterosexual
intercourse as a criminal act, fulfill their reproductive function in a
very mechanistic fashion. Like so many cows, they are herded to
hosed sperm collecting apparatuses which force them to ejaculate.
The men's bodies, then, are literally controlled by machines.
    A mandatory sperm service where the delicate sensibilities of
men are jolted by forced ejaculation in a 'laboratory full of machines
attended by women in white uniforms' is really quite humorous
(*RW*, p. 198). Not so for Connie's experience of becoming analogous
to a machine, an experience which routinely happens to poor
women:

How could anyone know what being a mother means who has
never . . . born a baby in blood and pain, who has never suckled
a child. Who got that child from a machine the way that couple,
white and rich, got my flesh and blood. All made up already, a
canned child, just add money. What do they know of
motherhood? (*WT*, p. 106).

Georgie's sperm is appropriated against his will; Connie's child is
appropriated against her will. She is also denied the subsequent
ability to give birth: 'They had taken out her womb at Metropolitan.
. . . Unnecessarily they had done a complete hysterectomy because
the residents wanted practice. She need never again fear a swollen
belly; and never again hope for a child' (*WT*, p. 45). Real women

who become surrogate mothers sell their children. Real women
are forced to relinquish their children to social agencies. Real
women are deprived of their ability to give birth. Women's
reproductive role sometimes becomes analogous to a biological
machine whose product can be purchased.

This fact helps to make the fantastic baby-making machines in
Woman on the Edge and *Regiment* appear to be more positive. In
Georgie's world, birth has nothing to do with a woman's body.
Watching a new life emerge is analogous to visiting a General
Motors factory:

> From a glass-enclosed balcony he [Georgie] and the visitors, all
> male, looked down on the ranks of stainless-steel incubating
> tanks. . . .
>
> A high spot of the tour had been the actual delivery of a baby.
> A technician checked the dials, threw a lever, opened a glass
> porthole of the type found in front-loading washers, and slid
> out a newborn child. Then she snipped off the plastic umbilicus
> that attached it to the tray.   (*RW*, p. 245)

Residents of Mattapoisett would believe that this cut and dried
procedure is a necessary and liberating sacrifice.

Luciente, Connie's link to Mattapoisett, explains that when
women no longer give birth, when everyone – males as well as
females – can become mothers, women enjoy equal relationships
with warm nurturing men (*RW*, p. 105). Hence, in Mattapoisett,
as in Georgie's world, 'mother' does not necessarily signify 'female'.
'Birth' becomes synonymous with 'machine':

> He [Bee] pressed a panel and a door slid aside revealing seven
> human babies joggling slowly upside down, each in a sac of its
> own inside a larger fluid receptacle. Connie gaped, her stomach
> also turning slowly upside down. All in a sluggish row, babies
> bobbed. Mother the machine.   (*RW*, p. 102)

'Mother the machine' is a good alternative to 'woman the machine'.
The latter phrase is also a good alternative to Connie's 'blood and
pain'. She – and readers – can be reassured because although
'birth' means 'machine' in Mattapoisett, 'nurture' does not mean
'nonhuman'. Luciente explains: 'Everyone raises the kids. . . .
Romance, sex, birth, children . . . isn't women's business anymore.

It's everybody's' (*WT*, p. 251). While Berger fails to explain exactly who raises children, Piercy creates an elaborate ritual where three 'mothers' publicly express their desire to accept and raise a child (*WT*, p. 250). One particular baby is mothered by an elderly woman, a lactating male and Connie, a woman who cannot give birth (ibid.). As more men realise that they should be responsible for more mothering, society will slowly move towards realising Percy's feminist Utopian vision.

'Mother the machine' is a useful feminist version of the biological manipulation which is already a routine method to ensure social control. Both novels reflect upon oppressive uses of changed human biology. Men in *Regiment* fear that they will be castrated by those in power; Connie and her fellow mental hospital inmates fear that they will be lobotomised by those in power. Those in power in our society do perform castrations and lobotomies. The potentially frightening spectre of the fictitious – and liberating – baby-making machine pales beside the truth of existing brutal biological manipulation.

III PEOPLE AS REGIMENTED AS ANIMALS

Aviva Cantor, another feminist voice, enters this section's discussion of the link between exploiting women, minority groups and animals. In her article in a popular feminist magazine, Cantor points out that vivisection and hunting trains men to act as oppressors: 'Hunting animals for sport is a training ground for callousness, cruelty, and insensitivity: it teaches men not to feel anything when they kill or maim a living creature.'[15] Such training might have made the power to castrate and lobotomise more acceptable to the novels' respective female and male psychiatrist villains, Berger's Doctor Prine and Piercy's Doctor Redding. Cantor explains that doctors have the power biologically to alter patients because of a power system analogous to patriarchy's oppression of animals:

Nowhere is patriarchy's iron fist as naked as in the oppression of animals, which serves as the model and training ground for all the other forms of oppression.
  Its three basic strategies – the club, the yoke, and the leash –

operate similarly in the oppression of women and minorities. The club strategy is to kill animals for gain. . . . It is domination through brute force. The yoke strategy is to domesticate animals to carry burdens. . . . It is domination through enslavement. The leash strategy is to tame animals to provide the psychic benefits of direct rule of master over pet. It is domination through deceit.[16]

The biological oppression suffered by Connie and Georgie can be understood in terms of Cantor's three categories.

A doctor maims Connie to practise hysterectomies. Another doctor imprisons Connie to practise a new brain electrode implantation procedure. Doctor Prine sexually abuses Georgie because she believes men should experience orgasm when women rape them with dildoes. She rapes him, violates him in terms of the club strategy: 'Another example of the club strategy of brute male power applied to human females is, of course, rape. Rape . . . strikingly resembles hunting'.[17] Both Georgie and Connie suffer from a form of the yoke. Cantor explains: 'Enclosing animals as prisoners in fenced-off areas led to the eventual loss of their survival skills. Limitation of movement produced similar results for the domestication of women'.[18] Connie is enclosed within her brother's house and within the mental hospital. After she manages to escape, like a stray dog, she is not equipped to survive in the outside world.

In addition to being imprisoned in a sperm collection facility, Georgie experiences limited freedom of movement on dark Manhattan streets. Further, he is 'leashed' and treated as a pet when he becomes the 'mattress' (read 'mistress') of an older female artist. Women of colour like Connie, however, are usually not treated as 'the pet-woman' by the patriarchy.[19] She does not have a male master to be her 'provider, protector, rescuer'.[20] Rather, Connie and her fellow inmates receive treatment analogous to Cantor's description of obedience training: 'the pet . . . requires obedience training in order to be responsive to *individual* owners. One of the thrills of being a pet owner is to show off "tricks" '.[21] Connie watches a patient who had undergone an electrode brain implantation perform 'tricks' according to a doctor's commands. Doctor Redding explains the procedure: ' "We can electrically trigger almost every mood and emotion. . . . We can monitor and induce reactions through the microminiaturized radio under the skull. . . . That concludes our little preview demonstration" ' (*WT*, p. 204).

Connie, whose body has been used as a reproductive machine, faces the possibility of having a similar electrode implanted within her head.

She visits an alternative to Mattapoisett which is a direct outgrowth of such casual abuses of individual patients' bodies. People in this second future are literally analogous to experimental animals: ' "It's not like they're people. They're diseased, all of them, just walking organ banks . . . and even half the time the liver's rotten . . . some are pithed for simple functions, but they live like animals" ' (*WT*, p. 291). In contrast, people in Mattapoisett respect animals and communicate with them through sign language (p. 99). Harriet, Georgie's eventual lover, shares this respect. She realises that vivisection leads to the biological alteration of people. She understands the relationship between degrading animals and degrading women: ' "You know why even a lot of women who have no objection to fishing disapprove of hunting?" . . . "We don't like to kill animals, . . . because they remind us of ourselves" ' (*RW*, p. 335).

IV JUGGLING GENDER IN MANHATTAN AND MATTAPOISETT – AND IN FEMINIST THEORY

Georgie and Connie at once reflect aspects of female marginalisation and inhabit different feminist spaces. Connie, whose experiences coincide with those of real disadvantaged minority women, is a part of feminist practice; Georgie, whose position as a literal feminised man is as yet possible only within the pages of science fiction, is a part of feminist theory. Georgie is a female impersonator who shares much in common with Stephen Heath's notion of a male theorist who reads as a feminist: 'There *is* a female impersonation in a man reading as a feminist'.[23]

Georgie, Berger and male feminist theorists all act as female impersonators, ersatz feminists. When Berger creates a fictitious female impersonator, he functions as an imperfect feminist reader, as Heath's male theorist reading as a feminist. Georgie's role as the fictive incarnation of a male feminist reader is more crucial than his role as an imperfect feminist woman. This character illustrates that male feminists are doomed to remain outside the female feminist perspective. Like the men in feminist theory, the men in feminist science fiction are outside, other, alien. They impersonate women experiencing patriarchy.

Paul Smith articulates the role reversal he shares with Berger and Georgie, the role of subordinate male engaging dominant female discourse: 'We're [men in feminism] not able to do quite the right thing. Even the fact that I'm perceived as understanding feminist theory . . . proves "difficult" for this female feminist [Jardine] because, finally, I do not have the right intonation and syntax. I don't have the native accent; I'm an alien.'[24] Georgie, in Smith's terms, is analogous to a real male theorist entering feminism, not to a real woman. Further, according to Smith's terms, Russ's hostility towards flasher novels is an example of a female feminist's difficulty accepting a male feminist. Russ defends feminist science fiction from being penetrated by a voice with the wrong intonation and syntax, the voice of the male feminist alien. Again, as men entering feminism, Georgie, Smith and Berger experience gender role reversal, a marginalised male stance before a dominant female system. Georgie is simultaneously a perfect impersonator of the male feminist as feminist reader and an imperfect impersonator of a female feminist.

Heath and Smith lead me to conclude that flasher novels can be understood best in terms of subordinate male feminism, not in terms of female feminism. Feminist science fiction is appropriately read in terms of female feminist theory;[25] flasher novels are appropriately read in terms of male feminist theory. Berger's sex-role-reversal plot provides an occasion for a science fiction text to merge with male feminist theoretical texts: Georgie and male feminist theorists (such as Smith and Heath) speak with one voice. Feminists (such as Russ) should at least refrain from completely dismissing flasher novels. Their attention would reflect feminist theory's agenda to elevate marginal discourses. After all, Berger and his fellow male authors of flasher novels – and male feminists theorists – have voluntarily reversed their customary dominant roles. They have chosen to become subordinate aliens who listen to female feminism. If Berger were given the opportunity to respond to Russ's '*Amor Vincit Foeminam*', his comments might resemble Smith's following thoughts about a male feminist's situation:

> These feelings, these fears, are in a large part the result of having to engage with a discourse whose laws I can never quite obey. I

recognize that such a discourse has its reasons for . . . not taking me in. . . . [I]t seems to me that it could still be useful to have men in feminism.[26]

As the male feminist theorist shares the unusual position of Berger and Georgie, the female feminist theorist customarily shares the position of the science fiction genre itself. Ursula Le Guin has discussed 'the feminization of science fiction'.[27] Because the female feminist theorist and the science fiction genre are both marginalised (or feminised), when 'men in feminism' is brought to bear upon 'women and men in feminist science fiction', gender merges with genre. Voluntary reversal enables the male feminist theorist to assume the position shared by both women and the science fiction genre: the feminised, inferior other. This analogy between men in feminism, feminism, and science fiction is, in the words of Heath, a discussion of 'matters of place and . . . exclusion or inclusion, [which] finishes in a series of ironic reversals in which men now occupy the dark continent, are the excluded other'.[28]

Women assume a dominant position within the realm of feminist discourse; men become the excluded other in feminist theory and in feminist science fiction. The male feminist – who is welcomed in Piercy's novel and barred from the feminist Utopias created by Russ, Tiptree and Charnas – can be understood according to a notion created by Russ: the female man. A series of ironic reversals allow the male feminist – like Georgie – to become the male woman, the reversal of Russ's female man: 'We must listen to the female man';[29] science fiction's feminists must listen to the genre's male women.

V CONCLUSION: FEMINISTS, FLASHERS AND CHANGED HUMAN BIOLOGY

The act of being reminded of oneself is one reason why flasher novels should be read by feminists. These novels' gender role reversals can help to illuminate patriarchal oppression whose occurrence is so routine it is often rendered invisible. Although Russ justifiably believes that flasher novels contain appalling male ignorance and soul-killing male wishes, I have sought to argue that these novels can be useful to feminists. I shall momentarily rely upon transactive criticism, my personal response, to explain further why my assertion is true.

Much science fiction has been characterised as male power fantasies. My own response signals that *Regiment* can be called a power fantasy for women. I enjoy entering a world where women have the upper hand. I am drawn to a novel which questions feminine behaviour: 'How men painted, adorned, and even mutilated themselves – for women?' (*RW*, p. 149). I have wondered about such feminine behaviour while viewing the televised graphic details of face lifts or, more frequently, while noticing pregnant women wearing panty hose during the heat of summer.

I do resent the novel's implication that women cannot run the world: 'the tyranny of women was exceeded only by their inefficiency' (*RW*, p. 175). However, *Regiment* also provides a clear picture of how men use gender as an excuse to deny women power. I sympathise with the fact that Georgie, who becomes a real man in the end, does not want to dominate anyone: ' "I don't want to be a boss." Cornell shouted. "Can't you understand? I just don't want to be bossed" ' (*RW*, p. 249). This attitude qualifies Georgie to participate in Mattapoisett's shared governmental power. If, while in the closing sex scene, he desires to 'be boss once in a while' (*RW*, p. 349), well, that's all right. Similarly, it is justifiable for Connie to commit murder. She wants to be the boss once in a while too. Georgie and Connie speak with and for each other.

Heath could be speaking for Berger:

> So there I am between a male writing as oppression and a male writing as utopia, and still I am . . . a male writing. All I can do is pose each time the question of the sexual positioning of my discourse, of my relations to and in it, my definition as man, and then through it to the practice and reality of men and women, their relations in the world. To do this . . . is, at least, to grasp writing as an involvement in an ethics of sexual difference, which is a start today towards another male writing. . . . [W]e [male theorists] can learn to read as feminists; that is, we can learn women's readings, feminist readings, we can make connections that we never made before, come back critically on our point of departure.[30]

Regiment is one start towards another male writing. Berger has learned feminist readings; feminists who read *Regiment* with an accepting rather than a rejecting approach make connections with a new male writing that they have never made before.

Russ concludes her article by stating, 'Strikingly, no Flasher book I was able to find envisioned a womanless world (or dared to say so); about half the feminist Utopias matter-of-factly excluded men.'[31] Those feminist Utopias which, like *Woman on the Edge*, include and tolerate both sexes, do not lean on the fantastic to eradicate a fundamental truth of our reality: our world consists of both feminists and flashers – and the potential for biological change which will alter gender roles. Women's lives, men's new roles and feminist fiction and theory authored by women and men must meet the challenges of these differences and changes. Connie's and Georgie's similar experiences exemplify that it is quite unnecessary to continue the literary gender war Tompkins describes. Feminists and flashers can logically ride off into the sunset, the realm of the western world's penchant for changed human biology and the new social roles resulting from these changes, together.

NOTES

1. Jane Tompkins, 'West of Everything', *South Atlantic Quarterly*, vol. 86 (1987) pp. 371, 374.
2. Joanna Russ, *'Amor Vincit Foeminam*: the Battle of the Sexes in Science Fiction', *Science Fiction Studies*, vol. 20 (1980) pp. 2–15; Alice Jardine and Paul Smith (eds), *Men in Feminism* (New York: Methuen, 1987).
3. Russ, '*Amor Vincit Foeminam*', p. 13.
4. Paul Smith, 'Men in Feminism: Men and Feminist Theory', in Jardine and Smith (eds), *Men in Feminism*, pp. 33–40; Stephen Heath, 'Male Feminism', ibid., pp. 1–32.
5. Smith, 'Men in Feminism', p. 33.
6. Ibid., p. 37.
7. For Russ's remarks about feminist Utopias see her 'Recent Feminist Utopias', in Marleen Barr (ed.), *Future Females: A Critical Anthology* (Bowling Green, Ky: Popular Press, 1981) pp. 71–85.
8. Suzy McKee Charnas, *Motherlines* (New York: Berkley Books, 1978); Joanna Russ, *The Female Man* (New York: Gregg Press, 1975); James Tiptree, 'Houston, Houston Do You Read?', in Vonda McIntyre and Susan Janice Anderson (eds), *Aurora: Beyond Equality* (Greenwich, Conn.: Fawcett, 1976).
9. Carolyn G. Heilbrun articulates this attitude: 'It is the Utopian mode that separates science fiction from the other categories of popular feminist fiction. Russ has brilliantly summarized that features of female Utopias: "the communal nature of the societies portrayed, the absence

of crime, the relative lack of government, and the diffusion of the parental role to the whole society". These are, indeed, longings from many female hearts, including mine. But I live here, where I must find the language to incarnate these things: whether through weakness of intellect or paucity of imagination, I am not content, nor even able, to dream them' (Carolyn G. Heilbrun, 'Why I Don't Read Science Fiction', *Women's Studies International Forum*, no. 7 (1984) p. 119).

10. Heath, 'Male Feminism', p. 5.
11. Ibid., p. 9.
12. Ibid., p. 24.
13. Thomas Berger, *Regiment of Women* (New York: Simon and Schuster, 1973) p. 128. Future references will appear in the text, preceded by the initials *RW*.
14. Marge Piercy, *Woman on the Edge of Time* (New York: Fawcett, 1976) pp. 134–5. Future references will appear in the text, proceded by the initials *WT*.
15. Aviva Cantor, 'The Club, the Yoke, and the Leash – What We Can Learn from the Way a Culture Treats Animals', *Ms* (August 1983) p. 27.
16. Ibid., p. 27.
17. In the discussion following Jane Tompkins's presentation of 'West of Everything: the Rise of a Male Mass Cultural Genre' (delivered at the Duke University Center for Critical Theory Conference, 'Convergence in Crisis: Narratives of the History of Theory', 24–7 September 1987) she asserted that women who derive power and status through the ability to inflict harm are not necessarily negative. Tompkins explained that the female discourse of love and peace is ignored, that powerful women sometimes have to be evil, that the good woman is powerless. Her argument supports the idea that Berger's powerful – and evil – women do not have to be seen as antifeminist. She provides an alternative view to the notion of some feminists that powerful women should not act like powerful men. Unlike the good women in Westerns, Berger's evil women have an opportunity to act. Furthermore, the protagonists of some feminist Utopias are not always good women. For example, the feminist tribes in *Motherlines* do not always behave peacefully and the feminist government in Katherine Forrest's *Daughters of a Coral Dawn* (Tallahasee, Fla.: Naiad Press, 1984) is not completely democratic.
18. Cantor, 'The Club, the Yoke, and the Leash', p. 28.
19. Ibid., p. 29.
20. Ibid.
21. Ibid.
22. Ibid.
23. Heath, 'Male Feminism', p. 28.
24. Smith, 'Men in Feminism', p. 36.
25. For an analysis of how feminist science fiction merges with feminist theory see Marleen Barr, *Alien to Femininity: Speculative Fiction and Feminist Theory* (New York: Greenwood Press, 1987).
26. Smith, 'Men in Feminism', p. 38.

27. Miriam Berkley, 'Ursula K. Le Guin', *Publisher's Weekly*, 23 May 1986, p. 2.
28. Heath, 'Male Feminism', p. 43.
29. Joanna Russ, *The Female Man* (New York: Gregg Press, 1977) p. 140.
30. Heath, 'Male Feminism', pp. 26–7.
31. Russ, *'Amor Vincit Foeminam'*, p. 14.

11

The Destabilisation of Gender in Vonda McIntyre's *Superluminal*

JENNY WOLMARK

The impact on science fiction of the cultural politics of feminism has resulted in recent years in the production of texts in which gender and sexual relations have been foregrounded as major issues in the narratives. If the genre now appears to have a less embattled relationship to feminism this is partly due to the way in which feminist science fiction, in challenging assumptions about gender, has also challenged the nature of the genre. By enabling and encouraging the production of stories that are inflected more towards a discussion of definitions of masculinity and femininity and of social and sexual relations generally, feminist science fiction has redrawn the boundaries of the genre. The process of cultural negotiation that this has involved has tested the limits of the dominant ideology by proposing alternative possibilities for social and sexual relations that are at odds with existing social structures and practices. But these kinds of cultural negotiations in popular narratives are complex and not without contradiction and the narratives which emerge are themselves often highly contradictory. The novel that I shall be discussing, Vonda McIntyre's *Superluminal*, is a striking example of a text which, because of its contradictions, has an ambivalent relationship both to feminism *and* to the science fiction genre.

This might seem surprising, since the narrative does contain a considerable critical reworking of those assumptions about gender that derive from culturally dominant definitions of masculinity and femininity. However, the science fiction genre is one in which the masculine is particularly clearly inscribed and the question that needs to be addressed is whether or not the narrative conventions of science fiction can be used to transgress the culturally dominant definitions of gender which are an integral part of the genre. It is also important to consider whether or not the expected pleasures offered by the narrative can be disrupted so that the process by

168

which such meanings are made becomes clear. I shall be arguing that McIntyre's *Superluminal* destabilises familiar representations of masculinity and femininity by challenging the identification of femininity with femaleness and masculinity with maleness and that this opens up the possibility that gender can be reconstructed in new and critically different ways. However, the destabilising of gender also has different and less radical resonances in the text. It is symptomatic of a broad cultural and political pessimism regarding the changed priorities and perspectives of late capitalist society, in which new types of consumerism rather than fundamental social change have resulted from technological advance. From this perspective, both modernisation and recession have disrupted the continuity between the values of the past that sustained the notion of the individual as the subject of history, and those contemporary values that appear to bear witness to the fragmentation of the subject within the socially and culturally alienating conditions of the present. Despite such a perspective, the radical result of the destabilising of gender in the text is that, by drawing our attention to the dissociation of the psychic and the physical in the human subject and to its divided and contradictory nature, the mythic nature of the unified subject of bourgeois liberalism is revealed. This is particularly significant where the female subject is concerned, since it enables the question of gender definition to be explored outside the confines of the traditional and seemingly unified categories or 'femininity' and 'masculinity'. But at the same time this questioning of gender has also to be seen as part of a whole range of social and cultural anxieties that are clearly both conservative and deeply pessimistic. On this level, *Superluminal* is as much about the perceived breakdown of social and temporal continuities as it is about the restructuring of gender. This is why the kinds of narrative and structural discontinuities that are present in the text have to be seen as complex indications of the ambivalence mentioned earlier towards both feminism and science fiction.

The ambiguous relationship of the text to the genre can be seen in the way in which, in order to move beyond the culturally dominant definitions of gender, McIntyre has to 'open up' the narrative conventions of science fiction and incorporate conventions from romance fiction. Romance narratives are written from a female point of view and are motivated by female desire. Romance fiction constructs a feminine subject and identification with that subject is part of the process and pleasure of reading a romance.[1]

This is very much at odds with science fiction, which remains a genre governed by the masculine. The narrative oscillates between the poles of representation familiar to romance and those familiar to science fiction, and in so doing offers the reader different subject positions from which to interpret the text. A radical instability is introduced into the narrative, which allows for shifts between the different subjectivities constructed by science fiction and by romance. This is why the novel is so interesting from a feminist point of view, since it is concerned to move away from the idea that women, and men, have fixed gender identities that are confirmed by popular narratives endlessly and without contradiction. It also suggests that, despite its predominantly masculine inflection, science fiction as a genre is well suited to the work of presenting culturally negotiable images of women because of the way in which it takes images of the present and re-presents them, as images of the future.[2] The defamiliarising effect of science fiction is particularly important where the cultural reconstruction of gender is concerned, since it provides the means by which the 'constant present' of culturally dominant representations can be made visible and therefore open to scrutiny. Their status as familiar and recognisable cultural memories can then be questioned. Since social and sexual relationships are never explored or explained within such cultural memories they are therefore assumed to have a coherence that they do not necessarily possess. The defamiliarising qualities of science fiction can break down that illusion of coherence and allow us to glimpse the ways in which such memories are constructed.

In *Superluminal*, this defamiliarisation is achieved not by the conventional means of providing detailed discussion of future cities, artefacts and cultures but by focusing the narrative unexpectedly and almost entirely on the psychic and emotional experiences of the characters. In fact, these experiences constitute the main narrative 'action', since the narrative revolves both directly and indirectly around the passionate love affair between the two central characters. McIntyre here moves out of conventional science fiction territory altogether and explicitly 'borrows' from the conventions of romance fiction. In this case, defamiliarisation occurs at the level of the genre itself and a radical instability is generated which allows for the disruption of expected narrative pleasures. For example, the opening sentence of the novel would be equally at home in romantic fiction: 'She gave up her heart quite willingly.' This is meant both literally and metaphorically in the narrative and it serves to throw the reader off-balance from the beginning, because it fails to provide a familiar and therefore secure narrative position. Although it quickly becomes clear that the familiar science-fiction theme of the effects of inter-stellar space flight on the human metabolism is being introduced in the narrative, what is also being signalled is the unusual fact that a female character is centrally involved.

The narrative assumes that the colonisation of space has long since taken place and the economic and political relationship between Earth and the colony planets is not presented as an issue. It is hinted that the economies of the colony worlds depend on exporting luxury items to Earth which has become a non-manufacturing consumer society with a service economy. This is, of course, the moment of late monopoly capitalism, thrust into the future to become the present of *Superluminal*. The computerised systems on automated space ships are no longer considered to be fast enough for shipping these luxury goods because they cannot achieve the navigational accuracy of human pilots. But human pilots cannot fly at the 'superluminal' speeds required for the shipment of such goods without being physically and mentally crippled by the inter-dimensional travel that is involved. The only way that humans have been able to travel at such speeds is by being anaesthetised for the entire journey. In the interests of profitability a solution has to be found to the problem of how to enable human pilots to overcome their dependence on normal space–time rhythms in order to endure inter-dimensional travel. That solution consists of replacing the human heart with a mechanical heart. The focus of the narrative is less on conventional narrative action and more on the social and emotional effects of such a solution. The pilots become an élite group, partly because the biological alteration they choose to undergo gives them a secure place in the economic structure, but also because it makes them physically incompatible with the rest of ordinary humanity. This dilemma is examined through the passionate love affair between the two central characters – Laenea Trevelyan, whose heart has just been removed to enable her to become a pilot, and Radu Dracul, who is an ordinary crew-member.

To return to the opening sentence of the novel: the reader is thrown off-balance by an ironic mixture of future technology and romantic involvement. This is very unsettling where the question of narrative authority is concerned, since the focus of the narrative is the love affair between the two main characters, and yet the reader is asked to identify with a female character whose characteristics are definitely not those of a conventional romance heroine. The point in the narrative at which their brief love affair ends is marked in the text by phrases that would appear to be more at home in romantic fiction: 'So Radu Dracul closed the door and walked away from Laenea Trevelyan, whom he had known for such a short time yet loved for so long.'[3] Some interesting ambiguities result from this fairly overt use of conventions from romance fiction in a science fiction narrative, particularly where the subject of the narrative is concerned. Laenea is not the divided subject that occurs in so many romantic novels, even though all the signals indicated that this was going to be the case. She is on the contrary a strong female character who is prepared to abandon her lover rather than give up her ambition to be a pilot. This is why the romantic implications of the reference to her 'giving up her heart' at the beginning of the narrative have to be entirely reconsidered in the light of the development of her character. She has indeed given up her heart, but not for love. She has chosen to undergo the operation so that she can become a pilot and do the job which 'ordinary' humans cannot tolerate because of the extreme dislocation of the normal space-time relationships which is involved in inter-dimensional travel. The crucial problem of how to avoid the situation in romance fiction where the female is expected to make some kind of ultimate sacrifice for the male is solved in the narrative through a stress on difference. As a pilot with an artificial heart Laenea's biorhythms are no longer compatible with those of ordinary humans. This becomes clear when she and Radu make love and discover that they both experience violently uncontrollable orgasms which quickly become life-threatening for them. In terms of romance fiction this has to be seen ironically, but in terms of the science-fiction narrative it is explained by reference to the technology that has provided Laenea with a 'new biological integrity' as a result of which:

> Her system and that of any normal human being would no longer mesh. The change in her was too disturbing, on psycho-logical and subliminal levels, while normal biorhythms were so compelling that they interfered with and would eventually destroy her new biological integrity. (*S*, p. 62)

She discovers this through the uncontrollable intensity of her lovemaking with Radu. As far as Laenea is concerned, her artificial heart sets her free from both biological and social constraints: it was the only way in which she could join the élite formed by the other pilots. Radu, in contrast, is unable to become a pilot because he is too firmly anchored to normal space–time rhythms. In narrative terms, the release from social and biological constraints enables Laenea to be placed both as the central character and as a strong female precisely because she has relinquished the social and cultural determinants of gender, and this ironically undermines the expectation generated by the opening of the novel and by the fact that the passionate love affair between her and Radu dominates the beginning of the narrative. In severing the link between sex and nature, the narrative is attempting to disconnect female sexuality from traditional female gender identities. By bringing the romance and science fiction genres, and the subjectivities constructed by the two kinds of narratives, into playful and ironic collision at this point, McIntyre is attempting to negotiate the ideological and cultural determinants of our social and sexual identities.

In contrast to those narratives in which the woman is the object of the male look and male desire, in this narrative it is the woman who perceives the male as the object of her desire. When she first sees Radu in the space crew lounge he is asleep, unaware of her gaze and therefore vulnerable in the particular way in which women are often portrayed as being. She says to Radu: '". . . I think you're beautiful and an admirable man"' (*S*, p. 45). Radu sees her as a hero in what appears to be a classic case of hero worship: '"I was frightened and full of grief and lost and alone. I needed . . . someone . . . to admire. And you were there. You were the only stability in my chaos, a hero . . ."' (*S*, p. 44). At this point in the narrative Radu is clearly not the subject of the narrative and is in a sense feminised as a character, at least in the terms of reference set by the conventions of romance fiction. This is only partly achieved by giving him those attributes not usually associated with 'strong' men in such fiction – for instance, he is often afraid and sometimes cries in frustration when in difficult situations.[4] It is more to do with the fact that not only is he the object of Laenea's desire but, as in romantic fiction, his 'completion' as a character depends on another: '"I hoped I would meet you, but I don't think I ever believed I would. And then I saw you again, and I realized

I wanted . . . to be someone in your life"' (*S*, p. 44). He is also the outsider who depends on someone else to give him a place and a definition. Initially this is Laenea's role, but it is also a task given to the other important female character in the narrative, Orca the diver. Part of Radu's textual feminisation is that he has to be rescued by Orca from threatening situations and the reason she is able to take on this role is that she, like Laenea, has been biologically altered and similarly freed from existing social and biological constraints. Orca's people are all divers, they can communicate with the other mammals in the sea and chose to be genetically altered in order to be able to live and breathe underwater. After a revolution that appears to have been motivated by a combination of unspecified political and ecological concerns, the divers have achieved social and political autonomy from the ruling body known simply as the Administration. Orca describes her people as 'more different than a race, but less different than a separate species' (*S*, p. 129). The emphasis on difference is an important aspect of the textual focus on the social and cultural construction of gender and sexuality. Radu's feminisation as a character is confirmed by the way in which he is placed within the context of such difference. In contrast to the strong female characters, he has undergone no deliberate physical and psychic change which would have marked him in the text as being at a critical distance from prevailing social and cultural norms.

However, with the ending of the love affair between Laenea and Radu, which occurs quite early on in the novel, the narrative undergoes a significant shift in emphasis away from romance and towards the more familiar science-fiction theme of the quest. To accommodate this shift, Radu becomes the central character. Why should such a major change have occurred? The reason lies in the narrative focus on the love affair between the two central characters and the destabilising of representations of masculinity and femininity. Both of these features are indicative of a crisis in the narrative not only at the level of representation but also at the level of culture. Running as an undercurrent all through the narrative is a deep unease which would appear to stem from anxieties about the decline of social and cultural authority. This precipitates a crisis in the narrative which can be located in the shifting subjects of the narrative as well as in the destabilising of gender representation. Although the character of Laenea is the central focus of the first part, that focus is transferred to Radu in the rest of the novel, when Laenea's ship is lost in space, in the seventh dimension to be precise, and he undertakes to find it when everyone else has given it and her up for lost. This causes some problems because of the way in which Radu has been 'feminised' as a character earlier in the narrative and yet now is expected to take on the role of hero that was previously attributed to Laenea. It also causes problems where the status of the female character is concerned, since this shift in the narrative effectively repositions her as a woman within the social constraints from which the narrative had earlier celebrated her breaking free. In other words she is placed outside the realms of culture, history, politics and production to become a passive onlooker, stuck in the seventh dimension, waiting to be rescued by Radu. Her only active participation in much of the rest of the narrative is on a psychic level because she is able to contact Radu telepathically while in the seventh dimension. It is the fact that only he can 'hear' her that spurs him on to try to find her lost ship. This particular development in the story allows her character to become somewhat tangential to the narrative as a whole and provides a means of resolving the crisis that has arisen because of the transfer of narrative authority from Laenea to Radu. It is resolved at the level of the psychic rather than the social and, while the need for social regeneration is not denied in the text, it can only take place at the psychic level precisely because of the prevailing sense of social dislocation and stagnation. This suggests that the contradictions in the text are resolvable only within the mythical space created by telepathy which is removed from any kind of social, sexual or political conflict. Their telepathic communication has the function of allowing the new narrative direction of the quest to be set in motion. Radu is able to take on the quest by virtue of his special abilities: not only can he hear Laenea telepathically but this also enables him to discover another exceptional quality, the fact that inter-dimensional travel has no adverse effect on him. He has to be made exceptional in order to fulfil the heroic role required to undertake the quest, while Laenea has to be rendered correspondingly powerless. Both are highly contradictory characterisations, which suggest the difficulties within the narrative of representing masculinity and femininity in alternative modes.

The particular problems that this causes for the characters of Laenea and Radu are recognised in the narrative handling of two other female characters – Orca and Kathell. Radu's attempts to treat them as if they are also clearly defined female identities within the familiar ideologies of masculinity and femininity is undermined by the narrative resistance of both these characters. At one point in the narrative, Radu and Orca are threatened by a group of pilots because the pilots are afraid that Radu's ability to withstand inter-stellar travel without biological alteration of the sort that they have undergone will undermine their own hitherto unique position. Although Radu seeks to protect Orca from the pilots, he ends up depending on her for his own protection. He underestimates both his own weakness and her strength, which is a product of her genetic alteration. His response is shown to be one which operates entirely within the confines of fixed notions of what constitutes masculinity and femininity: he tries to explain his attitude to her by saying: 'it's just that you're so small' (*S*, p. 148), thus reprodu-cing the usual dissociation of femininity and strength which the narrative consistently challenges. His encounter with Kathell takes a similar form. She is a minor and somewhat ambiguous character who is associated in the narrative with a kind of social decadence, since she epitomises the fact that the wealth of Earth is based on service, not production. In Radu's eyes that is synonymous with decadence, because the newly colonised world that he comes from depends on labour-intensive production or, as he puts it, 'hard work' (*S*, p. 13). She has a white tiger as a pet, and while others are impressed with its rarity value, Radu sees only its pitiful deformities: 'To Radu, the tiger was another example of the extravagance of earth, of things valued for their appearance rather than their usefulness or efficiency' (*S*, p. 70). But she is also highly independent, strong-minded and generous. She will do any favour asked of her but will accept none in return in order to remain free of obligation to anyone and in that way retain her independence. The only significant encounter between her and Radu occurs when he comforts her after her pet dies, and instead of thanking him she turns on him in anger because he has put her under an obligation to him, a situation she finds intolerable. He cannot understand her explanation for this attitude and indeed finds it intolerable in turn. But, interestingly enough, the narrative suggests that the fault is Radu's; as Kathell says: '"Don't insult me! . . . You're saying my reasons are meaningless and *they are not*!"' (*S*, p. 74). While the encounter initially appears to be a playing out of the dependency relation that women all too often find themselves in, whereby they are obliged to relinquish control of both them-selves and the situation, it becomes clear that it is Radu who is presented as being out of control and therefore unable to impose his definition of the world.

Although the narrative implies that it is Radu's masculinity that causes him problems in understanding Kathell's desire for absolute independence, this gender difference is displaced on to Radu's position as a social and cultural outsider who cannot understand the social and personal nuances of the situations in which he finds himself. The fact that Radu is from a new world, colonised from Earth, becomes significant at the point where he becomes the focus of the narrative, because his point of view is the one with which the reader would expect to identify. His position as a colonist, his attitude to the moral correctness of hard work, and his questioning of the moral validity of the Earth's social and economic structures, make his attitudes seem curiously outmoded. They seem to operate as an explicit reminder of an earlier period in American history, the inheritance of which is still so extraordinarily potent in contemporary social and sexual discourse. From this perspective his attitudes towards the women in the narrative begin to make some sense: his romantic idealisation of Laenea, his assumption that because Orca is small and female she is therefore helpless, and his complete incomprehension of the reasons for Kathell's rejection of his help when her pet dies, all become indications of a kind of nostalgia for a set of social relations that no longer exists, and indeed probably never did exist.

The use of an outsider like Radu enables the text to raise critical questions about the cultural construction of both social and sexual roles. His confusion and powerlessness can be seen as a direct result of his attempts to impose masculine solutions to problems – solutions which do not make sense either in terms of the character as he has been developed or in terms of the narrative. This means that the attempt to transfer narrative authority to the character of Radu causes some disturbance in the narrative, because he is at odds with the social behaviour and attitudes expressed in the rest of the narrative and, more importantly, because he has not been cast in a heroic and masculine mould. There is, therefore, a great deal of ambiguity about the kind of values that are being endorsed in the text and the wider culture that is implicated in these textual ambiguities.

The conflict between Radu's 'colonial' values and those of the consumer society of Earth are indications of the deep concerns in the text regarding the nature of late monopoly capitalism and the profound changes in the economic and political structures of society since the 1960s. The fact that Radu's values seem to be significantly out of place in this future version of our own present suggests that the text cannot fully endorse either their masculine bias or their conservatism. But at the same time this future society, based as it is on consumerism and economic exploitation, is tacitly associated with both social stagnation and moral decline. It is a world in which temporal continuities seem to have broken down to produce a radically disordered world with little sense of its own historical development or meaning. This is the probable origin of that strong undercurrent of pessimism in the text, which consistently undermines the progressive elements in the narrative regarding gender. Destabilisation in *Superluminal* is as much to do with the text's inability to negotiate the complexities of contemporary society as it is to do with the radical questioning of it.

The pessimism generated by this contemporary *impasse* is conveyed partly through the incomplete relationship between Laenea and Radu, the result being the kind of textual ambiguities that have already been discussed. It is also conveyed through veiled references to cultural and political institutions of which we get no more than a glimpse. The 'Administration' in particular stands for a totalising bureaucracy within which whole sets of relationships are subsumed rather than explored or explained. Since these disembodied institutions lack any kind of historical or even future-historical specificity, the text can avoid the painful necessity of having to come to terms with the political realities of its own time. The vacuum at the heart of the text is similar to that which exists in McIntyre's earlier novel *Dreamsnake* and stems from the attempt to shift gender relations into a more radical mode while leaving the social and political structures as fixed entities.[5] The resulting polarisation between gender and culture, while it is intended to generate criticism of contemporary structures, actually precipitates the sense of crisis in the narrative. Within the post-catastrophe society of *Dreamsnake* there is a seemingly untouchable social and political core, known as The Centre, which is rigidly hierarchical and based on the structures of an extended family. Changes in social and sexual relations take place only outside the literal and metaphoric confines of The Centre. Although the extrapolation from contemporary society is fairly obvious, the textual reliance on the rigid distinction between the actual and the possible inevitably suggests that change can take place only in terms of the individual rather than through social or political structures. *Superluminal* contains a more complex interweaving of the individual and the social in that the actions of the individual are granted some impact on the wider social structures; nevertheless, these changes are similarly presented as being incidental to those that take place in the individual psyche. There is an equally static socio-political structure in *Superluminal*, referred to as the Administration, which exists to administer an economic system in which new worlds have been colonised to the particular benefit of Earth, so that it has become a world of great luxury but little productivity. The narrative presents an image of a technologically advanced consumer society which is clearly being proposed as the logical development of our own contemporary post-industrial capitalist society. The narrative is primarily interested in the moral implications of such a society and Radu's reactions serve as a focus for this concern in the text. The wealth of Earth is associated in his eyes with puzzling and threatening sets of social relations and an exploitative economic relationship to the colony worlds. As the narrative has already made clear, his narrow and somewhat puritanical attitudes are associated with the hard and economically poor existence of a colony world. This is emphasised by Radu's decision that most of the wages he earns as a crew-member on the ships ferrying between the worlds should go towards paying off the national debt to Earth that his world has accumulated. This quixotic but morally correct gesture is used in the narrative as an important indication of individual character, and since Radu is not presented as a consumer he is therefore morally unimplicated in the social malaise produced by such an economic structure. He actually remains outside that structure, pure but distinterested, which leaves the larger system of social power untouched and fundamentally unquestioned in the narrative. In contrast, the abilities and freedoms of the three important women characters are attached irrevocably to a technologically advanced and economically wealthy Earth. They very clearly *are* members of this consumer society and have derived great benefit from so being. But to be a consumer is to be placed in the classic position that women are offered in capitalist society – always to be onlookers, always to be outside the power structures because they have no relation to production. Since the text presents the issue of social change solely as an individual concern, neither masculinity nor femininity are proposed as sites of social change and the critical questioning of gender identity is left incomplete.

The discontinuities in the text also emerge in the narrative position of the élite group formed by the pilots. Although their artificial hearts have freed them from normal space–time relationships, they are at the same time rendered physically and psychically incapable of relationships with anyone outside their own group. The pilots are insulated from the material world by their altered metabolisms, but they are also isolated from it. Their only function is to pilot spaceships for the shadowy structure known as the Administration, which developed the technology to replace their human hearts with artificial hearts. As a consequence of all this, the pilots experience a permanent sense of temporal and social dislocation. It is just such a sense of dislocation and discontinuity that is seen as the predominant characteristic of post-industrial society in which there is no sense of control of the object world by those who inhabit it.[6] The metaphor becomes obvious in the context of the textual anxieties about post-industrial society. There is a kind of nostalgia for a lost world of familiar certainties in which values were less disconcerting, more open to control by the individual.

Radu's relationship with Laenea is fraught with similar anxieties once the straightforwardly physical nature of their relationship has ended. He sets out to find her in the seventh dimension despite the fact that the concept of inter-dimensional travel is incomprehensible to him because he has such an overpowering sense of time and place. He is firmly rooted in the temporal world, anchored both by his colonial origins and by a more 'archaic' value system that is presented as being more authentic in comparison to the values of both the pilots and the Administration. Its authenticity lies in its association with a past which this future Earth has in some sense forsaken. In the end, the text attempts a compromise between these two seemingly opposed sets of values, one from a future past and one from our own future present. Radu is able to find Laenea because of the psychic link which opens up between them when Laenea is in the seventh dimension, but he is motivated by the stubborn love and loyalty he feels for her. The values that Radu enshrines can thus be endorsed by the text because they are actually enhanced and altered by his previously unrecognised psychic abilities. This allows them to be presented in relation to different and alternative modes of perception instead of being viewed as monolithic, unified and without contradiction. The significance of Radu's quest is changed as a result. Initially, it was clearly a quest for a different set of ethics which would re-establish some kind of moral authority and enable the reunification of the individual and society to take place. If the quest had succeeded without any psychic input this would have meant that the masculine and conservative values that cluster around the character of Radu were fully endorsed. Instead, it is the feminised characterisation of Radu that re-emerges through the development of his psychic ablity, and in this way the question of gender identity is restored to a position of central importance in the narrative. There is even an ironic return to the romance mode of the first part of the novel, when Laenea uses the mental link between herself and Radu to re-establish their sexual relationship but at a psychic, not physical, level.

The narrative focus on individual morality in much of the novel means that the degree of ideological contestation in the text is necessarily limited. It is by no means absent but it is confined to those areas which traditionally emphasise individual actions. Such an emphasis has to be seen as a response to the fragmentation of the different social and political constituencies or a post-industrial society. This produces conflicting social identities with correspondingly contradictory sets of priorities. The textual ambiguities in *Superluminal* are an expression of the contradiction between feminist, ecological and libertarian priorities in particular, each one of which is given primacy at different stages of the narrative, so that none of them ever becomes a completed project within the text. The generic shifts between romance and science fiction as well as the replacement of the female central character by a feminised male character are indications of the textual inability to resolve such contradictory constituencies. Within this context the destabilising of gender should be seen as a progressive account of the positive changes brought about by feminism as well as being an expression of deep-rooted anxieties about social and political fragmentation.

NOTES

1. For discussions of this perspective on romance fiction, see T. Modleski, *Loving with a Vengeance* (London: Methuen, 1984); J. Radford (ed.), *The Progress of Romance* (London: Routledge and Kegan Paul, 1986).
2. See F. Jameson, 'Progress versus Utopia: or, Can We Imagine the Future?', *Science Fiction Studies*, vol. 9 (1982) pp. 147–58.

3. Vonda McIntyre, *Superluminal* (New York: Pocket Books, 1984) p. 68. Future references will appear in the text, preceded by the initial *S*.
4. See the discussion of male characters in Gothic novels for women in Modleski, *Loving with a Vengeance*.
5. For a further discussion of this point, see J. Wolmark, 'Alternative Futures?: Science Fiction and Feminism', *Cultural Studies*, vol. 2, no. 1 (1988) pp. 48–56.
6. See F. Jameson, 'Postmodernism and Consumer Society', in H. Foster (ed.), *Postmodern Culture* (London: Pluto Press, 1985).

12

Man-Made Monsters: Suzy McKee Charnas's *Walk to the End of the World* as Dystopian Feminist Science Fiction

ANNE CRANNY-FRANCIS

> 'And if the Wild isn't empty after all?' he persisted. 'If there are monsters?'
> 'I am experienced,' she snarled, 'at handling monsters.'
> Suzy McKee Charnas, *Walk to the End of the World*

> 'For Christ's sake, Ruth, they're *aliens!*'
> 'I'm used to it,' she said absently.
> James Tiptree Jr, 'The Women Men Don't See'

Suzy McKee Charnas's dystopian novel, *Walk to the End of the World* and its sequel, *Motherline*, trace a particular trajectory in feminist genre writing – from fiction used to explicate the socialisation of women and men in a patriarchal society (*Walk*) to fiction used to explicate the role of fiction in that socialisation process (*Motherlines*).[1] It is arguable, however, whether *Motherlines* ever achieves the degree of self-consciousness attained by a text like James Tiptree Jr's 'The Women Men Don't See', which combines both explicatory functions, thus negotiating the contradiction between fiction as a 'representation' of 'life' (with all the naïve realist readings to which that gives rise) and fiction as a strategic intervention in the dominant discursive formations.[2]

Walk to the End of the World was first published in 1974. Like 'The Women Men Don't See', it reproduces the discourses which sustain sexism, estranging them from contemporary experience in order to render them visible.[3] The estrangement is a function of the setting of the story, a post-holocaust future in which men are dominant and women reduced to the level of the sub-human, denied their humanity. The means used to achieve this dehumanisation are those of past and contemporary western society, from witch-burning to ritual exorcism.[4] Charnas weaves this explanation of discursive practice into the four narratives which constitute the story. These narratives operate sequentially to develop the overall narrative, but refuse the simplistic reductionism of the quest narrative, in which the situation–complication–resolution structure becomes an affirmation of the unified coherent hero, a characterisation of this state of resolution and harmony. Charnas's more complex plot structure denies this ideology of closure, of the establishment and maintenance of a hegemonic discursive formation resistant to challenge from within or without. Instead, she characterises the character-types, and their corresponding discursive formations which sustain patriarchal ideology, not as coherent and unified, but as a set of strategic practices operating to sustain a particular power-formation, that is, the definition of humanity in exclusively male terms. More specifically, humanity in *Walk* is described in *white* male terms. Charnas's analysis extends beyond gender politics into the politics of race, though gender ideology remains the central focus of the text.

The main problem with Charnas's social critique in *Walk to the End of the World* is that she does not deal with class politics, which means that a major component of contemporary discursive formations is excluded from her analysis. This is problematic because none of these discourses – of gender, race, class – function independently. So if Charnas's text is read as operating in the dystopian mode, reproducing contemporary discursive formations in a displaced setting in order to render visible their delimiting and prescriptive categories, then this reductionist representation may be counter-productive. Rather than clarifying the discursive practice of sexism, it may serve to obscure its actual operation, which is inflected most subtly in terms of class and race (so, for example, it is often much more difficult to specify discrimination against middle-class women in a middle-class institution than it is to identify women's exclusion from traditional male trades). The danger with Charnas's pared-down version of contemporary gender discourse is that it may be read as an essentialist argument which condemns men virtually unequivocally and offers no hope for female autonomy beyond a total rejection of any society containing men (such societies forming the basis of Charnas's sequel, *Motherlines*). This separatist argument has very limited applicability to any critique of western society precisely because of the political economy which supports it, with its corresponding discourses of class and race. The more positive reading of the text, which this chapter outlines, traces Charnas's representations of the subject positions produced by a masculinist or sexist ideology. The process of constructing those positions is simultaneously their deconstruction since their determinants, the premises on which they are based, their ideological framework and the social practices they engender are made visible to the reader. Charnas's text is a succession of individuated narratives – Captain Kelmz, Servan d Layo, Eykar Bek, Alldera – each of which is an exploration of a gendered patriarchal subject, ending with the equivocally named 'Destination', in which Charnas speculates on the possibility of renegotiating patriarchal discourse.

PROLOGUE

In the Prologue to *Walk*, Charnas establishes the setting of her story, the time after the 'Wasting' when the world has been devastated by pollution, (environmental) exhaustion and (nuclear) war. Those who have survived the Wasting are not those who avoided it or worked against it, of course, but those who actively caused it: 'A handful of high officials had access to shelters established against enemy attack. Some of them thought to bring women with them' (*WE*, p. 3). So the survivors of the holocaust were its perpetrators and the women (partners? secretaries?) they took with them into the shelters. When the consequences of this Armageddon become visible, the men are unable to accept responsibility and so, in a familiar move, transfer it to those over whom they have power. 'They forbade all women to attend meetings and told them to keep their eyes lowered and their mouths shut and to mind their own business, which was reproduction.' When some of the women protest against this treatment, the men are delighted: 'they rejoiced to find an enemy they could conquer at last' (ibid.):

One night, as planned, they pulled all the women from sleep, herded them together, and harangued them, saying, remember that you caused the Wasting. It was a Black female's refusal to sit in the back of the bus that sparked the rebellion of the Blacks; female Gooks fought against our troops in the Eastern Wars; female terrorists made bombs side by side with our own rebel sons, whose mothers had brought them up to be half-men; female vermin of all kinds spewed out millions of young to steal our food-supplies and our living space! Females themselves brought on the Wasting of the world! (*WE*, pp. 3–4)

Charnas reproduces in another setting the reasoning which made women responsible for the original biblical fall of humanity. As Eve – and so all women – became the scapegoat for original sin, women are once again blamed for an apocalyptic fall – the Wasting of the world. And they are placed in this role because they are vulnerable, because these women and the men with them are the products of an unjust and inequitable social system which established men in positions of power – the power to destroy their environment and most of its inhabitants. Charnas does not conclude the Prologue with this reworking/deconstruction of the biblical story and its use within patriarchal discourse, however; she goes on to spell out the ways in which women have been and may be involved in the struggle against the patriarchal white supremacist order represented by the male survivors. Here Charnas uses a strategy characteristic of the dystopian text. She inserts into her fictional text references to the reader's 'real' world – the Civil Rights movement in the south of the United States and the Vietnam War. In this way the reader's 'real' and the fictional events of the text are placed in a dialectical relationship which constitutes an interrogation of the 'real'; that is, the avowedly fictional incidents of the narrative are consistently referred to the reader's own society and found to be the result of an identical discursive formation.[5] The shock experienced by the reader as a result of this identification is a function of the extreme brutality of the narrative – and of the corresponding recognition of the brutality inherent in her/his own society and its dominant discursive formation.

The other function of this identification of the role of women in liberation movements is a recognition of women's power, that women can and have acted in some of the most dangerous and volatile political situations involving the US of the early 1970s. As such it offers a reassurance about women's ability to act outside the gender role produced for them under patriarchy, a role which has as its major attributes passivity and compliance. The same kind of back-hand reassurance is offered by the catalogue of those hated by the 'men', the patriarchally-defined white supremacists who survive their own devastation of the world:

> They remember the evil races whose red skins, brown skins, yellow skins, black skins, skins all the colours of fresh-turned earth marked them as mere treacherous imitations of men, who are white; youths who repudiated their father's ways; animals that raided men's crops and waylaid and killed men in the wild places of the world; and most of all the men's own cunning, greedy females. Those were the rebels who caused the downfall of men's righteous rule: men call them 'unmen.' Of all the unmen, only females and their young remain, still the enemies of men. (*WE*, p. 4)

In other words, Charnas identifies those who are a threat to the white supremacist, patriarchal order and in so doing recognises their power, but she also specifies them as those most in danger from this discursive formation and so most likely to be destroyed – physically, socially – by it. In the dystopian world of Holdfast, most of the unmen have been physically destroyed as the result of starvation and fallout. In the dystopian world of contemporary western society most of these 'unmen' are destroyed by the negation of their humanity, by their exclusion from positions of power in which lie the ability to define the 'real'. At the same time Charnas identifies the process of exclusion, the way in which white men, because of their position of power – even a power bought at the cost of their world – are able to specify who is human, real, who may be accounted the rights and privileges of human status. And it is pertinent that Charnas describes the 'men' as aligning the non-white men and all women with animals, this strategy reinforcing the dehumanising of the former and the establishment of 'humanity' as a specifically white, male attribute. This same strategy is still in common use, and might perhaps have been particularly familiar to Vietnam-era readers of the early 1970s accustomed to hearing the North Vietnamese dehumanised as 'geeks' and to feminists of the same period still digesting writings such as *The Female Eunuch*, with its deconstruction of the language commonly used to refer to women (bitch, dog, pig, chick, bird and so on).[6]

In the Prologue, then, Charnas sets up the premises of the world she describes through the narratives of Captain Kelmz, Servan d Layo, Eykar Bek and Alldera. It is a world dominated by white men who treat women as reproductive mechanisms and deny their humanity since, for these men, humanity equals masculinity. It is also a world in which all non-white people and all animals have been destroyed/negated by those same men. And in this world the men blame all problems, including their own destruction of the pre-holocaust society, on the 'unmen', who include primarily women, but also the non-white races and animals. The discourses which describe this society are sexist and white supremacist, discourses which also describe, at least in part, the society in which the book was written, contemporary Western society. *Walk to the End of the World* explores fictionally the operation of sexism. What are the limits of this discourse? What practices does it validate as normal and natural?

CAPTAIN KELMZ

The narrative of Captain Kelmz explores the definition of masculinity in sexist discourse. The idea that male sexuality is *by nature* almost uncontrollable and extremely violent is given expression in the band of Rovers in the command of Kelmz as well as in the character of Kelmz himself: 'the captain's personal vice was to envision other men – even decent, manly men – in beast shapes' (*WE*, p. 8). Kelmz finds the beasts in men because he puts them there. Even though no animals remain in this burned-out world, Kelmz is so attracted by the idea of their power and apparent unpredictability that he searches the library for information about them. For him they are emblematic of the essential nature of men, which is also powerful and unpredictable. The Rovers are living proof of this view.

As a Rover Captain, Kelmz has under his command a group of extremely strong and powerful, but barely sentient, men. The Rovers are trained to obey commands without question, to lack any individual initiative. They are kept in check with doses of a drug carried by the Captain. The discursive positioning reproduced in this characterisation is that of the fighting man, the warrior, trained to kill without feeling and without question.

The two Rovers guarding the work-room and warehouse end

of the crescent came swinging down the gallery in step, bald-headed and thick-bodied like two rough clay men made from the same mold. That their features could not be discerned in the shadows of the thatch overhead seemed only fitting; their anonymous madness was their most formidable aspect. Servan knew from experience that they were nearly so soulless, like the mechanical men of Ancient legend, that they were a disappointment to kill unless fully aroused. (*WE*, p. 51)

And one way to rouse the Rovers is to put them near women, 'fems': 'He hummed part of a song concerning, "Rovers, red-handed, mad-eyes warders, dreadful and deadly to fems"' (ibid.). And yet, as one of the characters, Servan d Layo comments, the Rovers' motivation is not courage or sadism, but fear.

Once you figured out that they worked on the principle of the pre-emptive strike, it was easy to deal with them. Acting out of fear themselves, they interpreted others' fear of them as a presage of aggression and responded by attacking first. (ibid.)

The Rovers are even afraid of the enslaved women: 'To them, fems were drug-distorted demons' (*WE*, p. 55). And, of course, it suits their keepers to have them in this state of constant terror and, therefore, of potential violence; their lack of initiative makes them susceptible to skilful control and they will obey orders without regard to their own safety.

With the Rovers, Charnas constructs the subject position produced by the misogynistic, violent discourse of masculinity which defines men in terms of unpredictability, violence and insensitivity, *machismo* taken to its logical end. And this discourse has affinity with bourgeois discourse in its emphasis on the subject constructed as a coherent, autonomous individual; the Rovers are the heroes of many bourgeois narratives:

The imagined dangers dream-fixed in the Rovers' minds made them not only alert and fierce, but indiscriminately dangerous unless skillfully handled. Each Rover, in his isolated vision of himself as a hero constantly on guard, imagined all orders to be for his ears alone and himself to be the sole subject of all events. Rover-egotism was considered a sign of healthy, manly individualism and was encouraged, so that getting even two to work efficiently together as a brace was difficult.   (*WE*, p. 14)

Charnas also deconstructs that bourgeois, patriarchal discourse, revealing what it conceals – primarily that its motivation is fear. In her representations of the hapless Rovers missing their quarry through their inability to think laterally and of their mindless repetition of the actions of their controllers ('He slapped down the sandal he had taken off and began rubbing his foot. The Rovers imitated him' – *WE*, p. 71), Charnas describes both the limitations of that subjectivity and its potential for exploitation by those more brutal and more 'rational'; the soldier-of-fortune is revealed as the mere lackey of those more powerful than he. Charnas does not disguise the appalling brutality of the Rover, but she strips away its justification/appeal as an expression of 'natural' masculinity.

Captain Kelmz is obsessed by this construction of masculinity as beastlike. When his conscious defences are lowered by drugs, Kelmz hopes that he will see the beasts in men: 'real beasts, hot-hided, pungently scented alien beings' (*WE*, p. 46). Instead Kelmz becomes a beast:

> He couldn't understand the meaning of the upright-walking being that came toward him, sniffed at him, put its hot, smooth touch on him. Panicky, he reared back to escape, but there were barriers. He struck out. The tall-walker evaded him and withdrew. Alone, penned in, he squeezed his eyes half shut and swung his head away from the bright, flaring heat and burning smell. Deep tremors of fear shuddered through him. He swayed from side to side, nosing the air for a familiar scent. There was none.
>
> A sound found its way out of his throat, a whimper. He rocked his weight from shoulder to shoulder and moaned out his despair and isolation; but there came no answering voice.   (*WE*, p. 46)

Kelmz's beast is within; it is his own interpellation by the masculinist ideology of *machismo*. Kelmz's fantasies about the beasts in other men are the result of his own discursive positioning; his own subjectivity is constructed in these beast terms. When Kelmz looks for the beast in others, he is seeking a response to the beast in himself. That there is no reply attests to the mythic nature of Kelmz's desire, as well as to its power. There is no 'natural' man in the terms Kelmz desires; that desire is an effect of his discursive positioning, it has no material basis. Its power is the power of desire, never attainable, always out of reach, the ultimate consumer succubus. Kelmz is trapped within this desire, and within the discourse which describes it. So, while other Senior men have taken on administrative roles within the hierarchy of his society, Kelmz elects to remain a Rover Captain – to spend his life caring for and controlling these drug-sustained beast-men in whom he projects the myth of male *machismo* within which his own subjectivity is formulated.

Ironically, when Kelmz is mortally wounded, it is unclear whether he is acting out his own battle training, or attempting to save the renegade, Eykar Bek; the latter an action which contradicts that basic training. In many ways Bek is the antithesis of the beastly *machismo* Kelmz desires. Yet Bek has lived as an Entendant, one who gives elderly men the poison they need to end their lives, and he has deliberately drowned his Rover guards in order to leave the Endpath for a more pressing mission – to murder his father. Bek is a cool, deliberate killer, not a mindless psychopath. The attraction posited between Kelmz and Bek neverthless argues a compatibility between their discursive positions. Is this possible, or is it a fiction constructed by Servan d Layo, another renegade and ex-lover of Bek?

SERVAN D LAYO

Servan d Layo is known as the Darkdreamer because of his work as a drug supplier. Servan is a kind of interstitial tissue holding together the sociopathic Holdfast world. Rejected from the masculinist society of Holdfast in his youth, like Eykar Bek, Servan maintains himself by supplying the drugs needed to make life bearable. He supplies *manna* to the Holdfast males, the same drug used to control the Rovers. That his work is illegal makes it no less an essential part of Holdfast society, where practices (such as drug-dealing) which are designated as illegal – that is, described as being outside 'normal' social practice – are nevertheless necessary to the 'normal' operation of this discursive formation. This necessary illegality is itself indicative of the function of ideology as a mythic or imaginary set of relations by which the individual subject experiences the material 'real'; the 'normal' Holdfast male is positioned to perceive Servan as inimical to Holdfast society whereas he is, in fact, essential to it. Servan is an outcast from Holdfast social life, but not from the discursive framework which motivates it.

Servan is different from his fellow Holdfasters in another respect as well; he likes to have sex with women; he even likes to arouse them before penetration. In terms of Holdfast society this makes him a sexual pervert. But in other ways Servan's behaviour is typical of Holdfast men. Servan does not give the 'fem' Alldera any choice about having sex with him, even if he does attempt to arouse her in the process. And when he has finished with her, he brutalises her as effectively as any Holdfast male:

> Suddenly he jerked her head up by the hair and twisted, so that she had to turn on her belly or have her neck broken. She turned. He pushed her face against the wet, hard-packed earth.
> 'Eat,' he said.
> She bit at the mud. She coughed. Grit got between her teeth.
> 'What's the lesson?' he said.
> What he wanted was recognition of his god-like unpredictability. The trick was to furnish it without drawing attention to the fact that total arbitrariness was also an attribute of chaos and the void. It was not for a fem to point out paradoxes that men chose to ignore. The best Alldera could do at the moment was to mumble, through bruised and filthy lips, a stock response: 'The master is always the master, and he does as he pleases according to his will.'   (WE, pp. 144–5)

The essential element in Servan's treatment of Alldera is not sexual pleasure – whether or not he was able to arouse her – but power, his power, discursively formulated, to force her (violently or not) to be his sexual object.

The subjectivity Charnas formulates in the character of Servan d Layo is another familiar subject positioning from the late 1960s and early 1970s. Servan is a counter-culture member, a hippie, one who has rejected some of the discursive practices of her / his society, but who is nevertheless contained within that discursive formation. The existence of such subjects is evidence of the non-coherence, the contradictoriness, of the dominant discursive formation, and so of its capacity for change, for renegotiation. But they are also evidence of the power of the dominant formation, that it can contain such non-compliant subjects. And ironically, like Servan, they may even serve a useful function in terms of the dominant formation; their operation may be the means which enables it to survive. By supplying the drugs which enable compliant subjects to forget the contradictions they observe in the dominant formation, Servan positively contributes to the maintenance of his society. Charnas reinforces this interpretation by showing one of the means by which Servan is implicated within the dominant discursive formation, his compliance with the misogyny fundamental to its masculinist ideology. Servan may reject some of his society's practices but he enacts their fundamental power relation himself in his relationships with women. Servan is an example of the radical male of the late 1960s (and since) who recognises some of the contradictions within his society's discursive formation and so refuses to be contained by its definition of 'normality', but who, when it comes to refusing the power this same discursive formation grants him, will not do so. And this applies particularly in the areas of social interaction most necessary to his own function – in intimate relationships; the private / public dichotomy is most evident in the practice of this subject positioning. The feminist catch-cry, 'the personal is political' is as much a response to these so-called radicals as it is to the politically conservative patriarchal male subject.

Servan's interpellation within masculinist ideology is evident from the beginning of his narrative. Charnas uses his voice to explain further the discursive construction of femininity in Hold-fast:

It was hard to connect these crude mud walls and their stunted inhabitants with the great witch-fems who had overthrown the Ancients' mighty civilization. The Chants Historical told the tale: at the peak of their power the men of Ancient times had been so fascinated with their own technical prowess that they had neglected the supervision of their treacherous fems. . . .

The Moonwitch had not been destroyed by the missiles the Ancients had hurled; she had fought back through her minions, the fems. With her magic the fems had inspired the natural inferiors of the Ancients to join in a coalition to overthrow the rule of order and manly reason. There was some question as to the exact apportionment of blame for the rebellion of the Wasting among the various kinds of lesser beings (known collectively as the unmen). . . .

To the logical mind, however, the answer was obvious: there had been beast-fems, and fems among the Dirties, and the sons of men had turned Freak under the tutelage of their dams. The common denominator of corruption and rebellion among all the unmen had been fems.   (*WE*, p. 55)

Servan's conceptualisation of femininity mobilises familiar representations of women as witches, the holders of magical powers who can trick men into compliance, or overcome them with the aid of lesser beings, the witch and her familiar. These representations are displacements of male fear; that fear is projected on to women, or at least a patriarchal conceptualisation of women – *Woman*, which is thereby transformed into an even more threatening and evil concept, fem. The fem is degraded and degrading, fascinating and repulsive, and worthy of use and abuse (more correctly, a use which is abuse).

Here Charnas employs the familiar dystopian technique of defamiliarisation, that is, reconstructing a familiar discursive operation in an unfamiliar location in order to make it (that operation or practice) visible to a reader for whom it has been naturalised (that is, made to appear obvious or natural). So the image of the witch is recalled, along with the use to which it has been put in the domination and control of women. In the guise of fighting witchcraft, women have been tortured and murdered, their difference from men, which is a source of male fear, transformed by that fear into menace and evil, which men are morally correct to attack and destroy. What the reader is positioned to recognise is the way in which this discursive practice operates, to see the imaging of women in a particular role as part of a process motivated by a specific set of beliefs, here the un-humanity of women; that women are thereby misrepresented in a form which makes them vulnerable, and that this process of myth-making, of mystification, is the practice of ideology. Charnas continues this deconstruction of discursive practice in Servan's subsequent thoughts:

Even at the time, there had been names for fems indicating some understanding of the danger they represented. One Ancient book used in the Boyhouse mentioned fems as 'bra-burners.' Since 'bra' was a word in an old language meaning 'weapon,' clearly 'bra-burner' meant a fem who stole and destroyed the weapons of her masters. (*WE*, p. 56)

This apparently ludicrous misunderstanding of the meaning of 'bra' achieves two purposes. First, it illustrates further the delimiting effect of a discourse, here masculinist, that directs the thought/perception of its subject in ways which defy logic. So the masculinist Holdfast male would not do the research needed to establish the nature of the object 'bra' but would simply interpret the object in terms related to his understanding of the nature of 'fems'. Such apparent illogic, Charnas implies, is a measure of the power of discourses, such as the masculinist discourse of patriarchy. So Charnas positions the reader to ask how many other social practices, and particularly how many gendered social practices, are based on similar, illogical premises. Secondly, the passage serves to reinforce the early feminist deconstruction of such material practices as the wearing of bras; bras might well be regarded as weapons – of the 'masters' – if they are part of a discursive positioning of women which places them in a subordinate relationship to men.

Servan's narrative is a kind of bridge between that of Captain Kelmz, a subject interpellated unproblematically by the masculinist ideology of Holdfast, and that of Eykar Bek, an intelligent man who has found the contradictions within his social formation impossible to ignore. With Eykar Bek, Charnas moves from *machismo* through counter-culture to the intellectual.

EYKAR BEK

With the character of Bek, Charnas describes the intellectual basis of the masculinist ideology of Holdfast:

There was a theory that a man's soul was a fragment of eternal energy that had been split off from the soul of his father and fixed inside his dam's body by the act of intercourse. Being alien to everything that the soul represented, the fem's body surrounded the foreign element with a physical frame, by means of which the soul could be expelled. Seen from that perspective, a man's life could be regarded as the struggle of the flesh-caged soul not to be seduced and extinguished by the meaningless concerns of the brute-body.   (*WE*, pp. 102–3)

In the terms of this discourse, Woman, dehumanised as 'dam', represents the body, which is the site of worthless, valueless desires and cravings against which the essential masculinity of the soul must do battle. Again Charnas reproduces a discourse familiar to contemporary readers. Eva Figes traces the development of this discursive positioning of women in her book *Patriarchal Attitudes*. She concludes her critique of Schopenhauer's writing on women: 'Dominance is of course also the keynote in an analysis of the man–woman relationship where the male attributes are ones associated with mental thought and positive activity, whilst the woman is regarded as essentially passive, her role to be the receptacle of male sexual drive for the subsequent reproduction of the species.'[7] Hélène Cixous also records this dualism in her essay 'Where Is She?':

Activity / passivity,
Sun / Moon,
Culture / Nature,
Day / Night.

Father / Mother,
Head / heart,
Intelligible / sensitive,
Logos / Pathos.

Form, convex, step, advance, seed, progress.
Matter, concave, ground – which supports the step, receptacle.

Man
———
Woman

Always the same metaphor: we follow it, it transports us, in all of its forms, wherever a discourse is organized. The same thread, or double tress leads us, whether we are reading or speaking, through literature, philosophy, criticism, centuries of representation, of reflection.[8]

As Cixous notes, this dualising process is fundamental to Western thought and to Western ways of conceptualising gender. Further, the opposite sides of the dualities have their own metaphorical equivalences which are *not* equally valorised. These dualities are not equal opposites, but are discursively employed under patriarchy to produce / reinforce the dominance of the masculine. So, as Bek conjectures, woman is equated with the devalued, debased flesh; man with the pure, noble soul. The discursive positioning Bek explains for women is not only that of Holdfast; it is that of women in the reader's own society, another horrifying point of recognition, and another inflection of the dystopian genre.

When Bek recalls his youth, he remembers the ceremonies used to reinforce this patriarchal discourse, including 'the witch-burning which traditionally opened the dreaming ceremonies' (*WE*, p. 111). Unlike his contemporaries Bek feels sympathy for the women burned at the stake, a reaction he considers 'an involuntary sympathy rooted deep in the body-brute' (ibid.). When Bek describes the words chanted by the boys at these ceremonies, the reader is again confronted with misrecognitions of words in contemporary usage. So the 'Freaks' who helped cause the destruction of the world include: ' "Lonhairs, Raggles, Bleedingarts; Faggas, Hibbies, Fam lies, Kids; Junkies, Skinheads, Collegeists; Ef-eet Iron-mentalists," the last a reference to the soft-minded values of the Freaks, iron being notoriously less strong than steel' (*WE*, p. 112). This strange and contradictory mixture – long hairs, radicals, bleeding hearts, faggots, hippies, families, kids, junkies, skinheads, college kids, environmentalists – again signifies the power of a particular discursive formation to define and delimit the thought processes of the subjects it interpellates. Charnas then shows this process in operation in relation to women – and again the contemporary reader is confronted with a very familiar scenario:

> Finally, the chant came to the fems, huge-breasted, doused in sweet-stinking waters to mask uglier odors, loud and forever falsely smiling. Their names closed the circle for being beast-like ('red in tooth and claw,' as some old books said) they had been known by beasts' names: 'Bird, Cat, Chick, Sow; Filly, Tigress, Bitch, Cow. . .'. (*WE*, p. 112)

The mixture of prurience and disgust evident in a masculinist representation of women, with sexual characteristics emphasised, and the attribution to women of animal names, is a familiar feature of contemporary western life. And again Charnas employs the device of misrecognition to produce a reading position from which her deconstruction of these familiar images is apparent. So the contemporary reader knows that it was nature which was described in the nineteenth century as 'red in tooth and claw'; hence clarifying the equation of women and nature. Furthermore, the evolutionary theory which is figured in this expression was employed, ironically enough, by the patriarchal bourgeoisie to justify their behaviour towards both women and the working classes; namely, it is natural that the strong survive and so that women and the working classes (the weak) should be subservient. Again the inversion of familiar knowledge illustrates the power of ideological discourses, and challenges the reader to examine how many other 'natural' facts about gender are discursively produced. (The answer is: they all are – but we haven't quite reached that recognition yet.)

Bek's narrative takes the company to the Boyhouse Library where Bek once again sees the images of women which had so terrified him as a child: 'how was it, he mused, that he hadn't noticed that the fems in the pictures were not particularly huge breasted, nor magically alluring as the chants said?' (*WE*, p. 117). Bek is unable to explain his misrecognition: 'Baffled, Bek frowned at the pictures. Could he have been so blind with his terrors of this place as a boy that he had looked without seeing any of this? Then what of the Teachers?' (p. 118). Charnas emphasises her point that discursive positioning does not only determine what we see, but also *how* we see what we see; the compliant patriarchal subject sees women *as defined by that discourse*. Bek is a danger to Holdfast because he is no longer unproblematically positioned by its dominant discursive framework.

ALLDERA

The character of Bek is contextualised in the narrative which follows, that of the fem, Alldera. Through Alldera, Charnas describes the position of the non-compliant female patriarchal subject; that is, Alldera's whole existence is profoundly effected by the patriarchal discourse of Holdfast society but she nevertheless resists her interpellation by that ideology. Other women do not resist, or are unable to resist. The 'pet-fems', for example, collude with their 'perverted' masters who enjoy sex with women. For these women the collusion is a survival strategy, but Alldera notes: 'The trouble with pet-fems was that they came to take pride in their disfigurement – a technique of survival practiced by most fems to some extent' (*WE*, p. 142). The reference to contemporary debates concerning femininity is evident, particularly with Charnas's use of the label 'pet'. The women who are unable to resist are those so degraded by their treatment by men that they have little strength remaining beyond basic survival. They include the 'carry-fems' Alldera encounters on her journey with Bek and Servan:

> Though not matched for size like a proper crew, these fems carried the fully laden camper smoothly. Their ragged smocks showed dirty, scarred skin at the rents; their feet were pads of callous. Only Alldera's intelligence had saved her from being beaten into just such a shape herself. (*WE*, p. 141)

Even so, these carry-fems join Alldera in singing seditious songs against the 'masters'. They recall the millions of women whose labour is appropriated by men and who are so exhausted by this abuse that they have no strength to fight on their own behalf. Alldera acknowledges also those women who would brazenly oppose men and so call down the wrath of the 'masters' on all women; she explains that they are 'culled' by the older women in youth. Her world is a nightmare of intrigue, negotiation and cruelty, and every manifestation of that nightmare strikingly recalls aspects of contemporary western society: the strategies used by women to survive the white supremacist patriarchal bourgeois society of the West; the women who do not survive; and the women who are working to reconfigure that dominant discursive formation.

Alldera's rape by Servan d Layo has already been discussed, even more telling is her rape by Eykar Bek. Bek, after all, is an intellectual, a thinker, not a mere scavenger like Servan. This assault occurs after Bek has spent some time talking with Alldera, inducing her to talk about her life and her opinion of men. This unexpected opportunity to talk is both a relief and a danger to Alldera. It has enabled her to feel real, to feel autonomous, and she makes the mistake of allowing Bek to see her opinion of him in her face. Bek still does not act like an ordinary Holdfast male:

> Oh, these conscientious types, she thought. He needed an excuse to exercise his rage because he was ashamed of it. Instead of coming right to the point and beating her because her expression had angered him, he would give her orders and wait for the least sign of insubordination – which he would find, one way or another.   (*WE*, p. 161)

Alldera deliberately provokes Bek and then finds that her only defence is a familiar one: 'Alldera fell back. She spread her legs and clawed up her smock with both hands in the last, mindless defence: when threatened, present' (ibid.). Bek performs the rape despite his own fear: 'when he entered her, she heard his groan of mortal terror' (ibid.). Charnas thereby reinforces the point made earlier with the Servan rape, that this abuse is part of a particular set of power relationships. It is sexual, but is about a particular discursive configuration of sexuality; that is, sexuality defined by a misogynistic patriarchal ideology. It may be pleasurable for either or both partners, as it was in the Alldera–Servan rape, and yet still be a brutal, sadistic act of domination. Or it may be pleasurable for neither partner, as in the Alldera–Bek rape, and be equally brutal and sadistic, equally the demonstration of a particular power relationship. That relationship is described by Alldera as she reviews her own carelessness in allowing Bek to recognise her autonomy:

> A clever fem sometimes needed a reminder of her true position, and there was nothing like a good swift fuck to set firmly in her mind her relation to the masters again: the simplest relation of all, that of an object to the force of those stronger than she.
>
> Fem, she thought, you only think you think. The pitcher the man drinks from does not think. The camper that carries his weight does not think.
>
> She felt hollow in body, which was fitting in one who was merely a receptacle for the use of men; and she felt hollow in mind, for there was nothing that she might imagine, feel or will that a man could not wipe out of existence by picking her up for his own purposes. . . . That she could have a mission, a direction of her own – or that others like herself to whom she

was in some way bound could – was an absurdity. A man's usage conferred existence. (*WE*, p. 162)

Alldera reproduces the discursive positioning of the female patriarchal subject, a positioning she must know very well if she is to survive within a patriarchal society as either compliant or non-compliant subject. Charnas then uses this deconstruction of the female patriarchal subject to deconstruct the male patriarchal subject.

Eykar Bek learns a great deal from Alldera, primarily that the description of women which he has been taught since boyhood is not natural, but a discursive construct. Alldera explains the process by which both women and men are interpellated by the patriarchal gender ideology of Holdfast. Again Charnas uses the metaphor of witchcraft, as Alldera explains the attempts of some of the fems to 'rediscover' their witch powers, an endeavour which plays directly into the hands of the men who believe in this essential evil of women. Alldera explains that, like these naïve women, 'men were dupes of their own ideology' (*WE*, p. 173). Both women and men are constructed in terms of the dominant discursive framework of patriarchy, but this does not mean that women and men are equally treated, though they may, in some sense, be equally duped. As the witchcraft metaphor makes clear, patriarchy actively works against any possibility of an equal relatonship between women and men, since men are discursively defined as superior to women. When Bek attempts to reconstruct his relationship with Alldera in terms of equality – ' "Look around: where do you see 'men,' where do you see 'fems' in here? There's nobody but us, you and me" ' (*WE*, p. 176) – he is forced to this conclusion: ' "But it's worth nothing while I have the power of death over you. . . . Nothing that passes between us can be anything but rape" ' (ibid.). Again Charnas's argument refers specifically to contemporary debate within the Women's Movement of the early 1970s concerning the possibility of equal heterosexual relationships in a patriarchal society. Unless some way can be found to renegotiate the gender roles defined by patriarchy, no equality is possible.

DESTINATION

In the final narrative section of the book, 'Destination', Charnas concludes her study of the subject positions produced by the discursive configuration of Holdfast with an account of the meeting between Eykar Bek and his father, Raff Maggomas. Throughout the book Charnas presents her characters' debates about the transgressive relationship between Bek and Maggomas. The transgression lies in the fact that father and son know each other's identity. In Holdfast society this is forbidden, since it is a fundamental belief that father and son operate in direct opposition. This belief is represented by the crucifix which is interpreted as God's rightful punishment of his errant son:

> In all the Holdfast, no blood-ties were recognized. All men were brothers – that was the Law of Generations – though some were older brothers and some younger. Thus, men avoided the fated enmity of fathers and sons, who once known to each other must cross each other even to the point of mutual destruction. The sons of the Ancients had risen against their fathers and brought down the world; even God's own Son, in the old story had earned punishment from his Father. Old and young were natural enemies; everyone knew that. To know your father's identity would be to feel, however far off, the chill wind of death. (*WE*, p. 22)

This mis/interpretation is yet another of Charnas's contemporary references designed to demonstrate the power of an ideology as a meaning-making discourse; the symbol of peace and reconciliation from one ideology becomes a symbol of conflict in another ideology. The character most directly involved in this narrative is, of course, Eykar Bek, who is also the character with whom Charnas demonstrates the renegotiation of subjectivity. Bek does change his subject position in relation to women; he is no longer the compliant patriarchal male. Yet Bek is unable to renegotiate the father–son discourse of Holdfast. He kills Maggomas as much for his transgressive marking of his son as for his inhuman proposal to harvest women for food, a misogynistic version of Swift's 'Modest Proposal'. This act seals Bek's fate, but not before he assists Alldera to escape the ironically named city of Troi, Maggomas's stronghold. Bek's renegotiation of the gender discourse of Holdfast is still the major determinant of his death, however. His response to Maggomas's revelation that he and Servan have eaten fem-flesh is the blow that kills his father and ensures the downfall of Troi. In terms of the gender ideology which defines Holdfast, Bek has become an anomaly, a non-compliant male subject; he has no place in this world. So the ideology of Holdfast doubly determines the demise of Bek, the only reconstructive male subject in the book; his compliance with the father–son ideology of Holdfast ensures his death as effectively as his rejection of its masculinist discourse.

At the end of this narrative Troi falls and two people escape, both facilitated by Bek: Servan d Layo, the scavenger, and Alldera. When Bek warned Alldera of the monsters she may encounter in the wilderness outside Troi, Alldera's answer is instructive: ' "I am experienced," she snarled, "at handling monsters"' (*WE*, p. 211). This answer encapsulates Charnas's argument in *Walk to the End of the World*, that the discursive formation represented by Holdfast society produces monsters – men who act like monsters, women who are treated like monsters. Yet the conclusion is not hopeless since it is Bek's renegotiation of his own subjectivity which enables Alldera's escape from the (other) male monsters among whom she has lived.

The destination of this text may be that of a strategic intervention in contemporary debates about the possibility of renegotiating the gender discourse of the dominant ideological formation which is patriarchal (masculinist, sexist). By using the resources of the dystopian genre, Charnas presents a pared-down version of the discursive practice of patriarchy as it formulates particular subject positions – compliant and non-compliant male and female subjects. Conventions (used in both dystopian and Utopian texts) such as the misrecognition of words and objects familiar to contemporary readers, references to familiar social practices and, most importantly, the estranged representation of familiar discourses construct a text which positions readers to challenge the discursive practices of their own society, particularly in relation to gender. Charnas's multiple narratives work similarly to construct a reading position which interrogates the function of narrative closure; any new equilibrium reached is almost certain to reproduce discursively the initial position, so reinforcing the dominant discursive formation. Instead, *Walk to the End of the World* ends at a point of beginning; Eykar Bek remains in his father's cannibal city of Troi, which he surrenders to invading Holdfast forces; Servan d Layo is alone in the wilderness, a familiar position, and likely to find his way back to Holdfast; Alldera faces the wilderness, and its possible monsters, relieved to have left the known monsters who have brutalised her all her life; Captain Kelmz is dead. There is no comfortable point of closure but a hope of regeneration offered by the attempt of one Holdfast male to renegotiate his subject position, and the freedom he gains for one non-compliant female subject. But Bek also buys Servan's freedom and Servan is a compliant male subject like the rest of the male population of Holdfast.

Charnas's text describes the possibility of change, of renegotiation of the dominant discursive formation, and to this extent offers the reader some hope for the future. The mechanism of this renegotiation rests with the individual's recognition of contradictions within the discursive practices of her/his own society. As the Servan narrative makes clear, however, that recognition has to be reinforced by a desire for change; otherwise the power afforded by a particular discursive positioning will be irresistible. And it is not clear what produces that desire. Equally, it is significant that Bek does not dissociate himself from Servan, even though he recognises his brutality. Perhaps this is the sympathy of one renegade for another, or the remnants of love. Or it may signify the difficulty Bek faces in this radical renegotiation of his own subjectivity, that he is unable to reject the exploitative capability conferred on him by his discursive positioning; it lives on in Servan. And it is significant that Bek dies after performing the act made imperative by his positioning within the Oedipal ideology of Holdfast. The text suggests that renegotiation of individual subject positioning is possible; for Alldera it consists in a rejection of the degraded role in which she is positioned, but for men it involves a rejection of the power their positioning within patriarchal discourse affords them – and that is very difficult. In *Motherlines*, Charnas goes on to explore the difficulty for women in renegotiating the discursive framework in which they have been raised and in which their own subjectivity has been formulated. There are no men in *Motherlines*, and perhaps this is an answer to the question implicitly posed in *Walk to the End of the World* about the possibility of reformulating Holdfast society.

As noted at the beginning of this chapter, *Walk to the End of the World* does not achieve the comprehensive representation of the contemporary discursive formation characteristic of many Utopian and dystopian texts because Charnas does not deal with one of its major determinants, the class structure produced by the political economy of the capitalist state. Accordingly her representations of the gendered practices of that society are limited but she does show something of their operation – the kinds of subjects produced by a misogynistic, sexist ideology, the power of sexist discourse in naturalising certain kinds of behaviour (for example, *machismo*) and certain perceptions of women (that is, *fems*). She also offers some observations on the possibility – and difficulty – of change. For these reasons *Walk to the End of the World* is a useful contribution to the debate about the gender ideology of western capitalist society. But it is highly significant that both Charnas and that other great feminist science fiction writer, James Tiptree Jr, ended stories about the dominant gender discourse of the West in the same way, with the women leaving their own society altogether. The final words of the sexist narrator of 'The Women Men Don't See' are equally appropriate to Alldera as she flees the sociopathy of Holdfast:

> *We survive by ones and twos in the chinks of your world-machine . . . I'm used to aliens . . .* She'd meant every word. Insane. How could a woman choose to live among unknown monsters, to say good-bye to her home, her world?
>
> As the margharitas take hold, the whole mad scenario melts down to the image of those two small shapes [the female characters] sitting side by side in the receding alien glare.
>
> Two of our opposums are missing.[9]

NOTES

1. On this use of science fiction to explicate the socialisation of women and men in patriarchal society, see Pamela Sargent's 'Introduction' to *Women of Wonder: Science-Fiction Stories by Women about Women*, ed. Pamela Sargent (Harmondsworth, Middx.: Penguin, 1978). On the use of science fiction to discuss the role of fiction as a discursive practice see my discussion of James Tiptree Jr's 'The Women Men Don't See', in *Feminist Fiction: Feminist Revisions of Generic Fiction* (Cambridge: Polity Press, 1989). Suzy McKee Charnas, *Walk to the End of the World* (1977; rpt. London: Victor Gollancz, 1979). Future references to this work will appear in the text, preceded by the initials *WE*. Suzy McKee Charnas, *Motherlines* (1978; rpt. London: Victor Gollancz, 1980).

2. James Tiptree Jr. 'The Women Men Don't See', in *Warm Worlds and Otherwise*, with an Introduction by Robert Silverberg (New York: Ballantine, 1975).

3. This use of estrangement to make visible contemporary discursive practices is discussed in relation to science fiction in Darko Suvin, *Metamorphoses of Science Fiction: On the Poetics and History of a Literary Genre* (New Haven, Conn. and London: Yale University Press, 1979).

4. See Eva Figes, *Patriarchal Attitudes: Women in Society* (London: Virago, 1978) for a discussion of social practices, including witchcraft trials, used in the oppression of women.

5. This strategy is used in both Utopian and dystopian fiction. See my essay, 'The Education of Desire: Late Nineteenth-Century Utopian Fiction and its Influence on Twentieth-Century Feminist Fantasy', in *The Nameless Wood: Victorian Fantasies – Their Achievement – Their Influence*, Proceedings of the Second Annual Conference of the Mythopoeic Literature Society of Australia (Armidale, 1986) pp. 82–95, for a detailed discussion of its use in William Morris' Utopian romance *News from Nowhere*.

6. Germaine Greer, *The Female Eunuch* (London: Paladin, 1971).

7. Figes, *Patriarchal Attitudes*, p. 125. In chapter 5, 'Mind over Matter', Figes traces the contemporary manifestations of patriarchal attitudes particularly in terms of the oppositions voiced by Eykar Bek, and by Hélène Cixous, in her essay 'Where Is She?' in *New French Feminisms: An Anthology*, ed. E. Marks and I. de Courtivron (Brighton, Sussex: Harvester, 1981).

8. Cixous, ''Where Is She?', p. 90.

9. Tiptree, 'The Women Men Don't See', pp. 163–4.

Index

About, Edmond, 13
Aldiss, Brian W., 4n, 62, 88, 102n, 103n
Althusser, Louis, 123n
Amis, Kingsley, 4n
Anderson, Susan Janice, 165n
Asimov, Isaac, 62, 63, 64, 72, 78n
Astle, Richard, 52n

Ballard, J. G., 62, 75
Barron, Neil, 89, 103n
Barth, John, 75
Barthelme, Donald, 75
Barthes, Roland, 17n, 119, 123n
Bellamy, Edward, 11, 13, 14, 15, 102n
Belsey, Catherine, 123n
Benford, Gregory, 62, 67, 78n
Bentley, C. F., 54n
Berger, Thomas, 2, 153–66n
Berkley, Miriam, 167n
Bernal, J. D., 59, 62, 67
Besant, Walter, 12, 14–16, 17n
Biehl, Janet, 124n
Bleiler, Everett F., 102n
Blish, James, 63
Bloom, Clive, 53n
Borges, Jorge Luis, 82, 87n, 149n, 150n
Boyd, John, 63, 77n
Brecht, Bertholt, 16
Breza, Tadeusz, 83, 87n
Browning, Gavin, 66–9, 78n
Buber, Martin, 147n
Burne-Jones, Edward, 9
Burroughs, William, 75

Campbell, John W., 63
Cantor, Aviva, 159–61, 166n
Capek, Karel, 62
Carnell, E. J., 61, 62

Carson, Rachel, 106–8, 113–15, 117, 118, 120, 122n, 123n
Carter, Paul A., 4n
Chafe, William W., 122n, 123n
Chamberlain, Joseph, 33
Charnas, Suzy McKee, 2, 155, 163, 165n, 183–205n
Chatterton, Lady Georgina, 12
Cirlot, J. E., 87n
Cixous, Hélène, 196–7, 206n
Clarke, Arthur C., 61, 63, 70–1, 77n
Clute, John, 88, 102n
Cole, Thomas, 122n
Collard, Andrée, 124n
Collins, Wilkie, 51n
Conrad, Joseph, 3, 4n
Contrucci, Joyce, 124n
Cranny-Francis, Anne, 2, 53n, 54n
Crowther, J. G., 59
Csissery-Ronay, Istvan, 69, 78n
Curzon, Lord, 33, 52n

Darwin, Charles, 78n, 97, 117
Davies, A. Morley, 77n
Davison, Emily Wilding, 92
Delany, Samuel R., 63
Dering, Edward Heneage (Innominatus), 12–14, 16, 17n
Dick, Philip K., 63
Docherty, Brian, 53n

Einstein, Albert, 149–50n
Eliot, T. S., 2, 125, 138, 143, 144, 146, 146n–7n
Ellison, Harlan, 63–4

Farmer, Philip José, 90
Farson, Daniel, 51n
Fekete, John, 148n
Figes, Eva, 196, 206n
Flood, Leslie, 103n
Forrest, Katherine, 166n

207

Foster, H., 182n
Foucault, Michel, 2, 120, 123n
Freud, Sigmund, 52n, 59

Genet, Jean, 83
George, Henry, 10
Gernsback, Hugo, 62
Gibb, Jane, 53n
Gibson, William, 76, 78n
Goethe, Johann Wolfgang von, 71, 72, 78n
Gombrowicz, Witold, 83, 87n
Gooch, E. P., 51n, 53n
Gordon, General Charles George, 34
Greene, Graham, 50n
Greene, Hugh, 50n, 51n
Greer, Germaine, 187, 206n
Gregory, R. A., 61, 77n
Gunn, James, 78n

Haining, Peter, 51n
Haldane, J. B. S., 59, 62, 67, 73, 77n, 78n
Hardy, Thomas, 32, 52n
Hawthorne, Nathaniel, 60
Heath, Stephen, 154, 156, 161–4, 165n, 166n, 167n
Heilbrun, Carolyn G., 165–6n
Heinlein, Robert A., 63, 72
Heraclitus, 145, 150n
Herbert, Frank, 104–24n, 127, 148n
Hirsch, Walter, 64–5, 68–9, 77n
Hodgson, Godfrey, 122n
Homer, David, 149n
Hosty, T., 76n–7n
Hoyle, Sir Fred, 62
Hudson, W. H., 11, 15
Huntington, John, 148n
Huxley, Aldous, 61–2, 65
Huxley, Sir Julian S., 59, 61–2, 72–3, 77n, 78n
Huxley, T. H., 61, 78n
Hyndman, H. M., 9, 10
Hynes, Patricia, 122n

Innominatus (Edward Heneage Dering), 12–14, 16, 17n
Irving, Henry, 51n
Irving, Washington, 13

Jackson, Rosemary, 49, 54n
Jameson, Frederic, 2, 31–3, 51n, 181n, 182n
Jardine, Alice, 153, 162, 165n
Jeans, Sir James, 59
Jefferies, Richard, 11, 15
Jefferson, Ann, 123n
Joliot-Curie, J. F., 59
Jungk, Robert, 60, 77n

Kafka, Franz, 23, 29n, 83, 87n
Kagarlitski, Julius, 88, 102n, 103n
Keats, John, 13
Khouri, Nadia, 148n, 150n
King, Ynestra, 124n
Kitchener, Lord, 34, 45
Kropotkin, P. A., 148n
Kuncewitz, Piotr, 87n

Lacan, Jacques, 52n
Latham, Jean L., 122n
Le Guin, Ursula K., 2, 63, 67–8, 77n, 125–50n, 163, 167n
Lem, Stanislaw, 2, 3, 79–87n
Lenin, V. I., 59
Lessing, Doris, 1, 4, 4n
Lévi-Strauss, Claude, 118, 123n
Lewis, C. S., 65, 69
Lombroso, Cesare, 49
Lucian, 71
Ludlam, Harry, 51n

McCarthy, Joseph Raymond, 113
McCoubrey, John W., 122n
McIntyre, Vonda, 2, 165n, 168–82n
McNelly, W. E., 123n
Macnie, John, 13
Macherey, Pierre, 2, 111–12, 119, 123n
Marsh, Richard, 2, 30–52n
Marshall, Robert, 110
Marx, Karl, 16, 17
Masterman, C. F. G., 51n
Memmi, Albert, 34, 35, 52n
Millhauser, Milton, 65–6, 68–9, 77n
Mitchison, Naomi, 61–2, 73–4, 77n
Modleski, T., 181n, 182n
Molière, Jean Baptiste Poquelin de, 16

Monkhouse, Cosmo, 51n
Moorcock, Michael, 62
Moore, Patrick, 57, 60, 62, 76n
More, Thomas, 15
Moretti, Franco, 52n
Morris, James, 51n, 52n
Morris, William, 7–17n, 206n
Munslow, Alun, 123n
Myers, Victoria, 149n

Nash, Roderick, 122n
Nicholls, Peter, 76n, 88, 89
Nordau, Max Simon, 49
Nunan, E. E., 149n

O'Reilly, Timothy, 116, 122n, 123n
Orwell, George, 65, 134, 149n

Parkes, Lucas, 103n
Parrinder, Patrick, 2, 3, 4n, 123n
Parry, Benita, 35, 52n, 53n
Pearson, Karl, 51n
Piercy, Marge, 2, 148n, 153–66n
Poe, Edgar Allan, 60
Porush, David, 75–6, 78n
Potocki, Jan, 83, 87n
Proudhon, Pierre-Joseph, 17
Punter, David, 53n
Pynchon, Thomas, 75

Rabkin, Eric S., 4n
Radford, J., 181n
Rhodes, Cecil David, 33, 37
Robey, David, 123n
Rosebery, Lord, 33
Rousseau, Jean Jacques, 117
Russ, Joanna, 153–5, 162, 163–5,
    165n, 167n
Russell, Bertrand, 78n

Said, Edward, 38, 52n, 53n
Sale, Kirkpatrick, 124n
Sandison, Alan, 52n
Santarcangeli, F., 87n
Sargent, Pamela, 205n
Scarborough, John, 88, 89, 101–2n,
    103n
Schopenhauer, Arthur, 196
Scholes, Robert, 4n

Schulz, Bruno, 86
Scigaj, Leonard M., 122n
Sears, Paul Bigelow, 106, 108–15,
    117, 118, 120, 122n, 123n
Serf, Carol A., 53n
Shand, Keith, 53n
Shaw, George Bernard, 88, 95
Sheldon, Alice (James Tiptree Jr),
    155, 163, 165n, 183, 205, 205n,
    206n
Silverberg, Robert, 63
Simak, Clifford D., 97, 103n
Simmons, A. T., 77n
Skovorecky, Joseph, 3, 4n
Smith, Curtis C., 102n
Smith, David C., 77n
Smith, Paul, 153–4, 162–3, 165n,
    166n
Snow, C. P., 59, 64, 77n
Stableford, Brian, 76n
Stapledon, Olaf, 59
Stevenson, John Allen, 54n
Stevenson, Robert Louis, 65
Stoker, Bram, 2, 30–54n
Sturgeon, Theodore, 90
Suvin, Darko, 2, 4n, 206n
Swift, Jonathan, 65, 202

Thatcher, Margaret, 66
Theall, Donald, 147n
Thornton, A. P., 52n
Tiptree, James Jr (Alice Sheldon),
    155, 163, 165n, 183, 205, 205n,
    206n
Tompkins, Jane, 153, 165, 165n, 166n
Turing, Alan, 78n
Turner, Frederick Jackson, 120,
    123n
Turney, Jon, 76n
Twain, Mark, 60

Urbanowicz, Victor, 148n

Verne, Jules, 19, 60, 73
Victoria, Queen, 26, 30
Vonnegut, Kurt, 75, 76

Waddington, C. H., 59, 67, 77n
Wall, Geoffrey, 53n

Wasson, Richard, 53n
Watlock, W. A., 10, 17n
Watson, James D., 62, 74, 77n
Wells, G. P., 61, 77n
Wells, H. G., 3, 18–29n, 36, 59, 60–1, 62, 63, 65–6, 67, 73, 77n, 78n, 88, 97, 99, 102, 103n, 148n
Werskey, Gary, 77n
Whitehead, A. N., 59
Wiener, Martin J., 66, 78n

Williamson, Jack, 119–20, 123n
Williams, Raymond, 148n
Wylie, Philip, 90, 103n
Wyndham, John, 2, 88–103n

Young, Robert, 123n

Zeno the Eleatic, 137, 149n
Zinn, Howard, 122n